KOH-I-NOOR

BY THE SAME AUTHORS

by William Dalrymple
In Xanadu
City of Djinns
From the Holy Mountain
The Age of Kali
White Mughals
The Last Mughal
Nine Lives
Return of a King

by Anita Anand
Sophia

KOH-I-NOOR

The History of the World's Most Infamous Diamond

William Dalrymple
Anita Anand

BLOOMSBURY

LONDON · OXFORD · NEW YORK · NEW DELHI · SYDNEY

Bloomsbury Publishing
An imprint of Bloomsbury Publishing Plc

50 Bedford Square
London
WC1B 3DP
UK

1385 Broadway
New York
NY 10018
USA

www.bloomsbury.com

BLOOMSBURY and the Diana logo are trademarks of Bloomsbury Publishing Plc

First published in 2016 in India by Juggernaut Books, New Delhi
First published in Great Britain 2017

British Library Cataloguing-in-Publication Data
A catalogue record for this book is available from the British Library.

ISBN: HB: 978-1-4088-8884-1
          TPB: 978-1-4088-8886-5
          EPUB: 978-1-4088-8885-8

2 4 6 8 10 9 7 5 3 1

Typeset by Newgen Knowledge Works (P) Ltd., Chennai, India
Printed and bound in Great Britain by CPI Group (UK) Ltd, Croydon CR0 4YY

MIX
Paper from
responsible sources
FSC
www.fsc.org   FSC® C020471

To find out more about our authors and books visit www.bloomsbury.com. Here
you will find extracts, author interviews, details of forthcoming events and the
option to sign up for our newsletters.

Contents

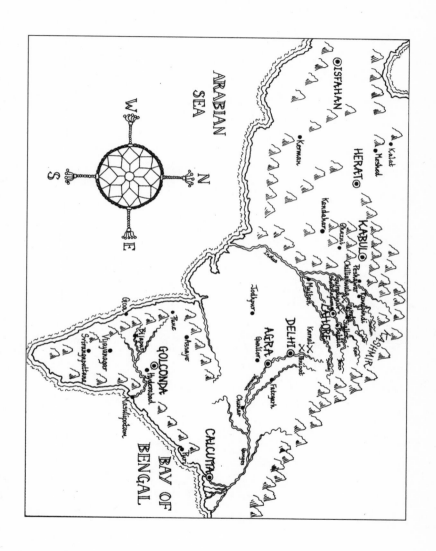

Introduction

On 29 March 1849, the ten-year-old maharaja of Punjab, Duleep Singh, was ushered into the Shish Mahal, the magnificent mirrored throne room at the centre of the great fort of Lahore.

The boy's father, Maharaja Ranjit Singh, was long dead, and his mother, Rani Jindan, had been forcibly removed some time earlier and incarcerated in a palace outside the city. Now Duleep Singh found himself surrounded by a group of grave-looking men wearing red coats and plumed hats, who talked among themselves in an unfamiliar language. In the terrors of the minutes that followed – what he later remembered as 'the crimson day' – the frightened but dignified child finally yielded to months of British pressure. In a public ceremony in front of what was left of the nobility of his court, he signed a formal Act of Submission, so accepting the punitive Terms offered to him by the victorious Company. Within minutes, the flag of the Sikh kingdom was lowered and the British colours run up above the gatehouse of the fort.

The document signed by the ten-year-old maharaja handed over to a private corporation, the East India Company, great swathes of the richest land in India – land which until that moment had formed the independent Sikh kingdom of Punjab. At the same time Duleep Singh was induced to hand over to Queen Victoria the single most valuable object not just in Punjab but arguably in the entire subcontinent: the celebrated Koh-i-Noor, or Mountain of Light.

Article III of the document read simply: 'The gem called the Koh-i-Noor, which was taken from Shah Sooja ool-Moolk by Maharaja Runjeet Singh, shall be surrendered by the Maharaja of Lahore to the Queen of England.'[1] When he heard that Duleep Singh had finally signed the document, the governor general, Lord Dalhousie, was triumphant. 'I had now "caught my hare",' he wrote.[2] He later added: 'The Koh-i-Noor has become in the lapse of ages a sort of historical emblem of conquest in India. It has now found its proper resting place.'[3]

The East India Company, the world's first really global multinational, had grown over the course of little more than a century from an operation employing only thirty-five permanent staff, headquartered in one small office in the City of London, into the most powerful and heavily militarised corporation in history: its army by 1800 was twice the size of that of Britain. It had

had its eyes on both Punjab and the diamond for many years.

Its chance finally came in 1839, on the death of Ranjit Singh, when Punjab had quickly descended into anarchy. A violent power struggle, a suspected poisoning, several assassinations, a civil war and two British invasions later, the Company's army finally defeated the Sikhs first at the bloody battle of Chillianwala on 13 January 1849, and then again, conclusively, shortly afterwards, at Gujrat – both now in the Pakistani Punjab – on 21 February. On 12 March, the whole Sikh army laid down its arms. Veterans shed tears as they dropped their ancestral swords and matchlocks on to an enormous pile of weaponry. One grey-bearded old warrior saluted gravely and, folding his hands, exclaimed: 'Aaj Ranjit Singh mar gaya' (Today Ranjit Singh has truly died).[4]

At the end of the same year, on a cold, bleak day in December, Dalhousie arrived in person in Lahore to take formal delivery of his prize from the hands of Duleep Singh's guardian, Dr John Spencer Login. The glittering white diamond remained in the Lahore Toshakhana, or Treasury, set still in the armlet that Maharaja Ranjit Singh had designed for it. To British eyes, used to modern European brilliant cuts of perfect symmetry, the strikingly irregular profile of the diamond made its shape seem distinctly odd: as its name, the Mountain of Light, suggested, it resembled a large hill or perhaps a huge iceberg rising steeply to a high, domed peak. Around the edge of this dome, the stone had been faceted into a simple Mughal rose-cut, leaving short but irregular crystal tails or azimuths sloping off, like saddles or declivities falling from a Himalayan snow-peak, gently on one side, but more steeply and cliff-like on the other. Login had found a way to compensate for this unexpected shape, and make the diamond glitter for his guests, by displaying it through a peephole, illuminated from below against a black velvet cloth, so enhancing its glitter. Dalhousie duly admired the stone, then took it from Login and placed it in a small, soft, kid-leather bag that had been specially made for the purpose by Lady Dalhousie. The governor general wrote out a receipt, 'I have received this day the Koh-i-Noor diamond,' to which all present then added their personal seals.[5]

Less than a week later, Dalhousie wrote to a junior assistant magistrate in Delhi, asking him to undertake some research on his glittering new acquisition.[6] Theo Metcalfe was not the most diligent or scholarly of East India Company officials. A noisy, convivial figure, he loved dogs and horses and parties, and since his arrival in Delhi had quickly accumulated significant gambling debts. Theo always had a tendency to cut corners and get into what his father described as 'scrapes', but he had a genuine interest in gems. He also had immense charm, and Dalhousie liked the boy. He therefore chose Theo to carry out an important and somewhat delicate task.

The Koh-i-Noor may have been made of the earth's hardest substance, but it had already attracted an airily insubstantial fog of mythology around it, and Dalhousie wanted to establish the solid truth about its history before dispatching it to his queen. Theo was instructed 'to collect and to record as much accurate and interesting information regarding the Koh-i-Noor' as he could from the jewellers and courtiers in Delhi in order to reconstruct as far as possible its history 'while belonging to the Emperors of Delhi, and to transmit it, as soon as he has obtained it, to the Government of India'.[7]

Theo went about his task with characteristically slapdash enthusiasm. But as the gem had been stolen away from Delhi during a Persian invasion a full 110 years earlier, his job was not easy. Even he had to admit that he had gathered little more than bazaar tittle-tattle: 'I cannot but regret that the results are so very meagre and imperfect,' he wrote in the preamble to his report. He nevertheless laid out in full his findings, making up in colour for what he lacked in accurate, substantiated research.

'First,' wrote Theo, 'according to the tradition of the eldest jewellers in the City of Delhee, as handed down from family to family, this diamond was extracted from the mine Koh-i-Noor, four days journey from Masulipatnam to the north west, on the banks of the

Godavari, during the lifetime of the [irrestible Hindu cowherd-God] Krishna, who is supposed to have lived 5,000 years since ...'[8]

Theo's report, which still exists in the vaults of the Indian National Archives, continued in this vein, sketching out for the first time what would become the accepted history of the Koh-i-Noor: a centuries-long chain of bloody conquests, and acts of pillage, looting and seizure. Theo's version of events has since been repeated in article after article, book after book, and still sits unchallenged on Wikipedia today.

Discovered in the deepest mists of antiquity, the great diamond was said to have been looted, probably from the eye of an idol in a temple in southern India, by marauding Turks. Soon, Theo's report continues, the 'jewel fell into the hands of the Emperors of the Ghoree dynasty, and from then successively of the [fourteenth-century] Tughluq, Syed and the Lodhi dynasties, and eventually descended to the family of Timur [the Mughals] and remained in their possession until the reign of Mohammud Shah, who wore it in his Turban'. Then, when the Mughal Empire crumbled under the invasion of the Persian warlord Nader Shah, 'the Emperor and he exchanged Turbans, and thus it became the property of the latter'. Theo went on to claim that it was named Koh-i-Noor by Nader Shah, and that it passed at his death to his chief Afghan bodyguard, Ahmad Khan Abdali. From there it spent nearly a hundred years in Afghan hands, before Ranjit Singh extracted it from a fleeing Afghan shah in 1813.

Shortly after Theo had delivered his report, the Koh-i-Noor was dispatched to England where Queen Victoria promptly lent it to the Great Exhibition of 1851. Long queues snaked through the Crystal Palace to see this celebrated imperial trophy locked away in its specially commissioned high-security glass safe, itself contained within a metal cage. Trumpeted by the British press and besieged by the British public, the Koh-i-Noor quickly became not only the most famous diamond in the world, but also the single most famous object of loot from India. It was a symbol of Victorian Britain's imperial domination of the world and its ability, for better or worse, to take from around the globe the most desirable objects and to display them in triumph, much as the Romans once had done with curiosities from their conquests 2,000 years earlier.

As the fame of the diamond grew, and as Theo's enjoyably lively but entirely unsubstantiated version of the stone's history circulated with it, the many other large Mughal diamonds which once rivalled the Koh-i-Noor came to be almost forgotten, and the Mountain of Light achieved a singular status as the greatest gem in the world. Only a few historians remembered that the Koh-i-Noor, which weighed 190.3 metric carats when it arrived in Britain, had had at least two comparable sisters, the Darya-i-Noor, or Sea of Light, now in Tehran (today estimated at 175 to 195 metric carats), and the Great Mughal Diamond, believed by most modern gemmologists to be the Orlov diamond (189.9 metric carats), today part of Catherine the Great's imperial Russian sceptre in the Kremlin.[9]

In reality, it was only really in the early nineteenth century, when the Koh-i-Noor reached Punjab and the hands of Ranjit Singh, that the diamond began to achieve its pre-eminent fame and celebrity – so much so that by the end of Ranjit's reign pious Hindus were beginning to wonder if the Koh-i-Noor was actually the legendary Syamantaka gem mentioned in the *Bhagavad Purana*'s tales of Krishna.

This growing fame was partly the result of Ranjit Singh's preference for diamonds over rubies – a taste Sikhs tended to share with most Hindus, but not with the Mughals or Persians, who preferred large, uncut, brightly coloured stones. Indeed in the Mughal treasury, the Koh-i-Noor seems to have been only one among a number of extraordinary highlights in the greatest gem collection ever assembled, the most prized items of which were not diamonds at all, but the Mughals' beloved red spinels from Badakhshan and, later, rubies from Burma.

The growing status of the Koh-i-Noor was also partly a consequence of the rapidly growing price of diamonds worldwide in the early and mid-nineteenth century. This followed the invention of the symmetrical and multi-faceted 'brilliant cut', which fully released the 'fire' inherent within every diamond, and which led in turn to the emerging fashion in middle-class Europe and America for diamond engagement rings – a taste which was eventually refracted back to India.

The final act in the Koh-i-Noor's rise to worldwide fame took place in the aftermath of the Great Exhibition and the press coverage it had engendered. Before long, huge, often cursed Indian diamonds began to make regular appearances in popular Victorian novels such as Wilkie Collins's *The Moonstone* and Prime Minister Benjamin Disraeli's *Lothair*, where the plot follows a bag of uncut diamonds acquired from a maharaja.

So it was that the Koh-i-Noor finally achieved in European exile a singular status it had never achieved before leaving Asia. Today, tourists who see it in the Tower of London are often surprised by its small size, especially when compared to the two much larger Cullinan diamonds kept in the same showcase: at present it is in fact only the ninetieth biggest diamond in the world.[10]

Remarkably, however, the Koh-i-Noor retains its fame and status and is once again at the centre of international dissension, as the Indian government – among others – calls for the gem's return. Even then, Indian officials cannot seem to make up their mind about the Koh-i-Noor's perennially foggy history: in April 2016, the Indian solicitor general, Ranjit Kumar, told the Indian Supreme Court that the Koh-i-Noor had been given freely to the British in the mid-nineteenth century by Maharaja Ranjit Singh, and had been 'neither stolen nor forcibly taken by British rulers'. This was by any standards a strikingly unhistorical statement – Ranjit Singh had been ten years dead in 1849, so could only have made this gift by Ouija board or astral projection – and the statement is all the odder given that its surrender to Lord Dalhousie in 1849 is about the one aspect of the diamond's history not in dispute. In the recent past, Pakistan, Iran, Afghanistan and even the Taliban have also all laid claim to the gem and asked for its return.

One hundred and seventy years after it was written, Theo's anecdotal version of the Koh-i-Noor's trajectory, based on Delhi bazaar gossip, has never been fully reassessed or properly challenged. Instead, the exact opposite has happened: as the other great Mughal diamonds have come to be forgotten by all except specialists, all mentions of extraordinary Indian diamonds in sources such as the *Memoirs* of the Mughal emperor Babur or the *Travels* of the French jeweller Tavernier have retrospectively come to be assumed to be references to the Koh-i-Noor. At each stage its mythology has grown ever more remarkable, ever more mythic – and ever more shakily fictitious.

Yet anyone who tries to establish the facts of the gem's history will find that unambiguous references to this most celebrated of gems are still, as Theo Metcalfe put it, 'very meagre and imperfect' – indeed they are almost suspiciously thin on the ground. For there is simply no certain reference to the Koh-i-Noor in any Sultanate or Mughal source, despite a huge number of textual references to outsized and immensely valuable diamonds appearing throughout Indian history, particularly towards the climax of Mughal rule. Some of these may well refer to the Koh-i-Noor but, lacking sufficiently detailed descriptions, it is impossible to be certain.

In fact, there are actually no clear and unambiguous mentions of the Koh-i-Noor in any historical document before the Persian historian Muhammad Kazim Marvi makes what seems to be the first extant, solid, named reference to the stone in his history of Nader Shah's invasion of India in 1739. This was written as late as the final years of the 1740s, a decade or so after the gem had been taken away from India. Significantly, Marvi's is the only contemporary chronicle, among a dozen or so detailed accounts left by Persian, Indian, French and Dutch eyewitnesses, specifically to mention the great diamond, and to do so by name, although most give detailed lists and breakdowns of Nader Shah's bejewelled loot.

Moreover, far from being a loose, singular gem that the Mughal emperor Muhammad Shah Rangila could secrete within his turban, and which Nader

Shah could craftily acquire by a turban swap – one of Theo's unsourced stories that is still repeated – according to Marvi's eyewitness account the emperor could not have hidden the gem because it was at that point a centrepiece of the most magnificent and expensive piece of furniture ever made: the Mughal emperor Shah Jahan's Peacock Throne. The Koh-i-Noor, he writes from personal observation, in the first named reference to the stone – until now untranslated into English – was placed on the roof of this extraordinary throne which cost twice as much as the Taj Mahal to build. Marvi writes:

> An octagon, shaped like a European hat, with circular brim, had its sides and canopy gilded and studded with jewels. On top of this was placed a peacock made of emeralds and rubies; on to its head was attached a diamond the size of a hen's egg, known as the Koh-i-Noor – the Mountain of Light, whose price no one but God Himself could know! The wings were studded with jewels; many pearls, each the size of a pigeon's egg, were strung on wire and attached to the pillars supporting the throne. Everything appertaining to this throne was adorned with gold and jewels ... and the ground was covered with a pearl-edged braid ... This throne and its railing were all in pieces, dismantled for transportation, and would be reassembled in order ... The present

writer saw this throne when the victorious armies had left Delhi and proceeded to the capital Herat, when it was, by royal command, propped up within Nader's royal tent, along with two other rare gifts: a diamond known as the Darya-i-Noor, the Sea of Light, and a ruby known as the 'Ayn al-Hur, the Eye of the Huri.[11]

There is one oddity in Marvi's eyewitness statement: in earlier accounts, the Peacock Throne is always said to have had not one but two peacocks. Possibly it had been reassembled differently by Nader Shah in Herat? Maybe the peacock containing the Koh-i-Noor had already been removed by the time Marvi saw it, so that Nader Shah could wear the jewel on his arm – as its subsequent owners did? Or did Marvi simply see the throne side-on? Whatever the truth, from the 1750s onwards, the Koh-i-Noor appears to have been detached from the Peacock Throne, and there are an increasing number of references to the passage of the gem – now worn as an armlet – in previously ignored and untranslated Persian and Afghan sources, and then after 1813 in a crescendo of Sikh chronicles and European travel accounts.

From these, and from new work by a team of modern gemmologists led by Alan Hart and John Nels Hatleberg, who have recently used laser and X-ray scanning technology to reconstruct the original form of the Koh-i-Noor before it was recut on its arrival in Britain, it has become possible to write an entirely new history of the diamond. What follows is an attempt to free the Koh-i-Noor for the first time from the fog of mythology which has clung to the stone since many of these stories were first propagated by Theo Metcalfe's report 170 years ago.

In the first part of this book, 'The Jewel in the Throne', William Dalrymple recounts the early history of the Koh-i-Noor. Tracing Indian ideas about diamonds in ancient texts, and through possible medieval and early modern sightings of the gem during Mughal times, to its clear emergence into history following its seizure by Nader Shah, he continues the story via Iran and Afghanistan to Punjab, and the Koh-i-Noor's temporary disappearance at the death of Ranjit Singh. By this time the diamond was more than an object of desire and had instead become a powerful symbol of sovereignty.

Anita Anand continues the Koh-i-Noor's story in the second part of this book, 'The Jewel in the Crown', giving the fullest account yet written of the most contested chapter in the diamond's history: how the Koh-i-Noor was taken from a boy who had lost his kingdom to a colonial power and so reached the British crown and the Tower of London.

The resulting narrative tells a tale not only of greed, conquest, murder, blindings, torture, seizure, colonialism and appropriation through an impressive slice of South and Central Asian history, but also of changing tastes and fashions in jewellery, ornamentation and personal adornment, and different understandings of the role, alchemy and astrology of precious stones. It reveals some unexpected and previously unknown moments in the diamond's history, such as the months the diamond spent hidden in a crack in the wall of a prison cell in a remote Afghan fort, and the years during which it languished unrecognised and unvalued on a mullah's desk, used only as a paperweight for pious sermons.

PART 1

THE JEWEL IN THE THRONE

The Indian Prehistory of the Koh-i-Noor

Until the discovery of diamond mines in Brazil in 1725, with the sole exception of a seam of black diamond crystals found in the mountains of Borneo, all the world's diamonds came from India.[1]

Ancient Indian diamonds were alluvial: they were not mined so much as sieved and extracted as natural crystals from the soft sands and gravels of ancient riverbeds. Originally ejected from the host rocks – kimberlite and lamproite – by primeval volcanoes, they were swept up by water and transported along rivers, until at last they came to rest when the river died, many millions of years ago. Most such alluvial diamonds are tiny, natural octahedral crystals. Very occasionally, however, a diamond as large as a hen's egg would be found. One such was the Koh-i-Noor.

As early as 2000 BCE, tiny Indian diamonds may have been used in polishing tools in ancient Egypt, and they were certainly in common use as abrasives across the Middle East and China by 500 BCE. Soon, diamond crystals were being coveted for their use in rings from the T'ang court through Hellenistic Afghanistan to Augustan Rome.[2] But in their Indian homeland, diamonds were not just valued for their usefulness and beauty: they were believed to be supremely auspicious objects, able to channel planetary influences, and so were given an almost semi-divine status. According to the *Garuda Purana*, a book of Hindu scriptures that reached its final form in the tenth century CE, the demon Bala had agreed to be sacrificed by the gods, and he 'yielded up his ghost for the good of the universe, and, behold, the severed limbs of his sacrificed body, were converted into the seeds of gems'. Heavenly beings, demons and naga snake deities all rushed to collect these gem seeds, and even the 'gods came riding in their aerial cars, and carried away the seeds of gems for their own use, some of which dropped down to earth, through the violent concussion of the air. Wherever they dropped, whether in oceans, rivers, mountains or wildernesses, there originated deposits of those gems, through the celestial potency of their seeds.'

These gems had magical, even divine, qualities: 'some are endowed with the virtue of expiating all sins, or acting as prophylactics against the effects of poison, snake bites and diseases, while there are others which are possessed of contrary virtues'. But the greatest of all gems were diamonds, 'the most effulgent of all precious stones ... Gods are supposed to dwell in a particle of diamond, wherever found, which is possessed of a clear, light shade, is smooth and divested of all threatening traits such as scratches, marks of crow's feet, or cloud-like impurities in its interior.'

The text then goes on to explain the wondrous effects that owning a good diamond can bring to the life of its owner: 'Prosperity, long life, increase of wives and progeny and domestic animals, and the bringing home of a teeming harvest all attend on the use of a diamond well marked in its points, clear in lustre and divested of baneful traits.' The *Garuda Purana* continues:

Dreadful poisons, secretly administered, prove inoperative in the wearer's system and all his possessions enjoy a sort of immunity from acts of incendiarism or erosion by water. The complexion of such a person improves in its glow and all his undertakings become prosperous and thriving. Serpents, tigers and thieves fly from the presence of a person wearing such a diamond.[3]

The *Garuda Purana* is possibly the only known text that imagines thieves flying away from diamonds. Certainly by the time of the *Bhagavad* and *Vishnu Puranas*, a hundred years later, enormously valuable gems were understood to be potential inducements not just to theft, but even to murder.

According to these two Puranas, the greatest of all gems was the legendary Syamantaka, 'the prince of gemstones', sometimes said to be a huge diamond, at other times a ruby, a gem that provoked envy, greed and violence in those who coveted it, exactly as the Koh-i-Noor would do, not in myth but in reality.

The Syamantaka was the brilliant jewel of the sun god, Surya, who wore it around his neck, and thereby gained his dazzling appearance. It was an irresistible object of wonder that everyone coveted – but also the first gem in Indian literature to leave a trail of havoc in its wake. For, according to the *Bhagavad Purana*, 'when worn by a clean man, it produces gold, but to an unclean person, it indubitably proves fatal'.[4] It is therefore the probable origin of a trope which in time would attach itself firmly to the Koh-i-Noor and follow it into English literature: the cursed gem.

In the *Bhagavad Purana*, the Syamantaka jewel came down to earth when Satrajit, the Yadava king of Dwarka, and an ardent devotee of Surya, finally encountered his patron deity while walking along the seashore near Dwarka. Unable to look directly at the god because of the brilliant glare of his radiance, King Satrajit asked him to appear in a less blinding form, explaining that he wished to perceive him with greater clarity. Surya then took the Syamantaka off his neck, and Satrajit knelt down and adored his god, whom he now saw was a surprisingly small figure with a body of burnished copper. 'After Satrajit had duly worshipped him, the divinity said, "Satrajit do you ask for some recompense for your merit?" Satrajit therefore asked for the gem. Surya accordingly gave it to him, as a token of his affection, and went away.'[5]

When Satrajit returned to Dwarka wearing the gem, the townsfolk mistook him for the sun god himself; Krishna alone realised that it was the Syamantaka which was responsible for the dazzling glow that now surrounded him. 'This is not the sun god,' he said, 'but rather Satrajit who is glowing because of his jewel.'

In due course, the jewel passed to Satrajit's brother. Shortly afterwards, he took it with him when he went out into the forest, where he was brutally mauled and killed by the lion he was hunting. The lion then seized the jewel, 'and was about to depart holding the gem in his mouth, when Jambavan, the mighty King of the Bears, slew him in turn, and took the spoil home to his cell and gave it to his son as a gewgaw [toy]'.[6]

When Satrajit's brother failed to return from his expedition, the townsfolk began to gossip: 'They concluded that Krishna had murdered him and appropriated the gem, he having been known before to have coveted it.' Eventually the grieving King Satrajit directly accused Krishna of killing his brother and stealing the Syamantaka. To clear his name, Krishna took a party of townsfolk with him out into the forest, following the trail left by the missing hunter, determined to find out what had happened.

The tracks led Krishna first to the mutilated corpse of the hunter, then to the great cave of the bear king where Krishna announced: 'It is for this jewel, O lord of the bears, that we have come to your cave. I intend to use the jewel to disprove false accusations against me.' But the bear king Jambavan refused to part with the Syamantaka, and a mighty battle took place between the invincible bear king and the beautiful man-god. Only after twenty-eight days of intense combat between the two did Jambavan finally realise that Krishna must be a deity. He bowed down, humbly begged forgiveness and offered Krishna the jewel.

On Krishna's triumphant return to Dwarka with the Syamantaka, King Satrajit – 'hanging his head in great shame' – was so overcome with remorse at having falsely accused Krishna that in recompense he offered him the hand of his beautiful daughter, Princess Satyabhama. It was a happy marriage but the Syamantaka continued to generate envy and bloodshed all around it.

Shortly after the wedding ceremony had been celebrated, three evil brothers, led by Prince Satadhanva, took advantage of Krishna's absence from Dwarka to plan a robbery, intending to seize the irresistibly brilliant gem. One night, they rode to Dwarka, entered the king's palace and killed him. Then they seized the

Syamantaka and escaped from the city. But Princess Satyabhama saw what had happened and fled in tears to her husband, demanding that he avenge his father-in-law and king. This Krishna did, tracking down and eventually killing Prince Satadhava, cutting off his head with his razor-sharp throwing disc, the Sudarshan Chakra.

This mythological trail of greed, theft and bloodshed so closely mirrored the actual murderous history of the Koh-i-Noor that, by the nineteenth century, many pious Hindus began to equate the diamond with the Syamantaka and the legends of Krishna.

The world's oldest treatises on gems and gemmology were written in ancient India, some predating even the Puranas. They often show remarkably detailed 'knowledge of the colour and hiding place of gems'.[7] In many of these early works, the qualities of gems are studied and analysed in great detail, from spinels 'the colour of pigeons' blood', through beryl 'flashing like parrots' wings' to diamonds that 'can fill the room with the fire of the rainbow'. Some of these texts – known collectively as *ratnashastras* – display impressive degrees of gemmological connoisseurship: for example, breaking down rubies into four classes, one of which has ten minutely varying shades, ranging from those the lustre of bees and the colour of lotus buds through to those resembling fireflies or the eyes of a cuckoo, to those the colour of pomegranate seeds, collyrium eyeshadow or the juice of the rose-apple fruit. Detailed information is also given to help the reader determine a fake: to test an emerald, for example, one early text advises the reader to take the gem on a Wednesday evening and stand facing the setting sun. A real emerald will emit green rays towards the holder.[8]

Gems do not just appear in the mythology and manuals of ancient India, they are also an almost obsessive theme in ancient Indian plays and poetry written in Sanskrit, where the jingle of jewelled ornaments is often used to evoke the favourite setting of the palace pleasure garden. Even Buddhist literature, despite its austere embrace of poverty and asceticism, is pervaded with gemmological imagery: gem doctrines, jewel bodies, diamond sutras and heavenly kingdoms and islands made up of jewels and precious stones.[9]

According to an early Tamil text called the *Tirukkailaya-nana-ula*, a lovely woman at the peak of her youthful beauty should never be entirely naked, even in bed; instead her body's beauty should be enhanced with gems:

> She adorns her feet with a pair of anklets
> And stacks her wrists with heavy bangles
> Thickly encrusted with gems.
> She decks her hair with an impeccable garland

Strung with gold thread
And enlivens her shapely neck with jewels,
Thus is she a match for Shri herself.[10]

This preference for bare, bejewelled bodies was shared throughout India. Many centuries later, the poet Keshavdas (1555–1617), who wrote the deeply sensuous *Kavi-priya*, or Poet's Delight, in the court of Orchha, just to the south of Agra, expresses similar ideas and is explicit that a woman's naked and unornamented body is uninteresting and unerotic compared to one hung with jewels: 'A woman may be noble, she may have good features. She may have a nice complexion, be filled with love, be shapely. But without ornaments, my friend, she is not beautiful. The same goes for poetry.'[11]

Early Indian sculpture shows the centrality of jewellery to Indian courtly life. In many ancient Indian courts, jewellery rather than clothing was the principal form of adornment and a visible sign of court hierarchy, with strict rules being laid down to establish which rank of courtier could wear which gem in which setting. Indeed in the earliest book of Indian statecraft, Kautilya's *Arthasastra*, written between the second century BCE and the third century CE, gemmology and the state's management of its gems are given an entire chapter – 'On Mines and Precious Stones' – alongside topics such as diplomacy, 'Rules for the Envoy', war, 'Misappropriation of Revenue by Officers and its Recovery', spies, intelligence and the use of subtle poisons, as well as the employment of skilled courtesans to administer them.[12]

The centrality of gems to ideas of beauty in pre-modern Indian court life is particularly apparent in the art and records of the Cholas of Thanjavur, who dominated the southern peninsula of India from the ninth to the thirteenth centuries. Here every queen and goddess sculpted in bronze is shown bare-breasted, but covered in a fabulous profusion of jewelled ornaments. On the walls of the temples are inscribed detailed lists of all the jewellery donated by such queens and their consorts, such as that which still lines the walls of the Great Temple at Thanjavur, recording the donation of Queen Kundavai, the sister of Rajaraja, the greatest of the Chola emperors, around 1010. She gave 'One sacred girdle adorning the hips, containing gold weighing 521.9 grams. Six hundred and sixty seven large and small diamonds with smooth edges set into it ... Eighty three large and small rubies, twenty two *halahalam* rubies, twenty small rubies, nine bluish rubies, ten unpolished rubies. Two hundred and twelve pearls ...'[13] The list of donated gems continues for several yards.

The quality and sheer quantity of jewels worn in pre-modern India is something that all visitors commented on, and all invaders coveted. The greatest poet of the Delhi Sultanate, Amir Khusrau (1253–1325), makes clear the allure held by the rich temples of India in his *Khazain al-Futuh*, or Treasures of Victory, composed for Sultan Alauddin Khalji (r.1296–1316). In one passage he describes the captured treasury of one temple:

> The diamonds were of such colour that the sun would have to stare hard for ages before the like of them is made in the factory of the rocks. The pearls glistened so brilliantly that the brow of the clouds will have to perspire for years before such pearls again reach the treasury of the sea. For generations the mines will have to drink blood in the stream of the sun before rubies such as these are produced. The emeralds were of water so fine that if the blue sky broke itself into fragments, none of its fragments would equal them. Every diamond sparkled brightly, it seemed as if it was a drop fallen from the sun. As to the other precious stones, their lustre eludes description just as water escapes from a broken pot.[14]

In a similar vein, Abdur Razzaq Samarqandi, the fifteenth-century ambassador sent to southern India by the Timurid ruler Shah Rukh of Herat, describes wide-eyed the gems he saw everywhere in the capital of Vijayanagara. This last great southern Indian empire

succeeded to much of the territories of the Cholas
between the fourteenth and sixteenth centuries, and
did so in some style, according to Samarqandi. He was
astonished by the remarkable profusion of jewellery
worn by men and women of every social class and by
the sophistication of the jewellers who dealt in such
gems: stalls selling pearls, rubies, emeralds and diamonds were, he says, everywhere on view.

Passing through gardens and orchards bubbling
with runnels of clear water and 'canals formed of
chiselled stone, polished and smooth', Abdur Razzak
was taken to an audience with the king, who wore 'a
necklace made of pearls of beautiful water and other
splendid gems ... on which a jeweller's intellect would
have found it difficult to put a price'. The throne, he
writes, 'was of an extraordinary size, made of gold
inlay encrusted with beautiful jewels and ornaments
with exceeding delicacy, dexterity and artistic refine-
ment ... It is probable that in all the kingdoms of the
world, the art in inlaying precious stones is nowhere
better understood than in this country.'[15]

Vijayanagara was also the supposed location of the
largest diamonds in India, according to one of the very
first treatises on the subject written by a European –
the remarkable Portuguese doctor and natural philos-
opher Garcia da Orta (1501–68), who was the author
of the third book ever printed in India, *Colloquies
on the Simples and Drugs of India*, published in Goa

in 1561.[16] Da Orta was a man of wonderfully broad interests, and his subjects range from the Indian names of chessmen and the different varieties of mangoes through the treatment of cholera and curious stories about the proclivities of cobras and mongooses, to the effects of *bhang* (cannabis).

Unknown to his rigorously Catholic compatriots, da Orta was in fact a practising Sephardic Jew, whose real Hebrew name was Avraham ben Yitzhak.[17] At a time when Jewish converts to Christianity were beginning to face persecution and torture in Portugal and Spain, da Orta took the decision to leave his position as Professor of Medicine at Lisbon University in 1534 and emigrate to the new colony of Goa specifically in order to escape the anti-Semitic attentions of the Inquisition. In the late 1540s when the Inquisition followed him to Goa, he took up a position beyond their reach as personal physician to Sultan Burhan Nizam Shah of Ahmadnagar (1503–53). In the end, his efforts to escape the Inquisitors proved successful, at least during his lifetime: the Inquisition caught up with him only after his death, when in 1580 his remains were posthumously disinterred and incinerated, then thrown into the Mandovi river in Goa.[18]

Deeply learned, scientifically rigorous, polyglot and fluent in Hebrew and Arabic, and so able to access the learning of India's Muslim *hakim*s (doctors) as well as that of his own Jewish community, da Orta gathered an unprecedented amount of information about the medical practices and natural sciences of India, and devoted an entire chapter of his work to clarifying the truth about diamonds.[19]

He begins by exposing 'many fables concerning diamonds and the working of diamond mines'. It is not true, he says, that you cannot smash a diamond with a hammer: 'they are easily broken'. Nor is it true, as Marco Polo and the Alexander Romance had alleged, 'that they are guarded by serpents that may not be extracted, and that people who own the mines throw poisoned meat in a certain place for the serpents to eat, while they in another place extract the diamonds at their will'. Diamonds are not poisonous, he continues, nor can they be used to test a man's fidelity by placing one beneath a woman's pillow: 'when she is asleep she will embrace her husband if he has been faithful, and if contrary avoid him – a thing I am unable to believe'.

After laying out at length the actual properties of diamonds, da Orta goes on to explain where they can be sourced. It is in Vijayanagara, he says, that India's biggest diamonds were to be found, and the richest deposits are located within its territories: 'there are two or three rocks which yield much to the King of Vijayanagara'.

The diamonds yield great income to the King of this country. Any stone which has a weight over 30 carats belongs to the King. For this a guard is placed over the diggers, and if any person is found with any, he is taken with all that he has ... The Gujaratis buy them and take them for sale in Vijayanagara, where these diamonds fetch a high price, especially those they call naifes, being those which nature has worked; while the Portuguese value those most which have been polished. The Canarese say that just as a virgin is more valuable than a woman who is not one, so this naife diamond is worth more than a cut one.

Da Orta then discusses the issue of unusually large diamonds:

As to what they say, that no diamond is larger than a filbert [hazelnut], neither Pliny nor any other writer is at fault. They only speak of what they have seen. The largest I have seen in this land was 140 carats, another 120, and I have heard that a native of this land had one of 250 carats. I know he had it, and made a large profit, though he denied it. Many years ago I heard from a person worthy of credit that he saw one in Vijayanagara the size of a small hen's egg.

Is this an early reference to the Koh-i-Noor, and did the great diamond once grace the throne room of the kings of Vijayanagara before finding its way to Delhi? It is quite possible, but, equally, unprovable.

2

The Mughals and the Koh-i-Noor

In April 1526, Zahir-ud-din Babur, a dashing Turco-Mongol poet-prince from Ferghana in Central Asia, descended the Khyber Pass with a small army of hand-picked followers. He brought with him some of the first cannon and muskets seen in northern India. With this new military technology, he defeated and killed the Delhi sultan Ibrahim Lodhi, at the battle of Panipat; a year later, he crushed the Rajputs. He then established his capital at Agra, where he began to build a series of irrigated paradise gardens.

This was not Babur's first conquest. He had spent much of his youth throneless, living with his companions from day to day, rustling sheep and stealing food. Occasionally he would capture a town – he was fourteen when he first took Samarkand and held it for four months. Generally he lived in a tent, a peripatetic existence that, although sanctioned by Timurid tradition, seemed to have little appeal to him. 'It passed through my mind', he wrote, 'that to wander from mountain to mountain, homeless and helpless, has little to recommend it.'¹

Babur not only established the Mughal dynasty, which ruled northern India for 330 years, he also wrote one of the most fascinating diaries ever written by a great ruler: the *Baburnama*. In its pages, he opens his soul with a frankness and lack of inhibition similar to Pepys, comparing the fruits and animals of India and Afghanistan with as much inquisitiveness as he records his impressions of the difference between falling in love with men and with women, or the differing pleasures of opium and wine.² Here he also makes reference to an extraordinary diamond that was among the wonderful richness of gems he had captured during his conquests.

As he noted in the *Baburnama*, when his son Humayun captured the family of Bikramjit, the raja of Gwalior, who were in Agra at the time of Ibrahim Lodhi's defeat, 'they made him a voluntary offering of a mass of jewels and valuables, amongst which was the famous diamond which [Sultan] Ala' ud-Din [Khalji] must have brought. Its reputation is that every appraiser has estimated its value at two and half days' food for the whole world. Apparently it weighs 8 misqals.'³ Another contemporary source, a small treatise on precious stones dedicated to Babur and Humayun, also refers to Babur's diamond: 'No private individual has ever seen such a diamond, or heard of it, nor is there any mention of it in any book.'⁴ These two mentions are often assumed to be early references to the Koh-i-Noor. They may well be – or not: the description is too vague to be certain, and there were clearly several very large diamonds circulating in India at this time.

Either way, Babur's diamond soon left India. Babur died in 1530, only four years after his arrival in India and before he could consolidate his new conquests. His dreamy and somewhat feckless son, Humayun, shared his father's poetic and cultural interests, but he had none of his military genius. He continued to build gardens and spent his days rapt in the study of astrology and mysticism, but his father's conquests crumbled and in 1540, after less than ten years on the throne, Humayun was forced into exile in Persia.

Throughout his diaries, Babur had shown a mixture of pride and extreme irritation with regard to his brave and intelligent but unfocused, unambitious and perennially unpunctual son; even an undertaking as important as the invasion of India was delayed by several weeks by Humayun failing to present himself on time in Kabul. He eventually turned up, three weeks late, which meant the invasion had to take place in the heat of summer. Both in his rule and during his exile Humayun demonstrated the same dreamy and unreliable nature.

Having lost his kingdom, and abandoned even his wives and infant son Akbar in his flight from India, the one asset Humayun kept with him was his glittering booty of gems from Agra. Rumours of this spread, and while passing through Rajasthan the fleeing emperor was approached by an envoy of Raja Maldev of Jodhpur, 'an officer in the guise of a merchant', who asked to buy his most valuable diamond. Humayun would have none of it, sending word to 'remind this purchaser that the likes of this valuable jewel cannot be bought. Either it will fall into his hands by means of glittering sword coupled with sovereign mind, or it will come about through the favour of exalted kings.'[5]

Yet even when his diamonds were all he had left, Humayun still showed a bewildering absent-mindedness, if not outright negligence, with regard to them. In July 1544, on his way to seek asylum at the court of the Safavid emperor Shah Tahmasp, Humayun was saved from potentially catastrophic inattention by the quick thinking of a boy named Jauhar.

Jauhar himself wrote many years later:

It was customary with his Majesty always to carry his valuable diamonds and rubies in a purse in his pocket. But when he was performing his ablutions, he generally laid them on one side. This time he had done so, and promptly forgot them: it so happened that when the king was gone, and the humble servant Jauhar was about to remount his horse, he saw a green flowered purse lying on the ground, and a pen case by the side of it: he immediately took them up, and as soon as he had overtaken the King, presented them. When his Majesty saw these articles he was amazed and astonished, and said, 'Oh my boy, you have done me the greatest possible favour; if these had been lost, I should have been subject to the meanness [*rezalet*] of this Persian monarch: in future please take care of them.'[6]

In due course, the diamonds saved Humayun. Though the staunchly Shia Shah Tahmasp initially gave the Sunni Humayun a cool reception, he was thrilled by the diamonds Humayun presented him with at their meeting. Jauhar recounts:

We remained several days encamped on the hunting grounds, during which time his Majesty ordered his rubies and diamonds to be brought to him; and having selected the largest diamond, placed it in a mother of pearl box; then he added several other diamonds and rubies; and having placed them on a tray, he gave them in the charge of Byram Beg to present to the Persian monarch with the message, 'that they were brought from Hindustan purposely for his Majesty'. When Shah Tahmasp saw these precious stones he was astonished, and sent for his jewellers to value them. The jewellers declared that

they were above all price; on which the Persian sig-
nified his acceptance.[7]

When Humayun eventually returned to India, he did
so at the head of a cohort of Shah Tahmasp's cavalry
which enabled him to recover his throne.

For reasons that remain unclear, however, shortly
afterwards, in 1547, Shah Tahmasp sent Babur's diamond to his Indian Shia ally, the sultan of Ahmadnagar,
one of the rulers of the Deccan. According to Khur
Shah, the ambassador of the rival Sultanate of
Golconda to the Persian court, 'it is notorious that a
connoisseur of jewels valued this diamond at two and
half days' subsistence of the whole world. Its weight
is 6½ misqals [a slightly lower estimate than that given
by Babur himself]. But in the eyes of his Majesty the
Shah, it was not of such great value. At last he sent
that diamond along with his envoy Mihtar Jamal, as a
present to Nizam Shah [of Ahmadnagar], the ruler of
the Deccan.'[8] It seems, however, that while the envoy
delivered the shah's letter, he failed to deliver the diamond, and the shah subsequently tried – and failed –
to have his absconding envoy arrested.[9]

Babur's diamond disappears from the record at
this point, presumably locked in the treasury of some
unknown merchant, noble or ruler in the Deccan: was
it, for example, the exceptionally large diamond, 'the
size of a small hen's egg', that Garcia da Orta heard

had made its way to Vijayanagara? It is impossible to know; indeed it is unclear not only if this much admired and much travelled diamond of Babur is actually the Koh-i-Noor, but also if, when or how it may have re-entered the Mughal treasury.

What is certain is that if it did eventually return to Delhi, it did not do so for at least a generation. Abu'l Fazl, the friend and biographer of the greatest of the Mughal emperors, Akbar, in his 1596 account of the imperial treasury, writes explicitly that the largest diamond in the treasury at that time was a much smaller stone of 180 ratis (1 rati is 0.91 metric carats or 0.004 ounces) – around half the size of Babur's diamond, which weighed around 320 ratis. It was not until much later that a massive diamond, of very similar weight to Babur's, returned to Mughal hands.[10]

The Mughals brought with them from Central Asia a very different set of ideas about gemstones to those then held in India. These ideas derived from the philosophy, aesthetics and literature of the Persianate world. Here it was not diamonds but 'red stones of light' that were given pre-eminence.[11] In Persian literature such stones were prized as symbols of the divine in metaphysics and of the highest reaches of the sublime in art, evoking the light of dusk – *shafaq* – that fills the sky immediately after the sun has set.

As Ferdowsi writes in his great *Shah-Nama*, or Book of Kings:

When the sun gave the world the colour of the spinel,
Dark night set foot on the celestial vault.[12]

Garcia da Orta is explicit that diamonds were not regarded as the pre-eminent gemstone by the Mughals – something which came as an enormous surprise to Europeans. In his *Colloquies*, da Orta has his interlocutor, Dr Ruano, remark that diamonds 'are the king of stones, for [they have] eminence over pearls and emeralds and rubies, if we believe Pliny'. Da Orta, however, corrects him: 'In this country ... they think more of an emerald or of a ruby, which have more value if they are perfect, and size for size, than of a diamond. But as they do not find other stones when perfect and of good water so large as diamonds, it happens that they often fetch a higher price. The value of the stones is no more than the will of buyers and the need for them.'[13]

Abu'l Fazl also gives pride of place to beautifully coloured and transparent red stones in his description of Akbar's imperial treasuries at the end of the sixteenth century: 'The amount of revenues is so great,' he writes, 'and the business so multifarious, that twelve treasuries are necessary for storing the money, nine for the different kinds of cash payments, and three for precious stones, gold and inlaid jewellery.' Rubies and spinels, divided into twelve classes, come first; diamonds – of which there are half the quantity of spinels and rubies – second, and these were kept mixed up with emeralds or blue corundum (sapphires), which the Mughals knew as blue *yaquts*. Pearls are in the third treasury: 'If I were to speak of the quantity and quality of precious stones' possessed by the emperor, he writes, 'it would take me an age.'[14]

The Mughals, perhaps more than any other Islamic dynasty, made their love of the arts and their aesthetic principles a central part of their identity as rulers. They consciously used jewellery and jewelled objects as they used their architecture, art, poetry, historiography and the dazzling brilliance of their court ceremonial – to make visible and manifest their imperial ideal, to give it a properly imperial splendour, and even a sheen of divine legitimacy. As Abu'l Fazl put it, 'Kings are fond of external splendour, because they consider it an image of the Divine glory.'[15]

Moreover, the Mughals were not just enthusiasts of the arts; by the time Akbar's reign was at its height, they also had unrivalled resources with which to patronise them. They ruled over five times the population commanded by their only rivals, the Ottomans – some 100 million subjects, by the early seventeenth century controlling almost all of present-day India, Pakistan and Bangladesh, as well as eastern Afghanistan. Their capitals were the megacities of their day. 'They are second to none either in Asia or in Europe,' thought the Jesuit Father Antonio Monserrate, 'with regards either to size, population, or wealth. Their cities are crowded with merchants, who gather there from all over Asia. There is no art or craft which is not practised there.'

For their grubby contemporaries in the West, stumbling around in their codpieces, the silk-clad Mughals, dripping in jewels, were the living embodiment of wealth and power – a meaning that has remained impregnated in the word 'mogul' ever since. In a letter from the court of Emperor Jahangir to the future King Charles I, Sir Thomas Roe, the first English ambassador to the court of the great Mughal, reported in 1616 that he had entered a world of almost unimaginable splendour. The emperor, he wrote, was:

> clothed, or rather laden with diamonds, rubies, pearls, and other precious vanities, so great, so glorious! His head, necke, breast, armes, above the elbowes, at the wrists, his fingers each one with at least two or three rings, are fettered with chaines of dyamonds, rubies as great as walnuts – some greater – and pearles such as mine eyes were amazed at ... in jewells, which is one of his felicityes, hee is the treasury of the world, buyeing all that comes, and heaping rich stones as if hee would rather build [with them] than wear them.[16]

As Roe realised, Jahangir (1569–1627) was an enormously curious and intelligent man: observant of the world around him and a keen collector of its curiosities – from Venetian swords and globes to Safavid silks, jade pebbles and even narwhal teeth. As well as maintaining the empire and commissioning great works of art, he took an active interest in goat and cheetah breeding, medicine and astronomy, and had an insatiable appetite for animal husbandry. But above all his other interests he was obsessed with gemmology and the beauty of precious stones, and he wore them lavishly on all state occasions – almost as if he was consciously turning himself into a bejewelled object. As the Flemish gem-trader Jacques de Coutre put it when he was admitted to an audience: 'He was seated on a most rich throne, and he had hanging around his neck many precious stones and large spinels, emeralds and all manner of large pearls on his arms, and many large diamonds hanging from his turban. In sum, he had so many jewels that he appeared like an idol.'[17]

Many of the pages of Jahangir's memoirs, the *Tuzuk-i-Jahangiri*, are devoted to his work admiring and collecting the greatest gemstones of the world. This process reached its climax each New Year, or Nau Roz, which Jahangir turned into an annual feast when all the nobles of the court were expected to shower him with gemstones – and he in turn would be weighed against gold and precious stones, which would then be distributed to the populace. The Nau Roz of 1616 was typical. Jahangir wrote:

> On this day the offering of Mir Jamal-ud-Din Husain was laid before me. What he offered was approved and accepted. Among other things was a jewelled dagger which had been made under his superintendence. On its hilt was a yellow ruby, exceedingly clear and bright, in size equal to half a hen's egg. I had never before seen so large and beautiful a yellow ruby. Along with it were other rubies of approved colour and old emeralds. Brokers valued it at 50,000 rupees. I increased the mansab [rank] of the said Mir by 1,000 horse ... Later, I'tmad ud-Daula [the prime minister] presented me with his offering, and I examined it in detail. Much of it was exceedingly rare. Of the jewels, there were two pearls worth 30,000 rupees, one qutbi ruby which had been purchased for 22,000 rupees, with other pearls and rubies. Altogether the value was 110,000 rupees. These had the honour of acceptance ... My son Baba Khurram at this blessed hour laid before me a ruby of the purest water and brilliancy, which they pronounced to be of the value of 80,000 rupees.[18]

And so on for several pages.

A year later, Jahangir records being given one of the largest gems in Mughal history by the governor of

Bihar, Ibrahim Fath Jung. The governor sent to court nine uncut and newly discovered diamonds from his province, one of which is recorded as being 348 ratis, so significantly larger even than Babur's diamond.[19]

Jahangir's passion for gems was one he shared with, and passed on to, his eldest son, Prince Khurram, the future Emperor Shah Jahan (1592–1666). To his father's delight, Khurram became one of the greatest connoisseurs of precious stones of his time. Over and again, Jahangir comments with pride on his son's eye for gems, calling him 'the star in the forehead of accomplished desires, and the brilliancy in the brow of prosperity'. He offers as an example of this an occasion when Jahangir had been given an especially fine pearl and wanted to find a pair for it. Prince Khurram took one look at the pearl and immediately remembered an exact match he had seen several years earlier, which lay 'in an old turban jewel and was of a weight and shape equal to this pearl. They produced the old sarpech [turban ornament] containing a royal pearl and indeed it was of exactly the same quality, weight and shape, lustre and brilliance; one might say they had been shed from the same mould. Placing the two pearls alongside the ruby, I bound them on my arm.'[20]

In due course Shah Jahan's love of beautiful and precious objects outshone even that of his father, as visitors noted. According to Edward Terry, Sir Thomas Roe's chaplain, Shah Jahan was 'the greatest and the richest master of precious stones that inhabits the whole earth'. The Portuguese Friar Manrique reported that he was so fascinated by gems that even when there appeared before him after a banquet twelve dancing girls decked out in 'lascivious and suggestive dress, immodest behaviour and posturing', the emperor hardly raised his eyes, but instead continued inspecting some fine jewels that had been brought to him by his brother-in-law, Asaf Khan. It has recently emerged that after apparently damaging his eyes through excessive weeping over the death of Mumtaz Mahal, Shah Jahan even commissioned two pairs of bejewelled spectacles, one with lenses of diamonds, the other with lenses of emeralds.[21]

It was not, however, just about beauty and luxury. Like the Mughals' miniature-painting ateliers, under Shah Jahan the imperial jewellery workshops were expected to put their work to the service of imperial and dynastic propaganda. A newly discovered sardonyx-hilted dagger that appeared recently on the London art market makes this particularly clear, giving a striking reflection of the imperial aspirations of Shah Jahan and his court: the cartouche reads unequivocally, 'The dagger of the king of kings, the defender of religion and conqueror of the world. The Second Lord of Happy Conjunction, Shah Jahan, is like the new moon, but out of its shining triumphs, it makes the world shine eternally like the rays of the Sun.' To his subjects Shah Jahan presented himself not just as the ruler; he wanted to be thought of as a centre of Divine Light, a sun king, in fact almost a sun god.

———

The largest diamond recorded as entering the Mughal treasury during the reign of Shah Jahan came as a gift from another of the great gem connoisseurs of the period. Mir Jumla was a Persian immigrant to the Deccan, who set himself up as a merchant and gem dealer. According to the Venetian traveller Niccolao Manucci, 'Mir Jumla initially went through the streets from door to door selling shoes; but fortune resolved to favour him, and little by little he rose to be a great merchant of much fame in the kingdom. Owing to his being very rich, with ships at sea, and also a man of much wisdom and very generous, he gained for himself many friends at court ... [and soon] filled various honourable offices.'

He continued to rise – ultimately to the rank of prime minister of Golconda – by presenting to the king and other key nobles valuable gifts of gems, 'jewels and diamonds which he extracted from the mines ... During his government in the Karnatik, Mir Jumla gathered together the great treasures which then existed in that province, in the ancient temples of the Hindu idols. Besides these, others were discovered by

his exertions in the said province, which for precious
stones is very famous.'[22]

The French diamond merchant Jean Baptiste
Tavernier (1605–89) gives a wonderfully revealing – if
chilling – portrait of Mir Jumla at the peak of his power.
Tavernier went to present his salaams one evening, and
found Mir Jumla sitting in his tent at the centre of the
camp in the Deccan countryside.

> According to the custom of the country, the Nawab
> [governor] had the intervals between his toes full of
> letters, and he also held many between the fingers
> of his left hand. He drew them sometimes from his
> feet, and sometimes from his hand, and he sent replies
> through his two secretaries, writing some also himself.
> After the secretaries had finished the letters, he made
> them read them; and he then affixed his seal himself,
> giving some to foot messengers, some to horsemen.[23]

While all this was going on, four criminals were
brought to the door of his tent. Mir Jumla paid no
attention to them for half an hour, but then had them
marched in, 'and after having questioned them, and
made them confess with their own mouths, he remained
nearly an hour without saying anything, continuing to
write and make his secretaries write', as a succession
of officers from the army came to pay their respects.
At this point, a meal was brought in, so he turned his
attention to the four prisoners, calmly ordering one to

have his hands and feet cut off and to be left in a field to bleed to death, another to have 'his stomach slit open and thrown in a drain' and the remaining two to be beheaded. 'While all this passed, dinner was served.'[24]

Throughout the 1650s, the Mughals increasingly focused on seizing the different kingdoms of the Deccan, at least in part so that they could possess the territory which produced the gems they were so obsessed with. In the words of the *Shah Jahan Nama*, the official history of the reign, 'This territory contained mines teeming with diamonds.'[25] At the same time, Mir Jumla fell out of favour with the sultan of Golconda, as rumours spread of his having had an affair with the queen mother. He therefore took the opportunity presented by a Mughal attack to defect to the service of Shah Jahan.

He sealed the pact, on 7 July 1656, by presenting Shah Jahan, within the newly inaugurated Red Fort of Shahjahanabad, with what Manucci describes as 'a large uncut diamond which weighed 360 carats', and what the *Shah Jahan Nama* calls 'an offering of exquisite gems, amongst which was a huge diamond weighing 216 *ratis*'.[26] Tavernier later called this stone 'that celebrated diamond which generally has been deemed unparalleled in size and beauty'. He said it was presented uncut at 900 ratis, or 787 metric carats, and added that it had come from the mines of Kollur (today in Karnataka).

Centuries later, many Victorian commentators identified this diamond both with Babur's diamond, which had disappeared into the Deccan a hundred years earlier, and with the Koh-i-Noor, which had by then come to be seen as the greatest of all Indian diamonds. Yet there is no suggestion in any of these texts that Mir Jumla was claiming to return to the Mughals their greatest family diamond, which had been lost to them since the time of Humayun – a claim he certainly would have made if this were true, given how much he wished to ingratiate himself with his new patrons.

Instead, it sounds as if this huge diamond – which Tavernier explicitly says was presented uncut, and for which our three different sources give widely different but very high weights – was a new discovery, and an unprecedented addition to the Mughal treasury.[27]

In 1628, at the height of his power, Shah Jahan brought the Mughal love affair with precious stones to its climax when he commissioned the most spectacular jewelled object ever made: the Peacock Throne.

Initially, it seems that the commission for a massive solid gold throne 'covered with diamonds, rubies, pearls and emeralds' was given to a French jeweller at the Mughal court named Augustin Hiriart.[28] Although the Mughals liked their diamonds cut differently from their contemporaries in the West – preferring to keep and celebrate the natural weight and shape of a stone rather than cutting to produce the smaller but more symmetrically cut gems favoured in Europe – at this stage in the seventeenth century European jewellers had established a slight technological edge on their Mughal rivals. There are references to emperors and other Indian rulers sending gems via the Jesuits to be cut in Goa, or even in the European merchant colony at Aleppo.[29] Hiriart was by no means the only Western jeweller to have found work at the Mughal court: an Englishman named Peter Mutton was also taken into the imperial *karkhana* (atelier).

Shortly afterwards, however, Hiriart left Mughal service and headed off to Goa, so it was Sa'ida-yi Gilani, an Iranian poet and calligrapher-turned-goldsmith and jewel-master, who started work on the commission afresh. The finished Peacock Throne was finally inaugurated at New Year 1635, on the emperor's return from his holidays in Kashmir.[30]

The Jewelled Throne – as it was initially known – was an object of the greatest magnificence, designed to resemble and evoke the fabled throne of Solomon. The Mughals had long surrounded themselves with the aura of the ancient kings – both historical and mythical – of the Middle East and Iran whom they had read about in the Quran and in epic poems like the *Shahnama*. Drawing on these exemplars, the Mughals claimed that their divinely illuminated kingship and their just rule would bring to the world a golden age of prosperity and peace. For Shah Jahan in particular, Solomon, the exemplary Quranic ruler and prophet king, was both a role model and a figure of identification, and he had himself celebrated by his poets as a second Solomon; Mumtaz Mahal, meanwhile, was praised as the new queen of Sheba.

Accordingly, the Jewelled Throne was made so that anyone who knew their Quran would immediately see it as an echo of Solomon's throne. It had four columns which carried a baldachin (ceremonial canopy), on which were depicted flowering trees and peacocks in gemstones. The columns had the form of tapering balusters, which the Mughals called cypress shaped, and were covered with green enamel or emeralds, to augment their treelike character. Above this were perched either one or, in most accounts, two freestanding figures of peacocks, a reference to the seat of Solomon which according to both Jewish and Islamic texts was decorated with jewelled trees and birds.

The best contemporary account we have of the throne is by the official court chronicler, Ahmad Shah Lahori, in the *Padshahnama*:

In the course of years many valuable gems had come into the Imperial jewel-house, each one of which might serve as an ear-drop for Venus, or would adorn the girdle of the Sun. Upon the accession of the Emperor, it occurred to his mind that, in the opinion of far-seeing men, the acquisition of such rare jewels and the keeping of such wonderful brilliants can only render one service, that of adorning the throne of empire. They ought therefore to be put to such a use that beholders might share in and benefit by their splendour, and that Majesty might shine with increased brilliancy.[31]

Lahori recounts how in addition to the jewels already stored in the imperial jewel-house, 'rubies, garnets, diamonds, rich pearls and emeralds, to the value of 200 lakhs of rupees, should be brought for the inspection of the Emperor, and that they, with some exquisite jewels of great weight, exceeding 50,000 miskals, having been carefully selected, should be handed over to Bebadal Khan [Sa'ida-yi Gilani's later title], the superintendent of the goldsmith's department'.

The outside of the canopy was to be of enamel work studded with gems, the inside was to be thickly set with rubies, garnets, and other jewels, and it was to be supported by emerald columns. On the top of each pillar there were to be two peacocks thick set with gems, and between each of the two peacocks a tree set with rubies and diamonds, emeralds and pearls. The ascent was to consist of three steps, set with jewels of fine water. This throne was completed in the course of seven years at a cost of 100 lakhs of rupees.

Given Mughal tastes, it is not surprising that the one stone that Lahori singled out for mention was not a diamond but a ruby:

> Among the jewels set in this recess was a ruby worth a lakh of rupees, which Shah 'Abbas, the king of Iran, had presented to the late Emperor Jahangir, who sent it to his present Majesty, the Sahib Kiran-i sani, when he accomplished the conquest of the Dakhin. On it were engraved the names of Sahib-kiran (Timur), Mir Shah Rukh, and Mirza Ulugh Beg. When in course of time it came into the possession of Shah 'Abbas, his name was added; and when Jahangir obtained it, he added the name of himself and of his father. Now it received the addition of the name of his most gracious Majesty Shah Jahan.

The ruby would, under various names – the Timur Ruby, the Ayn al-Hur, Eye of the Houri, and the Fakhraj – shadow the Koh-i-Noor and share its fate for the next two centuries. Only very much later, with changing tastes in the early nineteenth century, did the diamond come to be seen as more beautiful and significant than the ruby.

Shah Jahan's reign came to a dramatically premature end in 1658. Late in 1657 the Emperor suffered a stroke, and his son Dara Shukoh took over effective governance. Initially believing their father to be dead, the four royal princes began military manoeuvres that led Aurangzeb, eventually, to stage a skilful coup d'état, deposing his father and imprisoning him in the Red Fort of Agra, in a set of apartments looking out over the Taj.

Aurangzeb had headed north from the Deccan with a battle-hardened army, and defeated his rival brother Dara Shukoh at Samugarh, a few miles from Agra. In 1659, he had had his brother murdered a few days after capturing him. According to Manucci, he then sent his father a reconciliation present. When the old man opened it, it was found to contain the head of Dara.

It was shortly after this that we get one last glimpse of the Mughal treasury in all its glory before the empire collapsed and the Koh-i-Noor left India. In 1665 Jean Baptiste Tavernier was given by Aurangzeb (1618–1707) the unprecedented honour of being shown the highlights of the Mughal treasury. Encouraged by Louis XIV, Tavernier had made five previous journeys to India between 1630 and 1668, with a view to understanding more about diamonds, which he calls 'the most precious of all stones, and the article of trade to which I am most devoted. In order to acquire a thorough knowledge of it, I resolved to visit all the mines and one of the two rivers where diamonds are found.'

In his earlier journeys, Tavernier had brought back enough diamonds to win a baronetcy from Louis but it was only on his final trip that Aurangzeb finally gave his permission for Tavernier to see his private collection. 'On the first day of November 1665,' he wrote, 'I went to the palace to take leave of the Emperor, but he said that he did not wish me to depart without having seen his jewels and witnessing the splendour of his fete.'[32]

Shortly afterwards, Tavernier was summoned to the palace, where he did obeisance to the emperor, and was then ushered into a small apartment within sight of the Diwan-i-Khas.

I found in this apartment Akil Khan, chief of the jewel treasury, who, when he saw us, commanded four of the imperial eunuchs to bring jewels, which were carried in two large wooden trays lacquered with gold leaf, and covered with small cloths made expressly for the purpose – one of red and the other of green brocaded velvet. After these trays were uncovered, and all the pieces had been counted three times over, a list was prepared by the three scribes who were present. For the Indians do everything with great care and composure, and when they see anyone acting in a hurry or irritated they stare at him in silence and laugh at him for being a fool.[33]

Among the stones Tavernier was shown that day was the enormous gem he calls the Great Mughal Diamond and which he says was the gem given to Shah Jahan by Mir Jumla: 'The first piece that Akil Khan (Chief Keeper of the King's jewels) placed in my hands was the great diamond, which is rose cut, round and very high on one side. On the lower edge there is a slight crack, and a little flaw in it. Its water is fine, and weighs 286 [metric] carats.' He also mentions that the stone had been badly cut since Mir Jumla gifted it, and that thanks to the incompetence of the man responsible, Hortensio Borgio, the stone had lost much of its original astonishing size. Tavernier also saw two other great diamonds, one of which was a flat, pink stone in a table cut, which he calls the Great Table Diamond, and which from his drawing is clearly the major portion of the Darya-i-Noor, now in Tehran.[34]

Was the Great Mughal diamond the Koh-i-Noor? In the nineteenth century it was assumed that it must be, but most modern scholars are now convinced that the Great Mughal is actually the Orlov, which with its higher, more rounded dome looks much more like Tavernier's sketch of the Great Mughal. Moreover, the Orlov and the Great Mughal have the same type of cut, and the same pattern of facets.[35] None of the other stones seen by Tavernier looks at all like the Koh-i-Noor either.

How is it possible that Tavernier failed to see the Koh-i-Noor when the emperor explicitly gave permission for him to see his greatest gems? There are two possibilities. One is that the Koh-i-Noor was at this stage still in the collection of Shah Jahan, who in 1665 remained under house arrest in his apartments in the Red Fort of Agra. It is known from several sources, including Manucci and the *Shah Jahan Nama*, that the deposed emperor had not handed over all his personal diamond collection to his usurping son; indeed Aurangzeb got his hands on Shah Jahan's favourite gems only after his death.

But more probably, if Marvi's eyewitness account of Nader Shah's seizure of the Peacock Throne in 1750 is to be believed, the Koh-i-Noor was not in the imperial treasury because it was already lodged beyond Tavernier's close inspection, glittering on the top of the Peacock Throne, attached to the head of one of the peacocks which surmounted it. Tavernier certainly saw the Peacock Throne from a distance, and he describes the diamonds which covered it, but it seems he did not get close enough to see the stupendous size of the gems on its roof.

Was the Koh-i-Noor Babur's diamond? The weights are approximately right, and it looks on balance the most plausible and certainly the most seductive theory as to the origins of the Koh-i-Noor. However, given the absence of a full description of Babur's diamond, or an account of the gem's passage from the Deccan back into the Mughal treasury, until further evidence is uncovered in some forgotten Persian source, the mystery remains unsolved. Frustrating as it is, we simply do not know for sure the origin of the Koh-i-Noor and have no hard information about when, how or where it entered Mughal hands. We only know for sure how it left.

3

Nader Shah: The Koh-i-Noor
Goes to Iran

In January 1739, the Mughal Empire was still the wealthiest state in Asia. Almost all of the subcontinent was ruled from the Peacock Throne – with the Koh-i-Noor still glittering from one of the peacocks on its roof. Although it had been in decline for half a century, and often racked by internal conflict, the Mughal Empire still ruled most of the rich and fertile lands from Kabul to the Carnatic. Moreover, its decadent and sophisticated capital, Delhi, with two million inhabitants, larger than London and Paris combined, was still the most prosperous and magnificent city between Ottoman Istanbul and Imperial Edo (Tokyo).

Ruling this vast empire was the pleasure-loving Emperor Muhammad Shah – called Rangila, or Colourful, the Merry-Maker. He was an aesthete, much given to wearing tight, feminine *peshwaz* (long, open-fronted outer garment) and shoes embroidered with pearls; he was also a discerning patron of music and painting. It was Muhammad Shah who brought the sitar and the tabla out of the folk milieu and into his court. He revived the Mughal miniature atelier and employed master artists such as Nidha Mal and Chitarman, whose greatest works show bucolic scenes of Mughal court life: the palace Holi celebrations bathed in fabulous washes of red and orange; scenes of the emperor going hawking along the banks of the Yamuna or visiting his walled pleasure gardens; or, more rarely, holding audiences with his ministers amid the flower beds and parterres of the Red Fort.

In reaction to the harsh Islamic puritan militarism of Aurangzeb's era, under Muhammad Shah (1702–48), from about 1720 Delhi saw an explosion of unrestrainedly sensual art, dance, music and literary experimentation, with the city's poets writing some of the most unblushingly amorous Indian poetry to be composed since the end of the classical period a millennium earlier. This was the age of the great courtesans, whose beauty and notorious coquettishness were celebrated across South Asia. Ad Begum would turn up stark naked at parties, but so cleverly painted that no one would notice: 'she decorates her legs with beautiful drawings in the style of pyjamas instead of actually wearing them; in place of the cuffs she draws flowers and petals in ink exactly as is found in the finest cloth of Rum'. Her great rival, Nur Bai, was so popular that every night the elephants of the great Mughal *omrah*s completely blocked the narrow lanes outside her house, yet even the most senior nobles had 'to send a large sum of money to have her admit them ... whoever gets enamoured of her gets sucked into the whirlpool of her demands and brings ruin in on his house ... but the pleasure of her company can only be had as long as one is in possession of riches to bestow on her'.[1]

As in Restoration England, this sensuality was directly reflected in the painting of the period, which revelled in images of pleasure, partying and lovemaking: one celebrated image even showed the emperor *in flagrante* with one of his concubines – perhaps a muchneeded attempt to stress the potency and virility of a sovereign who was widely rumoured to be impotent.

But, whatever the situation in his bedroom, Muhammad Shah Rangila was certainly no warrior on the battlefield. He survived in power by the simple ruse of giving up any pretence of ruling: in the morning he watched partridge and elephant fights; in the afternoon he was entertained by jugglers, mime artists and conjurors. Politics he wisely left to his advisers and regents – though he was very skilful in keeping the revenue flowing in from the districts.

The dwindling of the power of the emperor was a process that had been going on for some time, as the empire began to decline after the death of Aurangzeb in 1707. Since then, three emperors had been murdered;

one was, in addition, first blinded with a hot needle; the mother of the third was strangled and the father of another forced off a precipice on his elephant. A fourth was strangled and thrown down the stairs. At one point during the reign of Emperor Farrukh Siyyar (1685–1719) his regents, the Syed brothers, had been so desperate for cash that they began to pick precious stones from the interior of the Peacock Throne and sell them off for cash to the Delhi moneylenders. The most magnificent stones of all – the Koh-i-Noor and the Timur Ruby – remained in place, however.

As Muhammad Shah's reign progressed, power ebbed slowly away from Delhi, and the Mughal emperor's regional governors increasingly began to take their own decisions on important matters of politics, economics, internal security and self-defence. Two rival regional strongmen in particular established their own discrete spheres of influence, and emerged as virtually autonomous rulers: Sa'adat Khan, the nawab of Avadh, became the main powerbroker in the north, with his base at Faizabad in the heart of the Gangetic plains; while to the south, Nizam ul-Mulk established himself as master of the Deccan, based in Aurangabad. The association of both men with the imperial court, and their loyalty to the emperor, was increasingly effected on their own terms and in their own interests. Both men would found dynasties that dominated India for a hundred years. They were deadly rivals, and their rivalry would soon prove fatal for the Mughal state they professed to serve.

In addition to sharing his sovereignty with two over-mighty governors, it was Muhammad Shah's ill fate to have as his immediate western neighbour the aggressive Persian-speaking warlord Nader Shah. Nader was the son of a humble shepherd who had risen rapidly in the army thanks to his remarkable military talents. He was as tough, humourless, ruthless and efficient a figure as Muhammad Shah was light-hearted, artistic, chaotic yet refined.

The finest pen portrait that survives of Nader was written by an urbane French Jesuit, Père Louis Bazin, who became Nader's personal physician. Bazin both admired and was horrified by the illiterate, brutal yet complex and commanding man he had agreed to take care of. The Jesuit wrote:

In spite of his humble birth, he seemed born for the throne. Nature had given him all the great qualities that make a hero and even some of those that make a great king ... His beard, dyed black, was in stark contrast to his hair which had gone completely white; his natural constitution was strong and robust, of tall stature, and his girth in proportion to his height; his complexion was sombre and weather-beaten, with a longish face, an aquiline nose, and a well-shaped mouth but with the lower lip jutting out. He had small piercing eyes with a sharp and penetrating stare; his voice was rough and loud, though he managed to soften it on occasion, as self-interest or caprice demanded ...

He had no fixed abode – his court was his military camp; his palace was a tent, his throne was placed in the middle of weapons, and his closest confidants were his bravest warriors ... Intrepid in combat, he pushed bravery to the limits of rashness, and was always to be found in the midst of danger among his braves, as long as the action lasted ... He neglected none of the means suggested by prudence ... Yet sordid avarice, the unheard-of cruelties which wearied his own people and eventually caused his downfall, and the excesses and horrors to which his violent and barbarous character led him, made Persia weep and bleed: he was at once admired, feared and execrated ...[2]

In 1732, Nader had seized the Persian throne, and shortly afterwards deposed the last infant Safavid prince. Seven years later, in the spring of 1739, he invaded Afghanistan and began besieging Kandahar. During the siege, a poet from Khorasan made the journey to present a poem of praise. He read his verses at dinner to the shah, but Nader liked them so little that he had a court usher take the poet around the camp and offer him for sale as a slave. Unfortunately for

Nader, there were no takers. Nader then asked, 'How did you get here?' The poet replied, 'On a donkey.' Nader then had the donkey offered for sale, while the poet was run out of the camp, to general derision.[3]

Unlike Muhammad Shah, Nader was clearly no great lover of the arts. He did, however, have a keen eye for jewels, and was determined to invade India with a view to replenishing his treasury's stock of Indian gemstones needed to pay his troops – something with which he knew that Mughal Delhi was overflowing.

Even before Nader Shah had taken Kandahar, there were rumours in Persia that he was secretly planning to mount a raid on the treasures of Mughal Delhi, 'to pluck some golden feathers' from the Mughal peacock.[4] Indeed he was already carefully cultivating two minor grievances as excuses to do so: the Mughals had recently given shelter to several Iranian rebels fleeing his tyranny, while some Mughal customs officials in Sindh had seized the effects of an Iranian ambassador and refused to return them. Nader Shah duly sent envoys to Delhi to complain that the Mughals were not behaving as friends, and to demand a full apology; but he received no redress. Advance warnings by Nasir Khan, the Mughal governor of Kabul, that Nader was clearly planning an invasion were also ignored by Muhammad Shah's government in Delhi.

On 10 May 1738, Nader Shah began his march into northern Afghanistan. On 21 May he crossed the border into the Mughal Empire, heading for the Mughal summer capital of Kabul, one of the empire's most strategic cities. In this way he began the first invasion of India since Babur's, two centuries earlier. The great citadel of Kabul, the Bala Hissar, surrendered at the end of June and, with no military resources at his command, there was little the Mughal governor could do to save it. As the Delhi courtier, poet and historian Anand Ram Mukhlis noted, the governor

had often written to Muhammad Shah concerning the want of money [to pay his troops], but none of his representations had been attended to. He now wrote to the effect that he himself was but a rose-bush withered by the blasts of Autumn, while his soldiery were no more than a faded pageant, ill-provided and without spirit; he begged that, of the five years' salary due to him, one year's salary might be paid, that he might satisfy his creditors and have some little money at his command.[5]

Receiving no reply to his pleas, the governor of Kabul decided to make a last stand at the Khyber Pass; but Nader Shah outmanoeuvred him and, using a forgotten trail, managed to encircle the Mughal forces, forcing them into a humiliating surrender. Nader Shah then descended the Khyber. Less than three months later, at Kurnal, 100 miles north of Delhi, he defeated three merged Mughal armies – one from Delhi, a second from Avadh and a third from the Deccan – in all, around 750,000 fighting men, with a force of only 150,000 musketeers.[6]

From the beginning it was clear that the Mughal army, though huge, was little more than an undisciplined rabble. The Dutch East India Company representative in Delhi reported the massive force gathering six miles outside the city, a sea of people 'two miles wide by 15 miles long. If this army were trained after the European model,' he noted, 'it could conquer the whole world. However, there is no order; each commander does as he pleases.' After years of ignoring the army and concentrating on music and art, Muhammad Shah was now paying the price for many years given over to the happy pursuit of pleasure.

In the days that followed it also became clear that the Mughal army was both incompetently led and painfully slow-moving, capable of advancing only five miles a day. 'If the army can defend itself, then Nader Shah has to be very lucky to defeat it,' continued the Dutch report. 'However, one has reason to fear that if the army of the Great Mughal does not put up an orderly defence, Nader Shah will not have too much trouble in defeating it … Many people look forward to Nader Shah's coming, because the Emperor is so weak in governing that nothing is really done. His soldiers

are badly paid, because the Hindu clerks steal everything and therefore are as rich as generals.'[7]

Nader Shah's job was certainly made much easier by
the increasingly bitter divisions between Muhammad
Shah's two principal generals, Sa'adat Khan and Nizam
ul-Mulk. Sa'adat Khan arrived late at the Mughal camp,
marching in from Avadh long after the Nizam had
encamped, but keen to show off his superior military
abilities, he decided to ride straight into battle without
waiting for his exhausted soldiers to rest. Around
noon on 13 February 1739, he marched out of the
earthwork defences erected by the nizam to protect
his troops, 'with headlong impetuosity misplaced in
a commander', against the advice of the nizam, who
remained behind, declaring that 'haste is of the devil'.[8]
The nizam was right to be cautious: Sa'adat Khan was
walking straight into a carefully laid trap.

Nader Shah lured Sa'adat Khan's old-fashioned heavy
Mughal cavalry into making a massed frontal charge.
As they neared the Persian lines, Nader's light cavalry
parted like a curtain, leaving the Mughals facing a long
line of mounted musketeers, each of them armed with
the latest in eighteenth-century weaponry: armour-
penetrating, horse-mounted swivel guns. They fired at
point-blank range. Within a few minutes, the flower of
Mughal chivalry lay dead on the ground.

Sa'adat Khan was wounded, and fought on until he
was captured by the Persians. When he was brought

before Nader Shah and told that his rival, Nizam ul-Mulk, had been promoted to his old offices, he took revenge on his own emperor for what he viewed as a personal betrayal and humiliation, after he had risked his life by heading into battle. He revealed to Nader the immense wealth held in the Mughal treasury and hinted that he should raise his demands for an indemnity and reparations a hundredfold.

A week later, as supplies began to run out in the encircled Mughal camp, Nader invited Muhammad Shah to pay a visit under flag of truce. The emperor accepted, and foolishly crossed the battle lines with only a handful of attendants and bodyguards. Invited for negotiations, and magnificently entertained, Muhammad Shah Rangila then found that Nader simply refused to let him leave. His bodyguards were disarmed, and Nader placed his own troops to stand guard over the Great Mughal. The next day, Nader's troops went to the Mughal camp, and brought over Muhammad Shah's harem, his personal servants and his tents. Once they had gone over, the Persians escorted the leading Mughal nobles across the battlefield to join their emperor. By evening they had begun removing the Mughal artillery as well.[9] The next day, the remaining Mughal troops, now starving and leaderless, were told they could go home.

'Here was an army of a million bold and well-equipped horsemen, held as it were in captivity, and all the resources of the Emperor and his grandees at the disposal of the Persians,' noted Anand Ram Mukhlis. 'The Mughal monarchy appeared to be at an end.' This was certainly the view of the ambassador of the Marathas to the Mughal court, who fled the Mughal camp under cover of darkness and made it back to Delhi by a circuitous route, through the jungle, only to leave the same day, heading south as fast as he could. 'God has averted a great danger from me,' he wrote to his masters in Pune, 'and helped me escape with honour. The Mughal empire is at an end, and the Persian has begun.'[10]

A week later, surrounded by elite Persian Qizilbash troops in their distinctive red headdresses, the two rulers marched towards Delhi side by side, and entered the city together. They made the journey seated on elephant-back, in an elevated howdah. Muhammad Shah marched into the citadel of Shahjahanabad in pin-drop silence on 20 March; the conqueror, mounted on a grey charger, followed on the 21st, the day of Nau Roz, with great fanfare. Nader Shah took over Shah Jahan's personal apartments, leaving the emperor to move into the women's quarters. 'By a strange cast of the dice, two monarchs who, but a short while before found the limits of an empire too narrow to contain them both, were now dwellers within the same four walls.'[11]

The following day was one of the most tragic in
the history of the Mughal capital. With over 40,000
of Nader's soldiers now billeted in the city, many of
them in people's homes, grain prices shot up. When
Nader Shah's soldiers went to negotiate with the grain
merchants at Paharganj, near the present-day railway
station, the merchants refused to budge and a scuffle
broke out. Shortly thereafter a rumour spread that
Nader Shah had been killed by a female palace guard.
Suddenly the mob began to attack Persian soldiers
wherever they found them; by midday, 3,000 Persians
had been killed.

Nader Shah responded by ordering a massacre of
the civilian population. He left the Red Fort at sunrise
the next day to supervise this in person. Dressed in
full battle armour, he rode out to the golden mosque
of Roshan ud-Daula, half a mile down the Chandni
Chowk from the Red Fort, to oversee the retribution
from the vantage point of its elevated terrace. The
slaughter began promptly at 9 a.m.; the worst killings took place around the Red Fort in the Chandni
Chowk, the Dariba and the Jami Masjid, where all the
richest shops and the jewellers' quarters were located.
'The soldiers commenced killing, moving from house
to house, slaughtering and plundering the people's
property, and carrying away their wives and daugh-
ters,' remembered the historian Ghulam Hussain
Khan. 'Many houses were set on fire. In a few days the

stench arising from so many unburied bodies, which were filling the houses and streets, became so excessive that the air was infected throughout the whole city.'[12]

In all, some 30,000 citizens of Delhi were slaughtered: 'The Persians laid violent hands on everything and everybody; cloth, jewels, dishes of gold and silver were acceptable spoil.' Many Delhi women were enslaved. Whole *mohallas* (walled neighbourhoods) around the Dariba were gutted. There was little armed resistance. 'For a long time the streets remained strewn with corpses, as the walks of a garden are with dead flowers and leaves. The town was reduced to ashes, and had the appearance of a plain consumed with fire.'[13] A Dutch eyewitness recorded the sickening thoroughness of the slaughter: 'The Iranians have behaved like animals,' wrote Mattheus van Leypsigh. 'It seemed as if it were raining blood, for the drains were streaming with it. As many as 10,000 women and children were taken as slaves.'[14]

Nizam ul-Mulk appealed to Sa'adat Khan to ask Nader to put an end to the violence. Sa'adat Khan ordered him out. That evening, Sa'adat Khan committed suicide by taking poison, horrified at the disaster he had helped unleash. The nizam then went bareheaded, with his hands tied with his turban, and begged Nader on his knees to spare the inhabitants and instead to take revenge on him. Nader Shah sheathed his sword and ordered his troops to stop the killing; they obeyed immediately. He did so, however, on the condition that the nizam would give him 100 crore (one crore = ten million) rupees before he left Delhi. 'The robbing, torture and plundering still continues,' concluded van Leypsigh, 'but not, thankfully, the killing.'[15]

In the days that followed, the nizam found himself in the unhappy position of having to loot his own capital city to pay the promised indemnity. Delhi was divided into five blocks and vast sums demanded of each. 'Now commenced the work of spoliation,' wrote Anand Ram Mukhlis, 'watered by the tears of the people ... Not only was their money taken, but whole families were ruined. Many swallowed poison, and others ended their days with the stab of a knife ... In short, the accumulated wealth of 348 years changed masters in a moment.'[16]

The Persians could not believe the riches that were offered to them over the next few days. They had simply never seen anything like it. Nader's court historian, Mirza Mahdi Astarabadi, was wide-eyed. 'Within a very few days, the officials entrusted with sequestration of the royal treasuries and workshops finished their appointed tasks,' he wrote. 'There appeared oceans of pearls & coral, and mines full of gems, gold and silver vessels, cups and other items encrusted with precious jewels and other luxurious objects in such vast quantities that accountants and scribes even in their wildest dreams would be unable to encompass them in their accounts and records.' Astarabadi went on:

> Among the sequestered objects was the Peacock Throne whose imperial jewels were unrivalled even by the treasures of ancient kings: in the time of earlier Emperors of India, two crores worth of jewels were used as encrustation to inlay this throne: the rarest spinels and rubies, the most brilliant diamonds, without parallel in any of the treasure of past or present kings, were transferred to Nader Shah's government treasury. During the period of our sojourn in Delhi, crores of rupees were extracted from the imperial treasuries. The military and landed nobility of the Mughal state, the grandees of the imperial capital, the independent rajas, the wealthy provincial governors – all sent contributions of crores of coined bullion and gems and jewel-encrusted imperial regalia and the rarest vessels as tributary gifts to the royal court of Nader Shah, in such quantities that beggar all description.[17]

For a month, hundreds of labourers were employed melting down and casting into ingots gold and silver jewellery and plates to facilitate its transport. Meanwhile Nader had accumulated such a profusion of jewels that he ordered his quartermaster general 'to make up arms and harness of every kind, inlaid with precious stones, and to ornament a large tent in the same manner. For that purpose, the best workmen that could be procured were employed a year and two months.'[18]

While all this was going on, Nader maintained a public attitude of paternal politeness and courtesy to Muhammad Shah, who was kept by his side as if he were Nader Shah's assistant and deputy, the two often appearing together in durbar. Finally, on 6 April 1739, Nader, the son of a humble shepherd, married his son Nasrullah to a great-great-granddaughter of Emperor Shah Jahan. As fireworks erupted along the banks of the Yamuna, Nader made a speech giving advice to the Mughal royal family on good government and promised to send a force from Kandahar if Muhammad Shah – the bride's uncle – ever needed help against the Marathas or any other enemy. A month later, on 12 May, Nader held a durbar and placed the crown of Hindustan back on the head of Muhammad Shah, effectively reinstating him as emperor, albeit shorn of his northern provinces to the west of the Indus, which Nader annexed, and ruling now through the grace of the Persian conqueror.

It was on this occasion, according to Theo Metcalfe, that Nader Shah discovered from the great courtesan Nur Bai that Muhammad Shah had hidden the Koh-i-Noor in his turban, and Nader won it by offering to swap turbans, as brother rulers and as a lasting memento of their friendship. It was then, according to Theo, that the great diamond gained its name – the Koh-i-Noor or Mountain of Light – as Nader held the stone in his hand, awestruck. Sadly, however, the story – wonderful as it is – is not referred to by any of the many contemporary sources, and appears only in much later accounts dating from the mid-nineteenth century onwards. It is almost certainly a myth, though one source, a Mughal courtier named Jugal Kishore, does mention Nader giving Muhammad Shah his own turban ornament, which was attached to the feather of an eagle, an act that may lie at the root of the myth.[19]

Instead, the one contemporary story about Nur Bai and Nader Shah has a rather more salty flavour. According to an eyewitness, Abdul Karim, a Kashmiri soldier who had enlisted with the Persian army, Nader was so taken by Nur Bai's dancing that he offered her half his fortune if she returned to Persia with him. Nur Bai was horrified and promptly took to her bed, claiming that she was too ill and feverish to leave Delhi. Asked afterwards why she had not taken advantage of Nader's generosity and gained access to his unlimited wealth, she is alleged to have replied that if she had slept with Nader, or gone off with him to Persia, 'I should feel as if the flower of my cunt had been complicit with his massacres.'[20]

On 16 May, after fifty-seven catastrophic days in Delhi, Nader Shah finally left the city, carrying with him the accumulated wealth of eight generations of imperial Mughal conquest. The greatest of all his winnings was the Peacock Throne, in which was still embedded both the Koh-i-Noor and the Timur Ruby.[21] The loot was loaded on to '700 elephants, 4,000 camels and 12,000 horses carrying wagons all laden with gold, silver and precious stones'.[22]

There was a haemorrhage of booty during the first weeks of the retreat, 'jettisoned by the wayside or carried off by the bare-bottomed peasants of the area', according to Nader Shah's court historian Astarabadi.[23] As the army passed over the bridge across the Chenab, every soldier was searched and, in order to avoid confiscation, many buried their treasures or tipped the gold and gems into the river, hoping to come back and retrieve their loot later. One camel loaded with jewels took fright and plunged into the river. Other pack animals carrying priceless loads of jewels and solid gold were lost fording the monsoon floodwaters, or fell down steep cliffs as the army wound its way through the Hindu Kush. But most of the extraordinary loot Nader Shah took from Delhi made it back to Khorasan, and was lost to South Asia for ever.

According to the Kashmiri soldier Abdul Karim, Nader Shah's 'own treasure, the jewel office, and the

Peacock Throne he sent to Herat'. On arrival the treasures were put on display, including:

> vessels richly inlaid with precious stones, jewelled horse harnesses, sword sheathes, quivers, shields, spear cases, and maces; and the fabulous tent Nader had had lined with jewels. The tent was ordered to be pitched in the Dewan Khaneh, in which were placed the *Tukht Taoussee*, or Peacock Throne, brought from Dehly, another jewelled throne known as the *Tukht Nadery*, along with the thrones of several other conquered monarchs. Publication was made by beat of the drum throughout the city and the camp, that all persons had liberty to come to his magnificent exhibition, such as never had been seen in any age or country.
>
> Its beauty and magnificence are beyond description. The outside of the tent was covered with fine scarlet broadcloth, the lining was of violet coloured satin, upon which were representations of all the birds and beasts in creation, with trees and flowers, the whole made of pearls, diamonds, rubies, emeralds, amethysts and other precious stones; and the tent poles were decorated in like manner.
>
> On both sides of the Peacock Throne there was a screen, upon which were the figures of two angels in precious stones. The roof of the tent consisted of seven pieces, and when it was transported to any

place, two of these pieces packed in cotton, were put into a wooden chest, two of which were a sufficient load for an elephant; and the screens filled another chest. The walls of the tent, the tent poles and the tent pins, which were of massy gold, loaded five more elephants; so that the carriage of the whole required seven elephants. This magnificent tent was displayed on all festivals in the Dewan Khaneh in Herat, during the remainder of Nader Shah's reign.[24]

Nader Shah's reign did not, however, last much longer. Two years later, on 15 May 1741, Nader was riding in the company of his women and harem eunuchs up a narrow wooded valley through the Alborz Mountains above Tehran when there was a loud report from an unseen musket. A lead slug grazed Nader's arm and hit his thumb where he was holding the reins, before plunging into the neck of his horse, killing it, and throwing the shah to the ground. In the weeks that followed, Nader became convinced that his own son and heir, Reza Qoli, had paid the marksman. He therefore ordered that Reza should be blinded, and his eyes brought to him on a platter. When it had been done, Nader looked at them and began to cry, shaking with grief, turning to his courtiers and screaming: 'What is a father? What is a son?'[25]

After this, the heartbroken and increasingly paranoid monarch descended rapidly into madness.[26]

Wherever he went, men were tortured and mutilated. The innocent were punished as cruelly as the guilty. Mass executions and grisly towers of severed heads began to mark the passage of his army.[27]

It was in 1746 that Père Bazin entered Nader's service. The two men had originally been introduced by the British East India Company representative at Isfahan which, following Nader's return from campaign in Central Asia, looked less like his capital city and more like 'a city which had been taken by assault and then given up to the fury of the conquerors'.

Each time the Jesuit left the royal palace he would pass the bodies of at least thirty men who had been murdered by Nader's soldiers or strangled on Nader's orders. Others were thrown into fires or had their severed heads erected in the grisly pyramids that marked the stages of Nader's progress: 'He was the terror of the Ottoman Empire, the conqueror of India, and master of Persia and of Asia,' wrote Père Bazin. 'He was respected by his neighbours, feared by his enemies, and lacked only the affection of his subjects.'

Nader was now in his early fifties, but was sick, probably with some sort of liver infection, and looked much older. In late March, Nau Roz, 1747, Bazin joined the royal camp at Kerman on its march through the barren wastes of the Dasht-e-Lut desert, and by

19 June they were approaching Kalat, in Khorasan, where what remained of Nader's Indian treasures were stored. Bazin was dazzled. 'Nothing could equal the riches he had heaped up at Kalat,' wrote the Jesuit.

The magnificence of his tents was way beyond anything that history relates about the luxury of the ancient monarchs of Asia.

One especially, embroidered with flowers on a gold ground, encrusted with pearls and jewels, was of considerable height and length. His thrones were magnificent; the one he brought back from India [the Peacock Throne] is, I believe, the richest one could ever see: there are columns embellished with diamonds and pearls, the roof is loaded with rubies and emeralds inside and out. His five other thrones were also most rich ...[28]

It was not, however, a happy homecoming. Nader knew that conspiracies were being hatched and that his life was in grave danger, but he was unsure from which direction the blow would come. 'It was as if he had a pre-sentiment of the misfortune awaiting him in this place,' wrote Bazin. 'Over recent days, he had a fully saddled and bridled horse kept ready for him in his harem.'

The most disaffected of Nader's courtiers were two of his relatives, Muhammad Quli Khan and Salah Khan: the former was head of the guards, the latter overseer of his household. Salah Khan caused him less concern, as he had no authority over the armed forces, but Muhammad Quli Khan was a man to fear: decisive, respected for his bravery, with great credit among the officers. He was chief suspect, and he was the one to be forestalled.[29]

Against this threat, Nader deployed a corps of 4,000 Afghan bodyguards: foreign troops who were entirely devoted to his person, and bitterly opposed to the Persians. On the night of 19 June, according to Bazin, he summoned their chief, Ahmad Khan Abdali. This young man he had first encountered rotting in the dungeons of Kandahar when he captured the citadel on the way to take Delhi. He agreed to train him and take him into his army. Abdali owed everything to Nader and was unquestioningly loyal. Nader now told him:

> I am not satisfied with my guards; but I well know your loyalty and courage. Tomorrow morning I want you to arrest all their officers and clap them in irons. Do not spare the life of any who resist! It is a question of the safety of my person – you are the only ones I trust to guard my life!

The Afghan chiefs were delighted at this display of respect and trust, and went to put their troops on the alert. The order, however, could not be kept secret, and it almost immediately leaked out. Within an hour,

Dancing celestial divinity, Chandela, Uttar Pradesh, 12th century.
In many ancient Indian courts, jewellery rather than clothing was the principal
form of adornment and a visible sign of court hierarchy, with strict rules being laid
down to establish which rank of courtier could wear which gem in which setting.

Krishna being given the Syamantaka gem by King Shatrajit. From a Bhagavad Purana manuscript, Rajasthan, c. 1520-40.

Sleeping King Shatrajit, the father-in-law of Krishna, is murdered by Prince Satadhanva in order to steal the Syamantaka. From a Bhagavad Purana manuscript, Rajasthan, c. 1520-40.

Babur with Humayun and courtiers.
From the Late Shah Jahan Album, 1640.

Akbar holding a sarpech.
From the Late Shah Jahan Album, 1640.

Prince Salim holding a jewelled mirror.
By Bichitr, c. 1630.

Jahangir with Asaf Khan.
From the Late Shah Jahan Album, 1640.

Portait of Shah Jahan as a prince,
holding a turban ornament.
By Balchand, c. 1616.

Shah Jahan on the Peacock Throne,
c. 1630.

Aurangzeb on the Peacock Throne,
c. 1680.

Jewellers examining royal ornaments.
By Payag, c. 1650.

Mohammad Shah Rangila making love, c. 1720. This celebrated painting may well been painted to counter the widespread rumour that Muhammad Shah was impotent.

Nader Shah. By Muhammad Reza i-Hindi, one of the Indian artists who Nader Shah took back to Iran along with the Koh-i-Noor and the Peacock Throne.
c. 1740, Isfahan.

Mohammad Shah and Nader Shah in the Red Fort, 1740.

Ahmed Shah Durrani, c. 1755.

Ahmed Shah Durrani, c. 1755.

Shah Shuja, c. 1830 (detail).

Ranjit Singh on an Elephant rides through the bazaars of Lahore, c. 1830 (detail).

the plotters had learned of it. Muhammad Quli Khan alerted Salah Khan and the two chiefs 'undertook not to forsake each other, and signed a document to that effect; they resolved to murder their common enemy that very night, as he had decreed their death on the following day'. They confided their plan to sixty officers who enjoyed their complete confidence, and assured them that they all had an interest in the success of this plan as they were all due to be arrested the following day by the Afghans. All signed the document and promised to turn up at the appointed hour, two hours after midnight, when the moon was setting, to carry out the plot. Bazin appears to have relied on the evidence of one of Nader's favourite women, Chuki, who survived the night and was able to give an eyewitness account of what happened:

Around fifteen of the conspirators were impatient or merely eager to distinguish themselves, and so turned up prematurely at the agreed meeting place. They entered the enclosure of the royal tent, pushing and smashing their way through any obstacles, and penetrated into the sleeping quarters of that ill-starred monarch. The noise they made on entering woke him up: 'Who goes there?' he shouted out in a roar. 'Where is my sword? Bring me my weapons!'

The assassins were struck with fear by these words and wanted to escape, but ran straight into the two chiefs of the murder-conspiracy, who allayed their fears and made them go into the tent again. Nader Shah had not yet had time to get dressed; Muhammad Quli Khan ran in first and struck him with a great blow of his sword which felled him to the ground; two or three others followed suit; the wretched monarch, covered in his own blood, attempted – but was too weak – to get up, and cried out, 'Why do you want to kill me? Spare my life and all I have shall be yours!' He was still pleading when Salah Khan ran up, sword in hand and severed his head, which he dropped into the hands of a waiting soldier. Thus perished the wealthiest monarch on earth.

After the bloody scene, the conspirators and their accomplices spread out through the camp, grabbing everything they could of Nader's possessions and sparing no one whom they suspected of ever having enjoyed his favour ... Twice I found myself in the midst of the fighting, gunfire and flashing swords, but somehow managed to escape.[30]

What happened to the Koh-i-Noor at this point has long been a mystery. But a previously untranslated Afghan source, the *Siraj ul-Tawarikh*, gives the answer:

One of Nader Shah's harem attendants immediately informed [his most senior Afghan general]

Ahmad Khan Abdali. With 3,000 Afghan troopers from the Abdali battalion and other troopers from the Uzbek battalion, Ahmad Khan stood guard until morning over the royal harem. At dawn, he clashed with a group of Qizilbash renegades and evil Afshar who were plundering the royal coffers, routed them, and took charge of all the money and valuables. As a reward for this service, the first lady of Nader Shah's harem gave Ahmad Khan the Koh-i-Noor diamond, one of two diamonds – the other being the Darya-i-Noor – which Nader Shah had seized from Muhammad Shah Rangila and which had been under lock and key in the harem, along with a peerless ruby [the Timur Ruby, which Nader had called the Ayn al-Hur, the Eye of the Houri]. Ahmad Khan then left with the Abdali Afghan cavalry and reached Kandahar in safety.[31]

The Peacock Throne had already been stripped of its two principal gems by Nader Shah, who towards the end of his life had begun to wear both the Koh-i-Noor and the Timur Ruby on his armband. Now the rest of the throne was picked apart by looters. Forty years later an old man told the Scottish traveller James Baillie Fraser that when Nader had been murdered his camp was plundered, and 'the Peacock Throne and the tent of pearls fell into our hands, and were torn in pieces and divided on the spot, although our chiefs themselves little knew their value; many of us threw away the pearls as useless, and our soldiers, ignorant of the value of gold, offered their yellow money in exchange for a lesser quantity of silver or copper'.[32]

It was at this point, presumably, that the other great Mughal gems went their separate ways. The Darya-i-Noor stayed in Persia. It was extracted from Shah Rukh, the grandson of Nader Shah, by especially gruesome torture. But long after Shah Rukh had told his captor, a sallow-cheeked former court eunuch named Agha Muhammad, the hiding place of the Darya-i-Noor and all his other crown jewels, the eunuch continued to torture him, asking him to reveal the hiding place of the one gem he did not have – the Koh-i-Noor. Frustrated in his designs, Agha Muhammad finally had Shah Rukh tied to a chair, and his head shaved. A crown of thick paste was built upon his bald pate. Then in a ghoulish coronation ceremony, reminiscent of an episode of *Game of Thrones*, Agha Muhammad personally poured a jug of molten lead into the crown.

Agha Muhammad was eventually assassinated by two of his personal servants, but not before he had performed an atrocity even more horrific than any carried out by Nader Shah. When he captured the southern Persian capital of Kerman which had revolted against him, he ordered that the women and children should be given over to his soldiers as slaves, and that any surviving men be killed. To make sure no one skimped on his orders, he commanded that the men's eyeballs be brought to him in baskets, and poured on the floor. He stopped counting only at 20,000.[33] Thirty years later, travellers still found hundreds of blind beggars stumbling around the region as living evidence of this atrocity. The Darya-i-Noor eventually found its way into the Qajar and Pahlavi crown jewels, where it remains, in the national bank in Tehran.

Meanwhile, the Great Mughal diamond found its way into the open market in Turkestan, where it was eventually purchased by an Armenian trader who shipped it to the emerging world centre of the diamond market in Amsterdam. Here it was purchased by Count Orlov, a dashing Russian aristocrat and lover of Catherine the Great. On his return to St Petersburg, however, he discovered that he had been supplanted in Catherine's bed by his rival Potemkin, and that in his absence his family had lost their position at court. He presented the gem to Catherine on her name day, full of hope – but while the diamond ended up in Catherine's sceptre, he remained as far from her bedchamber as he had been since his return from his travels. Having gone massively into debt to buy the stone, he soon realised he had ruined himself, and the count ended his days raving in a Russian lunatic asylum. The gem is now on show, amid the other Russian crown jewels, in the Kremlin.[34]

The Koh-i-Noor and its sister, the Timur Ruby, were both kept by Ahmad Khan Abdali on his person. He wore them both in an armlet in Kandahar when he took the throne to create what became in time a new country, and the home of the Koh-i-Noor for the next seventy years – Afghanistan.

4

The Durranis: The Koh-i-Noor in Afghanistan

Ahmad Khan knew he would be followed by his Persian enemies when he fled the violence and chaos of Nader Shah's camp with the Koh-i-Noor. He therefore took precautions, throwing off his 10,000 pursuers by sending a small diversionary force towards Herat, while he headed on to Kandahar, along with the bulk of his troops. The Persians fell for the ruse, and Ahmad Khan reached the safety of his tribal heartlands without having to fight, and with the Koh-i-Noor strapped safely on his arm.

Further good fortune followed. A caravan carrying huge amounts of gold, jewels and treasure intended for the salaries of Nader Shah's troops had just arrived at Kandahar, probably under the guard of Ahmad Khan's Abdali relatives. Ahmad Khan seized the bullion, and immediately put it to use to buy allies and influence. Within a few months, at a grand *jirga*, or gathering of the clans, held at the shrine of Sher Surkh near Kandahar in July 1747, the twenty-four-year-old Ahmad Khan was elected paramount chief, not just of his own Abdali clan, but of all the Afghan tribes. A celebrated Sufi holy man then placed some barley sheaves in Ahmad Khan's turban, crowning him Padshah, Durr-i-Durran – Emperor, and Pearl of Pearls.[1] From this point on, Ahmad Khan Abdali became known as Ahmad Shah Durrani.

Ahmad Shah's first conquests were Kabul and Herat. He then turned southwards, determined, like his hero Nader Shah, to fill his treasury with the plundered wealth of Hindustan. He seized Lahore, Multan and western Punjab, destroying the most sacred temples of the Sikhs at Amritsar and fixing the southern boundary of his empire at Sindh and at the great shrine of Sirhind in Punjab. He also invaded and took Kashmir.

According to the Orientalist and East India Company diplomat Mountstuart Elphinstone:

> For the consolidation of his power at home, he relied, in great measure, on the effects of foreign wars. If these were successful, his victories would raise his reputation, and his conquests would supply him with the means of maintaining an army, and of attaching Afghan chiefs by favours and rewards: the hope of plunder would induce many tribes to join him, whom he could not easily have compelled to submit ... In framing his government he appears

to have had the model of Persia before his eyes. The forms of his court, the great officers of state, the arrangements of the army, and the pretensions of the crown, were exactly the same as those of Nader Shah.[2]

Like Nader Shah, he also looted Delhi and massacred its citizens, leaving it in an even worse state than the Persians had done. Delhi – still much the richest city in Asia – recovered from Nader's visit in a few years. It took half a century for it to recover from Ahmad Shah's successive sackings. The poet Mir had fled from Delhi as Abdali's forces first closed in. When he returned several months later, he found the great capital despoiled and depopulated. He wrote:

What can I say about the rascally boys of the bazaar when there was no bazaar itself? The handsome young men had passed away, the pious old men had passed away. The palaces were in ruin, the streets were lost in rubble ...

Suddenly I found myself in the neighbourhood where I had lived – where I gathered friends and recited my verses; where I lived the life of love and cried many a night. But now no familiar face came to sight so that I could spend some happy moments with them. The bazaar was a place of desolation; the lane was a track of wilderness. At every step I shed tears and learned the lesson of mortality. And the further I went, the more bewildered I became. I could not recognize my neighbourhood or house ... Houses had collapsed. Walls had fallen down. The hospices were bereft of Sufis. The taverns were empty of revellers. It was a wasteland from one end to the other ... I stood there and looked at it in amazement, and was horrified. I swore I would never return to the city.[3]

After eight successive raids deeper and deeper into the plains of north India, Ahmad Shah finally crushed the massed cavalry of the Maratha Confederacy at the battle of Panipat on 14 January 1761, leaving tens of thousands dead on the field of battle. It was his greatest victory: Ahmad Shah along with his Mughal allies, in all an army 60,000 strong, had defeated 45,000 Marathas along a front seven miles long. The battle began with a cannonade that lasted until noon. Around 1.30 p.m., many of the Marathas, who had not eaten for a day, began wandering off in search of food and their line showed signs of cracking. All afternoon, massed Afghan swivel guns and a succession of brilliant cavalry charges cut down the Maratha horse. By evening around 28,000 Marathas lay dead, among them their general Sadashiva Rao, and the son of the head of the Maratha confederacy, the Peshwa.

The next day Ahmad Shah made a triumphant visit to the Sufi shrine of Sirhind with the Koh-i-Noor flashing on his arm.[4] He had won a crushing victory that definitively ended the dream of the emergence of an independent Maratha empire to replace that of the Mughals, and in the long term created a power vacuum that would leave India at the mercy of the armies of the East India Company. In the short term, however, it made Ahmad Shah the unrivalled warlord of his day. At its peak his Durrani Empire extended far beyond the boundaries of the modern Afghan state, stretching from Nishapur in Iran to Sirhind, and encompassing Afghanistan, Kashmir, Punjab and Sindh. After the Ottomans, it was the greatest Muslim empire of the second half of the eighteenth century. Yet though India was at his mercy, he never tried to rule in the place of the Mughals, and his gaze remained fixed on the mountains of the Hindu Kush. A poet as much as a warrior, he was clear where his heart belonged:

> Whatever countries I conquer in the world,
> I will never forget your beautiful gardens.
> When I remember the summits of your beautiful
>   mountains
> I forget the greatness of the throne of Delhi.[5]

Few possessors of the Koh-i-Noor have led happy lives, and while Ahmad Shah rarely lost a battle, he was eventually defeated by a foe more intractable than any army. From early on in his reign, his face began to be eaten away by what the Afghan sources call a 'gangrenous ulcer', possibly leprosy, syphilis or some form of tumour. Even as he was winning his greatest victory at Panipat, Ahmad Shah's disease had already consumed his nose, and a diamond-studded substitute was attached in its place. As his army grew to a horde of 120,000, and as his empire expanded ever wider, so did the tumour, ravaging his brain, spreading to his chest and throat and incapacitating his limbs. He sought healing in Sufi shrines, and consulted both Muslim Yunani *hakim*s and Hindu holy men, but none of this brought him the healing he craved.

We catch a small glimpse of the increasing desperation of Ahmad Shah in the mid-1760s, in the travel account of a peripatetic Indian holy man called Purn Puri. Puri, who had taken a vow to keep one hand in the air for the rest of his life, was on a pilgrimage in Afghanistan when he and his party encountered the army of Ahmad Shah, accompanied by 30,000 of his horsemen near Ghazni. The sadhus had reason to be apprehensive, since Ahmad Shah had destroyed both Hindu temples in Mathura and Sikh holy places in Amritsar, so they sat down to watch the army pass, keeping as inconspicuous as possible. Ahmad Shah, however, spotted them and that evening he sent for the party of pilgrims to join him.

In Purn Puri's words:

[The shah] had for some time been troubled with an ulcer in his nose: he therefore said to me, 'Fakeer! You are a native of India. Do you know of any remedy for this disease?' I told him, I was not acquainted with any remedy to remove that which had been inflicted by God. I also said, 'Recollect, O king! That ever since thou hadst this ulcer, thou hast been seated on the throne.' This assertion met with the king's approbation, as he knew it to be true: he consequently turned to his minister, Shah Wully Khan, and said, 'Let these fakeers be conveyed on the elephants which are going to Herat, and let written orders be granted to them, that they may be supplied with provisions at every village where they may halt, until they reach Herat.'[6]

As Ahmad Shah's health deteriorated, his Durrani Empire began to show the first signs of disintegration. The Sikhs whom he had repeatedly chastised, but always failed to cow, followed Ahmad Shah's armies closely on his last retreat from India in 1767 and, as he headed up the switchbacks of the Khyber, captured the greatest fortress in Punjab, Rohtas, and seized control of the land as far north as Rawalpindi.

By 1772, maggots were dropping from the upper part of Ahmad Shah's rotten nose into his mouth and his food as he ate. Having despaired of finding a cure, he took to his bed at Murgha in the Achakzai Toba hills, where he had gone to escape the summer heat of Kandahar.[7] As one observer put it, 'The leaves and fruit of his date palm then fell to the ground, and he returned whence he had come.'[8]

———

Ahmad Shah's diminutive son, Timur Shah, successfully maintained the heartlands of the empire his father had bequeathed to him. Born in Persia, in Mashhad, he never learned the Pashtun language, preferring Persian, and he disliked the rough manners of many of the Durrani nobles, surrounding himself instead with Persian Sufis, scholars and poets.

He moved the capital from Kandahar to Kabul, keeping out of the turbulent Pashtun heartlands, and looked to the Qizilbash – Shia colonists who had first come to Afghanistan from Persia with the armies of Nader Shah – for his royal guard. Like the Qizilbash, his court was Persian-speaking and culturally Persianised: in many ways Timur Shah looked to his Timurid predecessors – 'the Oriental Medici' as Robert Byron dubbed them[9] – for his cultural models.

A man of great taste and culture, Timur Shah designed the gorgeous pavilions and formal gardens of both the Bala Hissar forts – in Kabul, his summer residence, and Peshawar, where he preferred to spend the winter. He was inspired by the stories of his senior wife, a Mughal princess who had grown up in the

Delhi Red Fort with its courtyards of fountains and shade-giving fruit trees. Like his Mughal in-laws, he had a talent for dazzling display. 'He modelled his government on that of the great rulers,' records the *Siraj ul-Tawarikh*. 'He wore a diamond-studded brooch on his turban and a bejewelled sash over his shoulder. His overcoat was ornamented with precious stones, and he wore the Koh-i-Noor on his right forearm, and the Fakhraj ruby on his left. His Highness Timur Shah also mounted another encrusted brooch on his horse's forehead. Because he was a man of short stature, a bejewelled stepstool was also made for him. Wherever he rode, he would use it to mount his horse.'[10]

Like his contemporary Napoleon, similarly small-sized, Timur Shah was a remarkable general. Though he lost the Persian and Sindhi territories of his father's empire, he fought hard to preserve the Afghan core: in 1778–9, he recovered the rebellious city of Multan, returning with the heads of several thousand Sikh rebels laden on camels. The heads were then put on display as trophies.[11]

In 1791, a conspiracy against Timur's life was hatched in Peshawar and nearly succeeded. The welter of killings which Timur embarked on to destroy the conspirators, and the cold-blooded way he violated an oath to capture one of the ringleaders, cast a cloud over his final years. He died two years later in the spring of 1793, on his way from Peshawar to Kabul, probably from poison: as the historian Mirza 'Ata Mohammad put it, 'The wine server of fate served him the fatal cup.'[12]

Timur left thirty-six children, twenty-four of whom were sons, but he failed to nominate an heir. The prolonged succession struggle that followed his death – with all the competing claimants, many of them provincial governors, energetically capturing, murdering and maiming each other – undermined the last fragments of authority of the Durrani state Ahmad Shah had founded. Under Timur Shah's eventual successor, Shah Zaman, the empire finally disintegrated.

In 1795, Shah Zaman, like his father and grandfather, decided to revive his fortunes and fill his treasuries by ordering a full-scale invasion of Hindustan – the time-honoured Afghan solution to cash crises. He descended the Khyber Pass and moved within the walls of the Mughal fort of Lahore to plan his raid on the rich plains of north India, 'spreading his owl-like shadow over the Punjab'.[13]

By this time, however, India was increasingly coming under the sway of the East India Company. Under its most ambitious governor general, Lord Wellesley, the elder brother of the Duke of Wellington, the Company was expanding aggressively out from its coastal factories to conquer much of the interior; Wellesley's Indian campaigns would ultimately annex more territory than all of Napoleon's conquests in

Europe. India was no longer the source of easy plunder it had once been, and Wellesley was an especially cunning adversary.

Wellesley encouraged the Qajar Persian shah to attack Shah Zaman's undefended rear. In 1799, as the news of the Persian siege of Herat reached him, Shah Zaman was forced to retreat. In the process he left Lahore under the governorship of a capable and ambitious young Sikh, Raja Ranjit Singh. Ranjit's grandfather, Charat Singh, had been among the first Sikhs to build strong forts and defy the authority of the Durranis' lieutenants thirty years earlier. Ranjit Singh had also initially harried Shah Zaman's troops, but as the Afghan prepared to retreat he changed tack. Reaching out to make peace, he helped Shah Zaman save some cannon lost in the mud of the River Jhelum. By charming the shah, and impressing him with his efficiency, Ranjit Singh was given charge of much of Punjab, although he was only nineteen years old, blind in one eye from a childhood bout of smallpox, and commanded barely 5,000 horse.[14] He took charge of the citadel of Lahore on 7 July 1799, and held it for the rest of his life.

In the years that followed, as Shah Zaman tried to maintain his fracturing empire, it was Ranjit Singh who would slowly prise the lucrative eastern provinces of the Durrani Empire from his former overlord and take his place as the dominant power, eventually

ruling not just Punjab, but all the lands from Peshawar
to the borders of Sindh.

————

As the Sikhs consolidated their power, and as Durrani
Afghanistan retreated into tribal civil war, 800 years of
history – beginning with the invasions of Mahmud of
Ghazni (971–1030) – drew to a close: since 1799 no
Afghan has succeeded in invading the Punjab plains
or raiding the rich plains of Hindustan beyond. It was
during this period too that Afghanistan accelerated its
transformation from the sophisticated centre of learning and the arts, which led some of the Great Mughals
to regard it as a far more cultured place than India, to
the fractured war-torn backwater it was to become for
so much of its modern history. Already Shah Zaman's
kingdom was only a shadow of that once ruled by his
father. The great colleges, such as that of Gauhar Shad
in Herat, had long shrunk in size and reputation; the
poets and artists, the calligraphers and miniaturists,
the architects and tile-makers for which Khurasan was
famous under the Timurids, continued their migration
south-eastwards to Lahore, Multan and the cities of
Hindustan, and westwards to Persia.

'The Afghans of Khurasan have an age-old
reputation', wrote Mirza 'Ata Mohammad, one of
the most perceptive writers of the age, 'that wherever
the lamp of power burns brightly, there like moths

they swarm; and wherever the tablecloth of plenty is spread, there like flies they gather.' The reverse was also true. As Shah Zaman retreated, thwarted from plundering India, and hemmed in by the Sikhs, British and Persians, his authority waned as, one by one, his nobles, his extended family and even his half-brothers rebelled against him. The Durrani state was on the verge of collapse and Shah Zaman's authority rarely extended further than a day's march beyond wherever his small army of supporters happened to be camped.

The end of Shah Zaman's rule came during the icy winter of 1800, when the Kabulis finally refused to open the city gates to their feckless king. Instead, one cold winter's night, he took shelter from the gathering blizzard in a fortress between Jalalabad and the Khyber. According to the *Siraj ul-Tawarikh*:

Exhausted by the trip, the Shah stopped over at the fortress of a certain Shinwari named 'Ashiq, to get some much needed rest.

At first, 'Ashiq showed every sign of respect and fulfilled all the obligations of host. But just as the Shah was feeling comfortable, 'Ashiq summoned two hundred Shinwaris in the middle of the night and locked the gates of the fortress so that no one could get out. After manning the towers and ramparts with Shinwari musketeers, 'Ashiq sent his son as fast as he could ride to [Shah Zaman's rival] Prince

Mahmud, who had just seized Kabul. He brought the welcome news that Shah Zaman had been captured and obtained a reward from the prince for this service. Shah Zaman, meantime, now aware of his host's perfidy, tried every way possible to find the key to escape but was unable to unlock the door of 'Ashiq's hardheartedness and deception.[15]

Later that night, the Shinwaris murdered Shah Zaman's bodyguard, locked Shah Zaman in a dungeon and then blinded him with a hot needle: 'The point', wrote Mirza 'Ata, 'quickly spilled the wine of his sight from the cup of his eyes.'[16]

Before being blinded, however, Shah Zaman had succeeded in hiding his most precious gems. Some he dug deep into the prison floor with the point of his dagger. The Fakhraj ruby he had already hidden under a rock in a stream below the Shinwari fort; now he slipped the Koh-i-Noor into a crack in the wall of his cell.

The bookish Prince Shuja was only fourteen years old when his elder brother was captured, blinded and deposed. Shuja had been Shah Zaman's 'constant companion at all times' and in the coup d'état that followed troops were sent out to arrest him. But he eluded the search parties and with a few companions wandered through the snows of the high passes, sleeping rough and biding his time. He was an intelligent and literate teenager, who abhorred the violence around him, and in adversity sought solace in poetry. 'Lose no hope when faced with hardships,' he wrote at this time, while moving from village to village, protected by kinsmen. 'Black clouds soon give way to clear rain.'[17]

His moment came three years later, in 1803, when sectarian rioting broke out in Kabul. He was able to swoop down and seize power. Shuja forgave all who had rebelled against Shah Zaman, with the single exception of 'Ashiq Shinwari, the chieftain responsible for blinding his elder brother: 'Shuja's officers arrested the culprit, and his supporters, and razed his fort to the ground. They looted every possible thing, and dragged the man to Shuja's court. Then for his sins filled his mouth with gunpowder, and blew him up. They threw his men in prison, and brutally tortured them into a vegetative state until they became an example for those who claimed they were so fearless they were capable of resisting the exquisite pain of the torturer.'[18] Finally, they strapped the offender's wife and children to Shuja's artillery and blew them from the mouths of the cannon.[19]

After 'restoring the family honour', as the Afghans saw it, Shuja's first act was to search for his family's two most precious possessions. A court historian later recorded, 'Shah Shuja immediately dispatched a few of his most trustworthy men to find these two gems and advised them that they should leave no stone unturned in their efforts. They found the Koh-i-Noor with a mullah who in his ignorance was using it as a paperweight for his papers. As for the Fakhraj ruby, they found it with a Talib, a student, who had uncovered it when he went to a stream to bathe and wash his clothes. They impounded both gems and brought them back in the king's service.'[20]

The following year, an embassy arrived from the East India Company, and Shah Shuja received them in full durbar in his magnificent palace in Peshawar. He was wearing his two newly recovered gems on each arm, as his father had done before him: 'The King of Kabul was a handsome man,' wrote the Company's ambassador, the Scottish scholar-diplomat Mountstuart Elphinstone. He was, Elphinstone continued,

of an olive complexion, with a thick black beard. The expression of his countenance was dignified and pleasing, his voice clear, his address princely. We thought at first that he had on an armour of jewels; but, on close inspection, we found this to be a mistake, and his real dress to consist of a green tunic, with large flowers in gold and precious stones, over which were a large breastplate of diamonds, shaped like two flattened fleur de lis, an ornament of the same kind on each thigh, large emerald bracelets on the arms and many other jewels in different places. In one of the bracelets was the Koh-i-Noor ...[21]

A junior member of Elphinstone's staff, William Fraser, a young Persian scholar from Inverness, also wrote home to his parents about the impact Shuja had made on him. 'I was particularly struck with the dignity of his appearance,' he wrote, 'and the romantic Oriental awe which his situation, person and Majesty impressed on me.' He described the shah sitting in what appears to be a wooden replica of the now dismembered Peacock Throne:

On each side of the throne stood several eunuchs. The king sat under the domed pavilion on an elevated polygonal throne of gilt wood, but the distance we were at, and the great height he was elevated above us, prevented our being able to distinguish his features, dress or attendants, but he appeared to be magnificently clothed in the richest attire, covered with an armour of jewels.

His dress was superb, the crown very peculiar and ornamented with jewels. I believe it was hexagonal, and at each corner or angle a rich plume of black heron's feather about 8 or 10 inches long. The frame of the crown must have been of black velvet, but the feathers and gold so completely covered the ground that I could not accurately discover every precious stone that had a place, but it struck me that emeralds, rubies and pearls were most prevalent.

Next to the diadem, the collars were most rich, and he had, I think, some of the largest pearls I ever beheld. These were intermixed with the emeralds and rubies of extraordinary size and beauty. On each arm were bazoobunds [armlets] and amulets all richly set with the jewels. The stones which most prevailed were rubies and emeralds.[22]

The Company embassy did not yet realise it, but they were in fact witnessing the last days of the Durrani monarchy. Shortly after their departure, Shuja was defeated in battle and fell from power. At the end of June 1809, Elphinstone's embassy was encamped on the left bank of the Indus, under the sheltering walls of Akbar's great fort at Attock, when they saw a bedraggled royal caravan arrive on the north bank and hastily prepare to make the crossing. It was the blind Shah Zaman and Shuja's wife Wa'fa Begum, leading the family harem to safety: 'To describe to you the effect of such a meeting upon the minds of all our party would be as difficult as melancholy,' wrote William Fraser. 'Many with difficulty restrained their tears. The blinded monarch was seated on a low cot ... His eyes at a moderate distance would not be perceived to be defective, merely as if there was a speck on each, with a little irregularity of the surface. After we were seated, he welcomed us in the usual manner and said only that he regretted Shuja's present misfortunes, and trusted it would please God to favour him again.'²³

Both deposed monarchs now experienced a prolonged period of humiliation and exile. But Shah Shuja's wanderings were made all the more perilous by the fact that at his most vulnerable he was carrying on his person some of the most valuable jewels in the world.

Ranjit Singh was one among many leaders determined to get his hands on the great diamond, and did all he could to lure Shah Shuja to his court, sending friendly messages that he and his family were always welcome as his guests in Lahore. Shah Shuja met Ranjit briefly in 1810: the maharaja presented the appropriate gifts and, in return, Shuja gave him several precious gemstones from his store. But Shuja was suspicious of Ranjit Singh's offers, and moved north without taking up his offer. He did, however, leave his wife, Wa'fa Begum, in Ranjit Singh's hands, and secretly entrusted the Koh-i-Noor to her while he tried to find troops to regain his throne.

For several months Shuja visited the durbars of his allies, asking their help to mount a campaign against the usurper, Shah Mahmoud. One night, a former

courtier of his invited him to stay at the great fortress
of Attock, and there, according to Mirza 'Ata:

> They invited Shah Shuja to a private party where
> they served sweet water melons and started play-
> fully throwing the melon skins at each other. But
> the jest bit by bit turned to scorn and effront-
> ery, and Shah Shuja soon found himself arrested,
> held first in Attock then sent under close surveil-
> lance to Kashmir where he was kept prisoner in a
> fort ... The lancet was frequently held over his eyes;
> and his keeper once took him into the Indus, with
> his arms bound, threatening him with instant death
> if he didn't hand over the celebrated diamond.[24]

Shuja was handed over to 'Ata Muhammad Khan, who
incarcerated him in a fortress located high on the Kuh-i-
Maran mountains of Kashmir, then still a part of the fast-
fracturing Durrani empire. According to Shuja's own
Memoirs, "Ata Muhammad Khan, governor of Kashmir,
occasionally came to visit me, apologising that he had not
been true to his salt, that this disloyalty would disfigure
him till the Day of Resurrection, but also insinuating that
he could also one day be of service to us. So he begged of
us the Koh-i-Noor.'[25] But the governor of Kashmir was
not the only man after the great diamond.

When Shuja was captured, his wife, Wa'fa Begum,
was still in Lahore, and she soon found that Ranjit

Singh would go to almost any lengths to get his hands on the diamond. A British traveller who passed through the city shortly afterwards and who met both Wa'fa Begum and Ranjit Singh wrote with the greatest admiration of the way in which the defenceless queen protected herself while managing to secure both her own safety and her husband's interests. Wa'fa Begum, he wrote, was:

> a woman of most bold and determined character; and her counsel had often proved valuable to her husband, both in the days of his power and disaster.
>
> At Lahore, while at the mercy of the Sikhs, and absent from her husband, she preserved her own and his honour in a heroic manner. Runjeet Singh pressed her urgently to surrender the Koh-i-Noor which was in her possession; and evinced intentions of forcing it from her. He also sought to transfer the daughters of the unfortunate king to his own harem. The queen seized on the person who conveyed the message, and had him soundly chastised. She also intimated to the Maharaja that if he continued his dishonourable demands, she would pound the diamond in a mortar, and first administer it to her daughters, and those under her protection, and then swallow it herself; adding, 'May the blood of all of us be on your head!'[26]

Eventually, Wa'fa Begum managed to cut a deal with her host. If the Sikh maharaja would rescue her husband from his Kashmiri prison, she promised that the Koh-i-Noor would be his.

In the spring of 1813, Ranjit Singh duly sent an expedition to Kashmir, which defeated 'Ata Mohammad Khan and released Shuja from his dungeon, then brought the deposed shah to Lahore. Shuja was certainly grateful for his rescue but was determined if possible to hang on to his most valuable remaining possession. It took considerable pressure to pry the stone from his hands.

Upon arrival in Lahore, Shuja was separated from his harem, put under house arrest and told to fulfil the bargain made by his wife by handing over the diamond. 'The ladies of our harem were accommodated in another mansion, to which we had, most vexatiously, no access,' wrote Shuja in his *Memoirs*. 'Food was arbitrarily cut off, our servants sometimes allowed to go and sometimes forbidden from going about their business in the city.' Shuja regarded this as an ill-mannered breach of the laws of hospitality and, with all the hauteur he could muster, wrote, 'It was a display of oafish bad manners,' dismissing Ranjit Singh as 'both vulgar and tyrannical, as well as ugly and low-natured'.[27]

Slowly, Ranjit increased the pressure. At the lowest ebb of his fortunes, Shuja was put in a cage and, according to one account, his eldest son was tortured in front of him until he agreed to part with his most valuable possession. Mirza 'Ata wrote:

> Ranjit Singh coveted the Koh-i-Noor diamond beyond anything else in this world, and broke all the laws of hospitality in order to get possession of it. The King was imprisoned for a long time, and his guards left him out in the burning sun, but to no effect as he would not confess where the jewel was hidden. At length they took his young son, Prince Muhammad Timur, and made him run up and down ladders on the bare roof of the palace in the burning sun, with no shoes or head-covering: the child had been gently brought up and had a delicate physique which could not stand this burning torture, so he cried out aloud and seemed about to pass away. The King could not bear to see his beloved child suffer so.[28]

But even then Shuja sent word to Ranjit Singh that he would hand over the diamond only in return for a formal treaty of friendship, several lakh rupees and Ranjit Singh's aid in getting back his throne. As Shuja put it:

> The following morning, Ram Singh [Ranjit Singh's minister] came into our presence to request the Koh-i-Noor diamond. We answered that it was not

presently in our hands, but that whenever a firm treaty of friendship had been made between ourselves and Ranjit Singh, we would have no objection to bestowing it as a gift.

The same request and the same answer were repeated day after day: for nearly a month this continued. When the Sikhs realised that bad behaviour was not achieving the result they desired, Ranjit Singh sent several of his notables to ask what sum of money we might require, so that it could be got ready and handed over: we replied, again, that, on condition of a firm treaty of friendship and unity being signed, we would have no objection. So some 40–50,000 rupees were sent over in instalments to our lodgings – but still we gave the same answer.

Two days later, Ranjit Singh himself appeared at Shuja's residence:

Uttering words of friendship and unity, bringing a written document much to the same effect, dipping his hand into saffron water to print a paw-mark on the treaty, swearing by his sacred book, the Granth, and by his guru Baba Nanak, with his hand on the blade of his sword, that any troops deemed necessary by His Majesty for the reconquest of the province of Kabul and the punishment of the scoundrel rebels will be provided by the Sikh government.

Then turbans were exchanged as a sign of perfect amity, and Ranjit Singh exclaimed: 'Now we have performed all the ceremonies of undying friendship, can I please have the diamond?'[29]

According to Sir David Ochterlony, the British representative at the Company frontier town of Ludhiana, keenly watching events from just over the Sutlej river, which formed the border with the territories of the East India Company, Shah Shuja's conditions were improved slightly while the negotiations continued. 'The restrictions on Shah Shuja are a little diminished,' he wrote, 'on his having agreed to place some jewels in Runjeet's hands, as a pledge of a delivery of the Koh-i-Noor, within two months for which he is to receive two lakhs in ready money and a jageer [estate] of fifty thousand rupees.'[30]

Finally, on 1 June 1813, Ranjit Singh arrived again at Mubarak Haveli in the heart of the walled city of Lahore and waited upon the shah with a few attendants. He was received by Shuja:

with much dignity, and both being seated, a pause and solemn silence ensued, which continued for nearly an hour. Ranjit then, getting impatient, whispered to one of his attendants to remind the Shah of the object of his coming. No answer was returned, but the Shah with his eyes made a signal to a eunuch, who retired, and brought in a small roll, which he set down on the carpet at an equal distance between the chiefs. Ranjit desired his eunuch to unfold the roll, and when the diamond was exhibited and recognized, the Sikh immediately retired, with his prize in his hand.[31]

For the next thirty-six years the Koh-i-Noor would be in the possession of the Sikhs; indeed it would become in many ways a symbol of their sovereignty.

5

Ranjit Singh: The Koh-i-Noor in Lahore

Of all the owners of the Koh-i-Noor, none made more of the diamond than Ranjit Singh.

The great maharaja of the Sikhs was, in general, a man of unassuming tastes. A diminutive figure with a pockmarked face, he reminded one British observer who saw him in old age of 'an old mouse, with grey whiskers and one eye'.[1] He dressed in simple white robes and rarely took pains with his appearance. He did, however, love the Koh-i-Noor with a rare passion and wore it on all public occasions.

It was during his reign that the Koh-i-Noor first began to achieve real fame and gained the singular status it has retained ever since: up to this point, as a possession of Nader Shah and his Durrani successors, it had always been worn as part of a pair along with the gem known to the Mughals as the great ruby of Timur, to Nader Shah as the Eye of the Houri and to the Durranis as the Fakhraj. Now the Koh-i-Noor was

worn alone, quickly becoming a symbol of all Ranjit
Singh had strived for and the independence he had
fought so hard to achieve.

It was not just that Ranjit Singh liked diamonds,
and respected the stone's vast monetary value; the
gem seems to have held a far greater symbolism for
him. Since he had come to the throne he had won
back from the Afghan Durrani dynasty almost all
the Indian lands they had seized since the time of
Ahmad Shah. Having conquered all the Durrani territories as far as the Khyber Pass, Ranjit Singh seems
to have regarded his seizure of the Durrani's dynastic diamond as his crowning achievement, the seal
on his status as the successor to the fallen dynasty.
It may have been this, as much as the beauty of the
stone, that led him to wear it on his arm on all state
occasions.

When Ranjit Singh first took the great diamond in
1813, he suspected that Shah Shuja might have tried to
trick him. So he immediately assembled the jewellers
of Lahore to test the stone. There was much relief, and
even a little surprise, when they pronounced it genuine, and priceless. As an old courtier later recalled: 'The
Maharaja held a Durbar on his return to the Palace, and
the Koh-i-Noor Diamond was exhibited to the Chiefs
and people assembled there, and repeated congratula-
tions were offered his Highness on the attainment of
this valuable jewel.'[2]

Then:

> Having fully satisfied himself that the diamond which he had obtained from the Shah was the genuine Koh-i-Noor, he sent Shuja a lakh and twenty five thousand Rupees as a donation.
>
> The Maharaja then went to Amritsar and immediately sent for the principal jewellers of that City too to ascertain from them their opinion of the value of the Koh-i-Noor. Having carefully examined it, they replied that the value of a diamond of such great size and beauty was far beyond all computation. The Maharaja desired them to set the diamond in a handsome and suitable manner, and this work was executed in his Highness's presence, for he would not allow them to take the precious jewel out of his sight.
>
> The setting being completed, Ranjit Singh fixed the Koh-i-Noor in the front of his turban, mounted his Elephant, and accompanied by Sirdars and attendants, paraded several times up and down the principal streets of the City, in order that his subjects might see the Koh-i-Noor in his possession. The Koh-i-Noor was produced and worn by Ranjit Singh as an armlet on the Diwali, the Dusserah, and other great festivals, and it was always exhibited to visitors of distinction, especially to British Officers who visited his Court. Ranjit Singh took the Koh-i-Noor with him wherever he travelled to Multan, Peshawar and other places.[3]

Shortly after this, Ranjit returned to the diamond's old owners to try, yet again, to get an estimate of its real worth. Wa'fa Begum told him, 'If a strong man were to throw four stones, one to each of the cardinal points, North, South, East and West, and a fifth stone vertically, and if the space between were to be filled with gold and precious stones, they would not equal in value the Koh-i-Noor.' Meanwhile Shah Shuja, when asked the same question, is said to have replied, 'Good luck, for he who has possessed it, has obtained it by overpowering his enemies.'[4]

For the rest of his life, Ranjit Singh remained anxious that his precious jewel would be stolen. He was especially worried that, 'having partaken freely of his favourite and most potent beverage, as he was wont to do on occasions of great rejoicing, and feeling that his senses were fast yielding to its intoxicating effects, he evinced considerable anxiety for the safety of the Koh-i-Noor; for on a former occasion, when he had been indulging freely in like manner, a valuable jewel had been stolen from him'.[5]

When it was not being worn, therefore he had the gem hidden away in his high-security state treasury at the impregnable fortress of Gobindgarh, and he evolved an elaborate security regime for moving it from place to place. Forty camels with identical panniers would be assembled and great secrecy was maintained as to which was actually carrying the diamond, although invariably it would actually be placed in the first, immediately behind the guards. At other times the stone would be kept under a strong guard in the Gobindgarh treasury, or *toshakhana*.[6]

All the while, Ranjit Singh's state continued to prosper and expand. The maharaja took full advantage of the opportunity presented by the Afghan civil war to absorb almost all of the lands of the Durrani Empire between the Indus and the Khyber Pass, conquering Peshawar in 1818, and Kashmir a year later. At the same time he built a remarkably rich, strong, centralised and tightly governed Sikh state in its place, treating defeated chiefs with great generosity and absorbing them into his political system. As well as creating his remarkable army, Ranjit also modernised his bureaucracy, balanced his revenues, evolved an enlightened agrarian policy and ran a formidable intelligence network.

At its peak, his kingdom of Punjab and its province of Kashmir formed a unit with around thirteen million inhabitants, and Ranjit Singh seems to have been personally hugely popular: he made himself accessible to the humblest petitioner, generally respected the beliefs of non-Sikhs, visiting Muslim Sufi shrines and celebrating Hindu festivals, and was respected for his personal leniency and hatred of bloodshed – something that was observed by many visitors at court, and that dramatically distinguished him from most of his

Mughal, Persian and Durrani predecessors. As Emily Eden, the sister of the British governor general Lord Auckland, conceded: 'He is a very drunken old profligate, neither more nor less. Still he has made himself a great king; he has conquered a great many powerful enemies; he is remarkably just in his government; he has disciplined a large army; he hardly ever takes away life, which is wonderful in a despot; and he is excessively beloved by his people.'[7]

Emily Eden was not alone in her admiration of Ranjit Singh. The British generally got on well with him, but they never forgot that his army was the last military force in India which could take on the Company on the field of battle: by the 1830s, the Company had stationed nearly half the Bengal army, totalling more than 39,000 troops, along the Punjab frontier.[8]

The French traveller Victor Jacquemont penned a revealing portrait of the maharaja at this time. Like Emily Eden, he depicted Ranjit Singh as a wily, clever and charming old rogue – as disreputable in his private habits as he was admirable in his public virtues. 'Ranjit Singh is an old fox,' he wrote, 'compared with whom the wiliest of our diplomats is a mere innocent.' Jacquemont records several of his encounters with the maharaja. 'His conversation is a nightmare,' he wrote. 'He is almost the first inquisitive Indian I have seen, but his curiosity makes up for the apathy of the whole nation. He asked me a hundred thousand questions about India, the English, Europe, Bonaparte, the world in general and the other one, hell and paradise, the soul, God, the devil, and a thousand things besides.' Ranjit Singh regretted above all that 'women no longer give him any more pleasure than the flowers in his garden'.

To show me what good reason he had for his distress, yesterday in the midst of his whole court – that is to say in the open country, on a beautiful Persian carpet where we were squatting surrounded by a few thousand soldiers – lo and behold, the old roué sent for five young girls from his seraglio, ordered them to sit down in front of me, and smilingly asked what I thought of them. I said in all sincerity that I thought them very pretty, which was not a tenth what I really thought ...

But this model king is no saint: far from it. He cares nothing for law or good faith; but he is not cruel. He orders great criminals to have their noses or ears cut off, or a hand, but he never takes a life. He is extremely brave, and though he has been successful in his military campaigns, it has been by treaties and cunning negotiations that he has made himself absolute king of Punjab and Kashmir. He is also a shameless rogue who flaunts his vices as Henri III did in our country ... Ranjit has frequently exhibited himself to his good people of Lahore with a Moslem public woman, indulging in the least innocent of sports with her on the back of an elephant.

A little later, the British traveller and spy Alexander Burnes arrived in Lahore and was just as taken with Ranjit Singh as Jacquemont had been; indeed the two quickly became firm friends. 'Nothing could exceed the affability of the Maharaja,' Burnes wrote. 'He kept up an uninterrupted flow of conversation for the hour and a half which the interview lasted.' Ranjit laid on a round of entertainments for him. Dancing girls performed, deer were hunted, monuments visited and banquets thrown. Burnes even tried some of Ranjit's home-made hell-brew, a fiery distillation of raw spirit, crushed pearls, musk, opium, gravy and spices, two glasses of which was normally enough to knock out the most hardened British drinker, but which Ranjit recommended to Burnes as a cure for his dysentery. Burnes and Ranjit, the Scot and the Sikh, found themselves bonding over a shared taste for firewater. 'Runjeet Singh is, in every respect, an extraordinary character,' wrote Burnes. 'I have heard his French officers observe that he has no equal from Constantinople to India.'[9]

At their final dinner, Ranjit agreed to show Burnes the Koh-i-Noor: 'Nothing', wrote Burnes, 'can be imagined more superb than this stone; it is of the finest water, about half the size of an egg. Its weight amounts to 3½ rupees, and if such a jewel is to be valued, I am informed it is worth 3½ millions of money.'[10]

It was after Burnes's departure, on 17 August 1835, that Ranjit had his first major stroke. This left him partially paralysed in his face and right side; he could not speak for many hours. According to the doctor who attended him:

> The Maharaja retired to rest in a chamber where his body was freely exposed to a free circulation of air, the body being at this time in a rather profuse state of perspiration.
>
> In the middle of the night, he woke suddenly and found himself unable to move his tongue so as to articulate and his mouth distorted to a considerable degree. His attendants were alarmed at these symptoms and various recipes were prescribed by [his personal physician] Fakeer Azizuddin. By the end of these the Maharaja was able to articulate a little. His health likewise suffered a visible change. There was a loss of appetite, some heaviness in the head, heat on the palms of the hands and soles of the feet; thirst, frequently urgent, a general despondency and depression of the spirits.[11]

The German traveller Baron Hügel, who met Ranjit Singh in 1836, left an impression in his writings of a man now bowed down by disease, whose speech was so badly affected by his stroke that he was almost impossible to understand. He told the traveller, 'I begin to feel old. I am quite exhausted now.' A second stroke followed in 1837, paralysing his right side for six months, and forcing him to communicate through signs. Fakeer Azizuddin became an expert in interpreting and understanding his sovereign's stammering. He would put his ear close to Ranjit's mouth and if he understood would say, '*Eysh, eysh.*' If he failed to understand, he would shake his head and murmur, '*Nami fahman*' – I do not understand.[12]

The manoeuvres of the Great Game – that strategic, economic and political rivalry between Britain and Russia that had been growing more acute for two decades – continued throughout the late 1830s, with Burnes playing a leading role in first stoking and then moderating British fears of a Russian invasion of Afghanistan. By 1838, in response to further rumours of a Russian advance, the East India Company put into action an ambitious plan for the invasion of Afghanistan, a country which did not share a border with its territories. The Company's new governor general, Lord Auckland, therefore opened negotiations with Ranjit Singh, trying to draw him into ever closer alliance and to lure him into participating in a joint Anglo-Sikh invasion up the Khyber – something

Ranjit publicly applauded, while privately dragging his feet: the last thing he wanted was the Company encircling his territories to the north as well as to the east of his kingdom, yet he did not wish to come into conflict with his British allies and so could not publicly oppose the Company's plans.

In May 1838, Captain William Osborne arrived in Lahore on an East India Company official mission on behalf of his uncle, Lord Auckland, intending to change the maharaja's mind. Ranjit Singh received his British visitors, sitting:

> [c]ross-legged in a golden chair, dressed in simple white, wearing no ornaments but a single string of enormous pearls round the waist, and the celebrated Koh-i-Noor, on his arm – the jewel rivalled, if not surpassed, in brilliancy by the glance of fire which every now and then shot from his single eye as it wandered restlessly round the circle ... His chiefs all squatted around his chair, with the exception of Dheean Singh [his vizier] who remained standing behind his master. Though far removed from being handsome himself, Ranjit appears to take pride in being surrounded by good-looking people, and I believe few, if any other courts either in Europe or the East, could shew such a fine looking set of men as the principal Sikh sardars [noblemen].

As for the jewel itself, Osbourne judged it to be 'a most magnificent diamond, about an inch and a half in length, and upwards of an inch in width, and stands out from the setting about half an inch. It is in the shape of an egg … It is valued at three millions sterling, is very brilliant, and without a flaw of any kind.'

Osbourne, like many other visitors before him, was amazed by Ranjit Singh's restlessly inquisitive mind – despite his strokes, his mind remained as active and curious as ever. He wrote:

As soon as we were seated, our time was principally occupied in answering Runjeet's innumerable questions, but without the slightest chance of satisfying his curiosity.

It is hardly possible to give an idea of the ceaseless rapidity with which his questions flow, or the infinite variety they embrace: 'Do you drink wine?' 'How much?' 'Did you taste the wine which I sent you yesterday?' 'How much of it did you drink?' 'What artillery have you brought with you?' 'Have they got any shells?' 'How many?' 'Do you like riding on horseback?' 'What country horses do you prefer?' 'Are you in the army?' 'What do you like best, cavalry or infantry?' 'Does Lord Auckland drink wine?' 'How many glasses?' 'Does he drink it in the morning?' 'What is the strength of the Company's army?' 'Are they well disciplined?'

Such banter, he realised, was partly a smokescreen to disarm his interlocutor and disguise from them the acute political intelligence Ranjit always displayed in negotiation.

Seven months later, in December 1838, there followed a state visit by Lord Auckland. This marked the beginning of the first British invasion of Afghanistan with joint manoeuvres being enacted on the fields of Ferozepur by British and Sikh armies, bookended by a series of ceremonial levees and dinners. But the strain of the events began to show on the now ill and elderly Ranjit Singh: on 21 December, when the governor general's family visited Lahore shortly after the army had set off towards Afghanistan, 'the entertainments were on a scale of princely magnificence ... Runjeet insisted that his Lordship should take part in drinking, requiring each time that he should drain to the dregs a cup of fiery liquid he presented. The excesses committed by the Maharaja on this occasion produced a severe fit of apoplexy, and when Lord Auckland took leave of him, he was lying in his couch, scarcely able to articulate. But it is said that when his Lordship presented his host with a valuable jewel, his eye lighted up with all its wonted fire.'[13]

In this state Ranjit Singh was visited by the governor general's doctor, who reported back on the surprising austerity of Ranjit's personal living quarters. These consisted only of 'a little glass closet in a corner of his palace with a common charpoy to lie on, and no other furniture whatever, and hardly room for any'. From there Ranjit sent the Koh-i-Noor to entertain the governor general's sisters since he was too sick to do so himself. 'It is very large,' wrote Emily Eden, 'but not very bright.' Before they left, Emily reported a last, sad sighting of the great maharaja: 'He looked quite exhausted, almost dying.'[14]

Emily was right. Ranjit Singh was indeed nearing his end. He was eventually struck down by a third major stroke, in June 1839, and it became increasingly clear to everyone that he was not going to live much longer. Haunted by the imminence of death, Ranjit began to give away his most valuable possessions. He paid a last pilgrimage to Amritsar and donated large sums to religious charities: cows with gilded horns, golden rings, satin dresses and elephants with gold howdahs.[15] He then assembled all his senior officers and made them take an oath of allegiance to Kharak Singh, his eldest son.

As his health continued to worsen, a flood of other donations followed to religious institutions of different faiths: more cows with gilded horns, golden chairs and bedsteads, strings of pearls, swords and shields, a hundred caparisoned horses and hundreds of jewelled saddles – cumulatively worth a sum calculated by the newswriter at Ranjit's court to be around two crore rupees. It was at this stage, on 26 June, when Ranjit could only gesticulate but not speak, and as he was clearly beginning to fade away, that a major argument broke out around his deathbed as to the fate of his great diamond.

Ranjit Singh's head Brahmin, Bhai Gobind Ram, said that Ranjit had stated that 'The Koh-i-Noor had always been given away by the old kings and that none of the Sultans had taken it along with himself.' Apparently supported by the gestures of the mute, dying monarch, the Brahmin insisted that Ranjit had intended his jewels to go to the temple of Lord Jagannath in Puri, and that it should now be given away, just as he was now giving away his favourite pearls and horses.[16] But Ranjit Singh's chief treasurer, Misr Beli Ram, was equally insistent that the Koh-i-Noor belonged not personally to Ranjit but to the Sikh state, and should therefore go to Ranjit's heir, Kharak Singh. According to his court chronicle, the *Umdat ul-Tawarikh*, 'By a sign the Sarkar [Ranjit] pointed out that offerings should be made, and the stone should be sent over to Jagannathji.'

Kharak Singh was then ordered to fetch the great diamond; he in turn stated that the diamond was with the treasurer, Misr Beli Ram.

After that Jamdar Khushal Singh spoke to Misr Beli Ram, for its presentation; but he began to put forward excuses, and replied that the gem was in

Amritsar. After that the Jamdar [head of court pro-
tocol] also said that all the property, all the wealth
and all the material belonged to Kharak Singh. The
Sarkar [Ranjit] produced wrinkles [of disapproval]
on his forehead as he heard this discussion. After
that, two armlets with diamonds, worth Rs 2 lakhs,
several bejewelled ornaments, 8 top hats of the
Persian style, 2 elephants with gold howdahs and
Rs 5 lakh in cash were given away as temple offerings. The Sarkar put on all the ornaments and then
removed them from every limb of his body and,
making prostration by resting his head upon the
earth, gave them away with the remark that it was
his final wearing.[17]

He then had passages from the *Granth Sahib* read
to him and bowed deeply to the holy book, before
washing himself with Ganges water. His final act, that
of a dying soldier, was to give away his weapons. The
following day, 27 June, it was clear that the end was
very close.

The Sarkar's lips stopped and strength in his body
became suspended and his pulse left altogether its
normal course. Fakir Raza said with his eyes full of
tears and his heart full of anxiety, that he knew this
was the last hour. All began to weep and cry ... Bhai
Gobind Ram, the Brahmin, said into the ear of the

Sarkar, at the moment he was expiring, the words, 'Ram, Ram,' three times. The Sarkar repeated them twice, but at the third time, his lips did not open and his life went out of him. Up to the time of his expiring, his eyes had been fixed upon the picture of Laxmi and Vishnu. When the day had passed three quarters and three hours he bade farewell to this mortal world and got transferred to this everlasting universe. Kharak Singh and others began to weep and cry ...

The great maharaja was dead. Yet even as Ranjit Singh's cremation pyre was being kindled with sandalwood, the Koh-i-Noor – so visible throughout the latter part of Ranjit Singh's reign – was nowhere to be seen. Moreover, the issue of what to do with the great diamond remained wholly unresolved. Ranjit's successors were left with only a series of questions. Where exactly was the diamond? Had Misr Beli Ram hidden it? Had it already been sent off to the Jagannath temple in Orissa, as Ranjit Singh had apparently indicated? Was that really his wish? Had he been bullied into this last action by the manipulative Bhai Gobind Ram and the other Brahmins who surrounded him? Was the Koh-i-Noor Ranjit's personal property to give away as he pleased? Or did the stone actually belong to the state, and his successors, and in some way represent the independence of the Sikh kingdom?

These unanswered questions helped sow the seeds of dissension that would soon rend the entire Sikh empire and propel it into full-scale civil war. The diamond was nowhere to be seen, and yet – like the legendary Syamantaka, with which some identified it – it had lost none of its extraordinary ability to create discord all around it.

PART 2

THE JEWEL IN THE CROWN

SIMPLIFIED FAMILY TREE

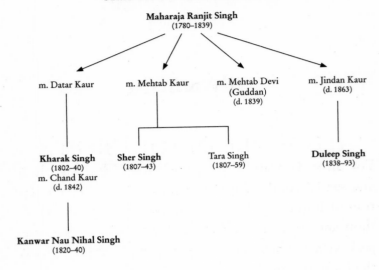

Maharaja Ranjit Singh
(1780–1839)

m. Datar Kaur   m. Mehtab Kaur   m. Mehtab Devi (Guddan) (d. 1839)   m. Jindan Kaur (d. 1863)

Kharak Singh (1802–40) m. Chand Kaur (d. 1842)   **Sher Singh** (1807–43)   Tara Singh (1807–59)   **Duleep Singh** (1838–93)

Kanwar Nau Nihal Singh (1820–40)

6

City of Ash

For three days and nights, the scent of burning flesh and sandalwood filled the palace grounds. The cremation of Ranjit Singh at the end of June 1839 attracted thousands from across Punjab. Death rites for maharajas have never been subtle, yet even by Indian standards the Lion of Punjab was sent off in spectacular fashion.

One of the most comprehensive accounts of the numerous ceremonies performed for the dead king comes from a European serving in the Lahore durbar. John Martin Honigberger, a doctor and adventurer from Austro-Hungary, had come to Punjab ten years earlier and had served at the pleasure of Ranjit Singh ever since. As a high-ranking official in the court, he had been required to keep his vigil while the cremation fire burned and the ashes cooled. Exhausted by the effort, he looked on as small sunburned men raked up ash and charred lumps of bone. This was all that remained of his once formidable patient. He felt nothing but disgust for his old patron now: Ranjit Singh's last rites filled Honigberger's mind with images he would rather forget.

Three days earlier, in the space between the palace and the outer walls of the Lahore Fort had stood a colossal pyre of wood. All Punjab seemed to have been drawn to the capital that day, a pulsing sea of grieving humanity, and Honigberger's ears had thrummed with the volume of noise which surrounded him.

Honigberger was shown to his place, in front of the neck-craning masses. Around him the nobles of the Sikh Sirdara stood barefoot and dressed in white. Everyone who mattered seemed to be there, except for the very highest-ranking Sikh nobles, who had the singular honour of accompanying their sovereign on the last journey he would ever make. Honigberger watched and waited for the funeral procession to come into view.

A double line of infantry, a quarter of a mile long, drove a wide furrow through the mourners. Through it, Honigberger saw Ranjit Singh's body, laid out on a golden platform made to look like a ship with spun-gold sails.[1] It was a fitting bier, for the maharaja's body seemed to be carried on waves of wailing. Musicians added to the cacophony with their drums and horns.

His senses battered, Honigberger then caught sight of the women in the maharaja's slipstream. Rani Mahtab Devi, known lovingly as 'Guddan', was held aloft on a golden chair, carried by sweating bearers.

Behind her followed three similar chairs, each filled by a queen.[2] Though he saw them all, he noticed only Rani Guddan. She and Honigberger had come to Lahore for the first time in the same year. Back then, he had been a young doctor, an adventurer determined to make his name and fortune. Guddan was a Rajput princess. Both she and her sister, Rani Raj Banso, had been betrothed to the maharaja.

Somehow Honigberger, who had always managed to charm his way in society, had inveigled his way into the royal wedding, one pale face lost among thousands. He remembered that Guddan had a reputation for great beauty then, a rumour he was unable to verify. Guddan had been veiled for her marriage and every day since. Only now, ten years later, on the day of her death, could she show her face in public. Honigberger saw that she was beautiful still.

As Guddan and the three other ranis were carried closer to the pyre they removed their bracelets, and threw them to the numerous hands that stretched towards them. Honigberger kept his arms resolutely by his side.

His fellow members of the Sikh durbar assured Honigberger that these ranis (four among Ranjit Singh's seventeen wives) were willing participants in this age-old ritual. Nevertheless he felt sickened by what was about to unfold. These women were *satis*,[3] devoted to their husband in life and beyond, and their public suicide – or murder, depending on your point of view – was being celebrated all around him. The royal historian, Sohan Lal Suri, whose job it was to record events in Ranjit Singh's court, would later report that the ranis had been willing victims, filled with unfettered joy as they dressed for their funeral, 'dancing and laughing like intoxicated elephants'.[4] Honigberger saw nothing of that in the wretched women's faces.

The maharaja's head and shoulders had been placed on two of the ranis' laps, to make it look as though he was sleeping, while the other two carried the weight of his torso. They sat perfectly still around his corpse, with their eyes tightly closed. Though they did not see the crown prince, Kharak Singh, carry the torch to the pyre, they would have felt his presence as he drew closer with the flames. If the women screamed, Honigberger could not tell. As the fire consumed them all, drums and the roar of the crowd confounded his senses. Honigberger was not the only one to be overwhelmed. A pair of pigeons, perhaps startled by the noise, flew into the climbing column of flames. Wings alight, they plummeted on to the pyre, causing the crowd to crescendo in a frenzy of ecstasy. It was said the birds were also willing *sati*s for Ranjit Singh.[5]

After the funeral pyre had burned for two days and nights, even after the last piece of sandalwood had crackled and crumbled, Honigberger was forced to maintain his vigil for almost twenty hours more. Senior members of Ranjit Singh's court were expected to attend their master until the river took his ashes. When the mound was cool enough for calloused fingers, the Doms, a caste of sweepers who handle corpses, began their work. How they knew where the maharaja's remains ended and his wives' began was a mystery. For centuries, commoners and kings had passed through the Doms' skilled fingers and their methods were never questioned. As they sorted the ash into five neat piles – for the maharaja and his queens – nobody seemed to care that the remains of seven slave girls were also mixed in with the powdered grey. Like the ranis, they too had burned with their maharaja. Unlike their mistresses, they had been expected to walk to their deaths on their own two feet.

The sight of the slave girls cowering as a heavy oil-soaked reed mat was lowered over their heads would remain vivid in Honigberger's mind for the rest of his life.[6] Nobody mourned for them, and Honigberger did not even know their names. Consumed with revulsion, and a degree of self-pity, he watched the 'abominable ceremony'.[7] When asked later why he had not left Punjab before the funeral, Honigberger liked to quote the words of General Jean-François Allard, a friend and fellow European in Ranjit Singh's court: 'It is very difficult to get an appointment here, but still more so to get one's dismissal …'[8]

Back in 1829, at the age of thirty-four, Honigberger had been a fresh-faced physician from Imperial Austria, filled with unconventional ideas of how medicine ought to be practised. A well-travelled young man, he arrived in Lahore armed with a box full of tinctures and a letter of recommendation. Despite ambitiously high hopes, his progress was frustratingly slow. Maharaja Ranjit Singh refused to let the *gora* doctor anywhere near him, so instead Honigberger contented himself with treating minor officials on the periphery of the durbar. Only when enough of them survived was he summoned to the palace.

Though Honigberger did not expect his first royal patient to be the maharaja himself, he did at least expect that patient to be human. Instead a horse, a creature 'of uncommon height',[9] was brought before the baffled physician. The stallion had been given as a token of friendship by King George IV of England and, though coddled in the royal stables, the beast had developed painful leg ulcers. *Hakims* had tried their best, but when their cures failed Honigberger was called in as a last hope. He worked hard to save the horse, but it died, convulsing at his feet. Such a result might have ended a man's future in Lahore, yet something in the tenderness Honigberger had shown the stricken animal impressed Ranjit Singh. The maharaja granted the young doctor a position, allowing him to practise on humans and earn healthy rewards for his efforts. Despite his generosity, Honigberger secretly harboured an unflattering opinion of his benefactor, describing Ranjit Singh as a man of 'very low stature'[10] who, on horseback, looked like 'an ape on an elephant'.[11]

The maharaja even offered the doctor command of an artillery battalion. Other white men had proved very useful in Ranjit Singh's army,[12] and he had come to look upon them as lucky talismans. Honigberger shrewdly turned down the position: 'I refused [the maharaja] deeming that I had not sufficient abilities to execute such an office properly ...'[13] Not one to be thwarted, the maharaja countered with a second proposition. In lieu of an active military post, he offered to make Honigberger superintendent of his royal gunpowder factory, a title which came with wealth and influence. Honigberger accepted, though secretly he never intended to stay in Punjab for long. He was homesick from the very start, and wanted to return to Europe: 'I was so occupied by this idea, that if they had offered me the Koh-i-Noor to remain there for the remainder of my life, I would have refused it.'[14]

Ten years had passed and he was serving at the pleasure of the durbar still.

The men clearing the maharaja's cremation site were permitted to keep any of the warm gems and heat-tortured gold they found in the ashes. Few begrudged them, especially since the one gem that truly mattered was safe from their grubbing fingers. Rumours about the Koh-i-Noor's whereabouts swirled through the court like smoke. Some said it had been spirited away to Kashmir, while others claimed that the wily master of the *toshakhana* (royal treasury), Misr Beli Ram, had stolen it. The most persistent rumour concerned a Hindu deity in a far-off province. Apparently Lord Jagannath's statue in Orissa would soon be wearing the Mountain of Light on its forehead like a priceless third eye.

Many devout Hindus believed that the Koh-i-Noor was in fact the Syamantaka gem, closely associated with Lord Krishna in the legends of the *Bhagavad Purana*. Lord Krishna was an avatar of Lord Jagannath, therefore returning the gem to the deity would restore some balance to the universe – at least that was what the Brahmins surrounding Ranjit Singh told him. In the weeks leading up to the maharaja's death they had been whispering almost constantly in Ranjit Singh's ear, persuading him to swap his earthly riches for heavenly blessings. Though the maharaja was a Sikh, part of a religion that did not hold with such karmic bargaining, the Hindu priests still managed to convince him to part with a fortune in gold and jewels. Too weak to resist, he had been robbed of speech by a stroke, and by the end was capable only of nodding his head. With one such inclination Ranjit Singh was said to have given away the Koh-i-Noor to the Jagannath pundits.[15] The Brahmin priests were understandably jubilant; the crown prince of Punjab less so.

As the next in line, Ranjit's eldest legitimate son, Kharak Singh, had grown up seeing his father with the Koh-i-Noor strapped to his bicep. The potential loss of such a prize was fraught with bitterness and Kharak Singh was not the only one left struggling with the deathbed bequest. Thousands of miles away in England, news of the Koh-i-Noor's fate was also causing upheaval. Intelligence reports had been shuttling between Fort William in Calcutta and Whitehall in London.

Since he arrived in Ludhiana in 1823, British agent Captain C. M. Wade had been keeping a close eye on the maharaja and regularly sending back intelligence reports to his masters in the East India Company. Though Wade learned of the maharaja's death immediately, his official report took more than five months to reach British headquarters in the Bengal Presidency, thanks to unrest in the region blocking its progress en route. Wade's letter finally arrived in Calcutta only on 4 December 1839: 'Although the Right Honourable the Governor General will have received the melancholy intelligence of the demise of Maharajah Runjeet Singh before my report of that event can arrive, I deem it my duty to announce that His Highness expired at

Lahore on the 27th of June.' The letter suggested that the diamond had been sent to Orissa, as per the maharaja's final wishes:

> During the last few days of his illness His Highness is declared to have bestowed in charity money, jewels and other property to the supposed value of fifty lakhs of Rupees. Among his jewels he directed the well-known Cohi nur diamond to be sent to the temple of Jagur nath. He observed that no one carrys away with him his worldly wealth and that such a bequest would perpetuate his name.[16]

Though the intelligence was received by the 'secret' division of the Company's foreign department in Calcutta, the matters disclosed were hardly classified. Word of the old Lion's death had already made it into the British papers. As news of his demise sank in, attention turned to his legacy. What was he leaving behind? On 20 October 1839, an indignant letter appeared in the *Era*, a popular British weekly newspaper:

> So, Mr Editor, after many previous unfounded reports which have been in circulation for the last nine months past, it has been fully and officially confirmed that the Lion of the Punjaub is no more: – that fierce oppressor, so long, an eyesore to the East India company, is numbered with his

departed ancestors, and the Koh-i-Noor Diamond
or 'Great Mountain of Light' has been bequeathed,
by the dying tyrant, to the pundits of the Juggernaut,
wherewith to bedeck a senseless idol. The richest,
the most costly gem in the known world, has been
committed to the trust of a profane, idolatrous and
mercenary priesthood ...[17]

The author called himself 'A Voice from Cashmere'
and clearly had insider knowledge of the Sikh court.
India crawled with invisible players of the Great Game;
it is not clear whether 'A Voice' worked for the British
government or for the East India Company, but one
thing was certain: he was more than a little obsessed
with the Koh-i-Noor, which he believed to be the key
to the whole Kingdom of Punjab.

'A Voice' urged his countrymen to seize the
moment and the fabled diamond: 'Either the East India
Company must tamely submit to the insolent appetite of "Khurruck Singh", the present representative
of the throne of Lahore, in his retaining possession of
the above valuable prize, as a portion of his patrimony
... or they must defend the claim of [Juggernaut] and
commence hostilities against him.'

Either way, 'A Voice' argued, the British must follow
the diamond. He urged a swift British alliance with the
crown prince. With the loss of the Koh-i-Noor immi-
nent, English laws of inheritance would look attractive

to Kharak Singh. They automatically made the diamond his property, superseding any spurious deathbed bequest of Ranjit Singh: 'if the Company could even persuade "Khurruck Singh" that English law must pass current in the Lahore country as well as in the ceded provinces of Hindoostan', he maintained, everything else would follow smoothly. Kharak Singh would open the door to British jurisprudence, then to British influence; and when the time was right, he would have no power to resist British domination. To make the proposal more attractive to Kharak Singh, continued 'A Voice', agents could offer to harass the Jagannath priests, forcing them to give up their claim of their own volition:

> The priests are the immediate dependents of the Company ... Who furnishes, let me ask, the necessary paraphernalia to support the pageantry attendant upon the festivals of the idol of Juggernaut? The East India Company!! Who endows the Temple of Juggernaut with large grants of land? The East India Company!! Who is it that employs agents to drive in force from their peasant homesteads the poor, wretched, half-starved to the abominable city of juggernaut during their Ruthyatra? The East India Company.

The British were excellently placed to win the crown prince's gratitude. In the letter-writer's estimation, the

Lion's son and heir Kharak Singh was an intemperate weakling, and this was a good thing: Kharak Singh's shortcomings would make it easy to prise the Koh-i-Noor away. If the gem ever went to Jagannath, it would fall into the hands of saffron-clad thieves and be lost to Britain for ever. 'A Voice' warned the British that the priests would simply sell the stone to the highest bidder and benefit from the proceeds. 'Would the wary Brahmins long suffer the Koh-i-Noor to bedeck the hobgoblin effigy of the idol to whom it was bequeathed?' he asked; 'the dazzling gem, which once graced the mighty arm of the "lion of the Punjaub" and which previously added weight and dignity to the house of Caboul, will be substituted by some valueless glass ball, as a miserable trophy of Hindoo credulity and superstition ...'

Though his letter was peppered with derisory comments about Indians, some of the writer's assessments were factually accurate. Kharak Singh was a weak and greedy man, and even the nobles of his court regarded him as a fool. Frequently drunk, the crown prince was more interested in wine and women than in matters of state. He imbibed copious amounts of opium and had little time for royal advisers. The prospect of serving such a man did not sit easy with the durbar. To those who knew the inner workings of Lahore, the plan put forward by 'A Voice' was not implausible. However the British never had the chance to implement this plan, or any other. Weeks before the *Era* published the letter, the Koh-i-Noor's fate had already been decided – by a mere servant of the Sikh court.

The master of the *toshakhana*, Misr Beli Ram, had served Ranjit Singh as guardian of the jewel-house for decades. He was one of the most trusted and respected men in all Lahore. Beli Ram's father had served in the *toshakhana* before him, and four of his brothers held high positions in the Imperial army. It was hard to find a family more dedicated to the maharaja.

Other than Ranjit Singh himself, Beli Ram was the only man in the kingdom permitted to handle the Koh-i-Noor. Twisting the long pearl-embellished tassels of the diamond's elaborate mount around his fingers, Beli Ram treated the Koh-i-Noor as if it was a living, dangerous bird of prey. When the maharaja visited the far reaches of his kingdom, Beli Ram took care of the most sensitive arrangements. He hid the Koh-i-Noor in a plain unobtrusive casket, and placed two exact glass replicas in two identical caskets. These boxes would be loaded on to different camels in Ranjit Singh's heavily guarded train. Nobody but Beli Ram knew which camel carried the real diamond.[18] If they struck camp for the night, the three caskets were chained to Beli Ram's bed. Thieves who might break through the tight rings of security outside his tent would then have to cut all three boxes free to be sure they got the right gem. Not that it ever came to it, but Beli Ram would have slit their throats before they got near his master's diamond.

So loyal was Beli Ram to the maharaja that he managed to alienate the most powerful and dangerous man in the kingdom. Punjab's vizier, or prime minister, Raja Dhian Singh, had once asked for a selection of crown jewels to be sent to his home, wishing to impress some visiting dignitaries. Dhian Singh knew better than to include the Koh-i-Noor in his request; nevertheless Beli Ram flatly refused, telling Dhian Singh to produce written permission from the maharaja first. The vizier's rage at such insolence was supressed but never forgotten. Four years later, with Maharaja Ranjit Singh gone, Dhian Singh would take his revenge, imprisoning Beli Ram and his brothers in his stables, chaining them up like animals, starving and beating them for days, only to have them strangled one by one when he tired of the torture.

In 1839, however, as 'A Voice' goaded his countrymen into making a move on the Koh-i-Noor, Beli Ram was at the height of his powers. His master might have been dead, but his sense of duty was very much alive and Beli Ram was all that stood between the diamond and the Jagannath temple. In a move that was completely out of keeping with his loyalty to his king, Beli Ram failed to honour Ranjit Singh's dying bequest. With the curses of the Jagannath priests ringing in his ears, he hid the Koh-i-Noor in his vaults and refused to send it to Orissa. Though he knew he might be accused of stealing the gem and insulting his master, Beli Ram's strong belief in the ancient principle of Chakravartin[19] gave him the strength to resist men, priests and even their gods. Dating back to the Mauryan Empire (322–185 BCE), Chakravartin encapsulated a code of kingship that obliged monarchs to rule benevolently. Centuries before Machiavelli was dispensing his own brand of cunning to Italian princes, an Indian emperor named Chandragupta Maurya was setting out his own Chakravartin philosophy, according to which it was the crown and not the king that mattered.

In Beli Ram's mind, the rules of Chakravartin made the Koh-i-Noor a jewel of state, an emblem of power, not the personal property of the Lion of Punjab or his anointed cub. Beli Ram therefore could not in all conscience honour the Jagannath bequest. The Koh-i-Noor belonged to Punjab and in Punjab it would stay, ready to be worn on the bicep of the next maharaja, whoever he might be. Of course it helped that Kharak Singh, the crown prince, and Raja Dhian Singh had also made their wishes abundantly clear: the Koh-i-Noor should, under no circumstances, leave Lahore.[20]

The thirty-seven-year-old Kharak Singh might have been the eldest of Maharaja Ranjit Singh's eight sons, but he was also the least able. The physician John Martin Honigberger despised him even more than he did Ranjit Singh, describing his coronation on 1 September 1839 as a dark day: 'Kurruck Sing ascended the Guddee [throne], who, besides being a blockhead, was a worse opium eater than his father. Twice a day he deprived himself of his senses and passed his whole time in a state of stupefaction.'[21]

Though his coronation came later, Kharak Singh had assumed the title of maharaja immediately after his father's funeral in June 1839, and proceeded to gorge himself on the trappings of power. He threw lavish parties, got drunk for days on end, ignored his vizier (the unforgiving Dhian Singh) and alienated the most powerful nobles in his realm. The religious Khalsa grew to despise his louche behaviour, and they were not alone. The new maharaja's generals and advisers were also disgusted with him, more because of his inability to focus on matters of state than because of his love of drugs, drink and dancing girls. A plan was hatched, just four months into his reign, to murder Kharak Singh.

Sapheeda kaskaree (white lead) and *rus camphor* (a compound of mercury) made their way into the maharaja's daily food and wine.[22] At first, the poison simply mimicked drunkenness, and Kharak Singh's speech became a little more slurred than usual, and his co-ordination clumsier for longer periods of time. Then the maharaja started to go blind as some kind of mysterious and merciless itch took over his body. Within weeks, Kharak Singh's joints burned with pain, and bleeding skin lesions opened up all over his body. Six months after the poisoning began, his organs started to shut down. Confined to his bed, Kharak Singh lay in unremitting agony, waiting to die.

The slow murder took eleven months in all, during which time Kharak Singh's eighteen-year-old son, Nau Nihal Singh, was recalled to the capital. A handsome young man and a brave soldier, Nau Nihal had little experience of court politics, and had been forced by his father's incapacity to return to Lahore and govern in his name under the direction of the vizier. Though it was never proven, most believed that same man, Dhian Singh, to be the mastermind behind the poison plot.

There was no suggestion, however, that Nau Nihal had any hand in his father's murder, although he did behave callously towards him. While he clung yet to life, Kharak Singh begged to see his son every day. But, as Honigberger noted tersely, the crown prince rarely visited his father. When death finally came to Kharak Singh on 5 November 1840, it was a mercy. The official announcement blamed a sudden mysterious illness, making no mention of the months of suffering that had passed. It seemed to Honigberger that nobody really missed the dead king or questioned the manner of his death.

Once again, the foreign physician found himself with a ringside seat at a Punjabi state funeral. Describing the event curtly in his memoirs, Honigberger said: 'Three of his wives were burnt with him; and I was present at that horrid, yet remarkable spectacle ...'[23] Eleven slave girls also burned to death that day, but Honigberger, perhaps inured to the horror of *sati* now, failed even to mention them.

As Kharak Singh had lit his own father's pyre, so Nau Nihal performed the last rites for Kharak Singh. In contrast to his father, he looked every inch a king as he did so. Popular with the court and the masses, he had already proven himself a natural leader during his father's 'sickness'. Though only eighteen, he possessed a maturity beyond his years, and to those who had longed for leadership, Nau Nihal seemed worthy to wear the Koh-i-Noor.

As his father burned, the new maharaja led his courtiers, including Honigberger, to the river Ravi, 'to perform their ablutions, according to the custom of the country ...'[24] Unnoticed, the doctor took the opportunity to slip away. He had tolerated Punjab's 'horrid' rituals for long enough and one of his patients needed his attention. Back at home, barely had he commenced his examination when a pageboy arrived from the palace in a state of great agitation. Nau Nihal and his companions had been returning from the river to the palace via the Hazuri Bagh, a tranquil garden built in 1818 by Ranjit Singh to celebrate the capture of the Koh-i-Noor. As the royal party passed beneath the Hazuri Bagh gate, a large elaborate structure, a heavy block of stone had fallen mysteriously from the archway. The masonry had struck Nau Nihal and two of his companions, killing one of them on the spot. Nau Nihal, thankfully, was not badly hurt, and according to the page had walked away from the scene.

Honigberger grabbed his box of balms and rushed to the palace, expecting to attend to a shaken, slightly bruised young maharaja. Instead, ashen-faced nobles greeted him. Raja Dhian Singh, the vizier, beckoned Honigberger to follow:

> The minister conducted me to a tent, where I saw the prince; but he enjoined me, in the most energetic manner, not to speak about that event to anyone. The prince was on his bed, his head most awfully crushed, and his state was such that no hope of his recovery existed. With that conviction I left the tent, and whispered to the minister, in so low a tone that no one else could hear it, 'Medical art can do nothing to relieve this unfortunate prince.'

The circumstances of Nau Nihal's 'accident' were far from clear, and eyewitness reports varied wildly. It had been the vizier's own nephew who was killed instantly by the falling masonry, and in contrast to the page's account, Dhian Singh swore that Nau Nihal's grievous injuries were also sustained in the Hazuri Bagh just like his nephew's. Alexander Gardner, an American mercenary-turned-artillery colonel in Ranjit Singh's army, told a very different story.[25] Gardner had been just a few steps behind the prince when the structure collapsed, and his own men had stretchered the wounded Nau Nihal to the palace. As Gardner told it, the prince was conscious and well enough to walk away, asking for water. Only upon Gardner's insistence was he stretchered to his bed.

What Honigberger saw shortly afterwards was not a man capable of walking or even talking. Nau Nihal's skull had caved in and the sheets were covered with blood and brain tissue. So severe were his injuries that he died hours later, though the news was kept from the people for three days. While sandalwood was collected in secret for his pyre, nobles in the durbar scrambled to fill the empty *gaddi* or throne before panic took hold in a rudderless Punjab.[26]

When news of the 'freak accident' finally got out three days later, Gardner fanned speculation by reporting that of the five artillerymen who had carried Nau Nihal to his bed, two died in mysterious circumstances, two asked for leave and never came back, and one simply and inexplicably disappeared. Nau Nihal, like his father before him, seemed to be the victim of surreptitious regicide.

As Punjab prepared itself for yet another royal funeral, the third in two years, thoughts turned towards the Koh-i-Noor. Its violent history, coupled with the belief that the diamond was in fact the Syamantaka stone, the gem of the gods, had always linked the diamond with dark powers in the minds of Indians. According to ancient Hindu scripture, the gem rained misfortune on unworthy mortal custodians. The Koh-i-Noor may have overlooked the great Lion, but it seemed intent on picking off his weaker heirs one by one.

On 9 November 1840 Nau Nihal was cremated and two of his teenage wives went with his body to the flames. His eldest wife, in the early stages of pregnancy, was spared. Another young girl was also saved from the fire when Nau Nihal's uncle, Sher Singh, interceded on her behalf. Honigberger recorded the incident: 'Two beautiful young ladies became victims of the flames with him [Nau Nihal Singh]. One female of the age of twelve years was detained ... owing to her not yet being ripe for the ceremony of suttee ...'

The child's saviour, Sher Singh, was the half-brother of Kharak Singh. Stout and striking, with a thick jet-black beard and piercing glare, he had the authority to pull a child from the pyre, but not to stake his own claim to the throne and the Koh-i-Noor. Now, as he watched his young nephew Nau Nihal burn, Sher Singh might have been forgiven a degree of satisfaction.

7

The Boy King

One of twins, Sher Singh was the second eldest son of Ranjit, born in 1807, five years after the now dead Kharak Singh. Minutes separated Sher Singh from his twin brother Tara, but an abyss lay between both boys and the throne of Punjab. Their mother, Maharani Mehtab, had been betrothed to Ranjit Singh when she was four and he only six years of age. She had been named Mehtab, the Persian for 'light of the moon', because of her fair, clear complexion. Her charm made her seem mismatched for the skinny, rough boy Ranjit Singh, who had already lost an eye and been scarred by smallpox. Nevertheless, they were married in 1796.

The marriage was not a happy one. Mehtab Kaur, a proud woman born to rich parents, found that Ranjit Singh paid her scant attention, spending the decade after his marriage battling to become the undisputed maharaja of all Punjab. His one eye had also taken to wandering: as the maharaja took more lovers, a humiliated Mehtab returned to her mother's estates in Batala, sixty miles north-east of the capital. Though Ranjit Singh continued to visit Mehtab at his in-laws' home, the couple were, to all intents and purposes, estranged. In the years that followed, Ranjit Singh married several other women and kept a large harem of beautiful girls. When Kharak Singh was born to his other wife Datar Kaur, Mehtab's mother urged her to reconcile with her husband. The new baby threatened her position in court, and the fortunes of Mehtab's entire family rested on her favour with the maharaja.

The reconciliation must have worked, because in 1803 Mehtab gave birth to a child, Ishar Singh. However the boy died soon after his first birthday. Distraught, Mehtab was pushed again by her mother to woo the maharaja. By this time, seduction was no easy task. Ranjit Singh was now captivated by a beautiful Muslim dancing girl called Mauran, who seemed to have eclipsed all others in his affections. Nevertheless, three long years later Mehtab finally fell pregnant, giving birth to twin boys, Sher Singh and Tara Singh. Despite the double good fortune, jubilation in Batala was short lived.

Vicious rumours drowned out the babies' first cries. There were allegations that Mehtab had conceived a daughter and secretly given her away, knowing that a girl would have no claim to the throne. She stood accused of taking two commoner children in the girl's place, one the baby of a weaver, the other of a carpenter. True or not, Ranjit Singh refused to acknowledge the boys as his legitimate heirs. However, he chose not to disown them either: though they would live as princes of Punjab, Ranjit Singh's rebuking silence meant that neither Sher Singh nor his brother would ever be king. They were condemned by their father to grow up rich, powerful but ultimately shamed.

———

At the sudden death of Nau Nihal, the durbar split. One faction proclaimed Sher Singh the rightful heir and the other positioned itself behind Nau Nihal Singh's mother and Kharak Singh's widow, the dowager Maharani Chand Kaur. It was hoped she might hold the throne till Nau Nihal Singh's pregnant wife gave birth to a son. When a baby boy emerged six months later, he was stillborn, and as grief overwhelmed his mother, panic gripped Lahore. The dowager maharani ordered the gates of the capital locked, realising that her personal tragedy would now embolden Sher Singh. The cloud over his legitimacy might have marred his chances before, but as the eldest living son of Ranjit Singh, with no Nau Nihal line to thwart him, his way now seemed clear. It also helped that he had a fully mobilised army at his disposal. In desperation, Chand Kaur called an emergency meeting of the aristocratic families of Lahore, and begged them to support her as ruler of the Sikh Empire, but it was too late. Even as the nobles debated their options, Sher Singh was on the move.

He had left his estate in Batala as soon as news of the stillbirth reached him. A 70,000-strong army marched behind Sher Singh and, upon finding the gates of the citadel locked, they laid siege to Lahore. For five days, Batala troops looted and terrorised the bazaars in the surrounding area enthusiastically, making their strength in numbers clearer with every passing day. Ultimately the desperation of her people forced Chand Kaur to open the gates. This she did only in exchange for a generous settlement and safe passage from the palace for herself and her grieving daughter-in-law.

With the Koh-i-Noor strapped to his arm, Sher Singh was anointed maharaja of Punjab, on 18 January 1841. As he sat on the golden throne, the unquestioned ruler of Punjab, he perhaps realised that as long as Chand Kaur lived, she remained his greatest threat.

On 11 June 1842, Chand Kaur was found dead in a pool of blood at her palace. Like her son, Nau Nihal, the dowager's skull had been crushed. This time there was no way of mistaking her death for any freak accident. Chand Kaur's own maids had beaten her to death with bricks as they brushed her hair. Apprehended by guards as they attempted to flee the scene, the women were dragged to Sher Singh's palace to await judgement, all the while protesting their innocence.

Sher Singh was away on a hunting trip at the time, far from any accusation of complicity, so it was left to his vizier, Dhian Singh, to punish the women. He ordered their noses, ears and hands to be cut off, before having their bleeding but yet breathing bodies thrown out of the city. Dr Honigberger noted wryly that perhaps he should have ripped their tongues out too, since they left Lahore screaming that they had only been obeying their maharaja's orders.

Though he might have thought he had shored up his position, Sher Singh's days were also numbered. A year later, on 15 September 1843, the maharaja was greeted at his hunting lodge by two trusted cousins, Ajit Singh Sandhanwalia and his brother Lena Singh. Knowing Sher Singh's great passion for weaponry, they had come to show him a new type of gun, 'a double-barrelled fowling-piece'.[1] The gun went off while it was pointing at Sher Singh's chest. Though the maharaja's cousins insisted that the shooting had been accidental, there was little explanation as to how and why it might have gone off a second time in his face,[2] nor why his beloved ten-year-old son was also found dead, 'cut into pieces with sabres',[3] at the Padhania gardens nearby. Dhian Singh, the scheming vizier who had survived three maharajas, was also murdered shortly afterwards.

In the four years that followed Ranjit Singh's death, Punjab had lost three maharajas, two crown princes, one dowager queen and numerous aristocrats. By December 1843, the last man standing was no man at all, but a tiny doe-eyed child by the name of Duleep Singh. Desperate for a symbol of unity, the entire durbar united behind Ranjit Singh's five-year-old son.

Born on 8 September 1838, Duleep Singh never knew his father. Barely a year old when Ranjit Singh died, Duleep found himself spirited away from Lahore before his father's funeral. Recognising the approaching succession storm, Rani Jindan, his mother, had taken her baby to Jammu where they could remain out of sight, far away from murderous minds. In retrospect, the infant prince was lucky to have had the protection of one such as Jindan. What she lacked in breeding, she more than made up for in brute survival instinct.

Born in 1817, Jindan had been brought up around ferocious hunting dogs. Her father, Manna Singh Aulak, had been the kennel-keeper in charge of Maharaja Ranjit Singh's hounds, and almost from the time of Jindan's puberty Aulak had thrust his pretty young daughter at the Lion. A wily and ambitious man, Aulak coaxed and cajoled the ageing one-eyed king to take Jindan as his wife, saying that she might put fire back into his loins. In 1835, Ranjit Singh, at the age of fifty-five, finally gave in, and his marriage to the eighteen-year-old Jindan made her his seventeenth wife.

Beautiful Jindan, with her oval face, aquiline nose and large, intense, almond-shaped eyes, was said to move with the grace of a dancer. Her innate sensuality unnerved many of those who met her, and she attracted admirers and detractors in equal measure. In contrast, war and the pressures of state had taken their toll on her husband: his long hair and chest-length beard were snowy white, and his tanned and pockmarked face deeply weathered and wrinkled. Paralysis had frozen his right side, and the pair looked deeply incongruous together. When Jindan fell pregnant two years later, the court gossips could barely contain themselves.

Just as they had destroyed Sher Singh's reputation in the cradle, so whispers set about the new baby from the moment he was born. How could the gnarled maharaja have fathered a child at his age and with his infirmities? Jindan must have slept with one of her servants. The gossips singled out one of her water-bearers for suspicion, a good-looking boy who was frequently caught locking gazes with the low-born queen. Surely the baby was too delicate and pretty to be of the Lion's loins?

In an unusual move, Maharaja Ranjit Singh took the step of officially and publicly declaring Duleep Singh his legitimate child, silencing rumours of Jindan's impropriety. By doing so, he quashed any notion that he was gullible enough to be cuckolded, while simultaneously confirming his own virility. Grudgingly, the court made room for Jindan and her baby, never thinking for a moment that he might one day be their king, and that she might sit on the throne of Punjab.

———

When they anointed the five-year-old Duleep Singh as maharaja of Punjab on 18 September 1843 the nobles of the durbar hoped they had found a puppet king to do their bidding. But the twenty-six-year-old Jindan, ill-educated, with no aristocratic family behind her, had other plans. The kennel-keeper's daughter scandalised the court by leaving the purdah of the women's quarters and declaring that she would govern Punjab herself in her boy's name.

With the Koh-i-Noor strapped to his soft, plump arm, Duleep sat in his mother's lap while she ruled over one of the most powerful empires in all India. The outrage provoked by her decision was made worse when Jindan appointed her brother, Jawahar Singh, the new vizier. He was one of the most detested men in the realm, wearing his coarseness like armour. Jawahar knew that his new-found wealth and status depended entirely on his sister, and as soon as he became vizier he set about destroying any challenge to her authority.

His intrigues were tolerated for a while. But on 11 September 1845, just two years into his nephew's reign, Jawahar went too far. Duleep's half-brother, Prince Pashaura Singh Kanwar, one of the only other surviving sons of Ranjit Singh, was restive. The twenty-three-year-old prince lacked the all-important stamp of legitimacy bestowed on Duleep, the boy king. Yet, having seen his half-brother Sher Singh shrug off his own similarly unlegitimised status, Pashaura Singh grew convinced that he too could seize power. Openly challenging Duleep for the throne, Pashaura amassed an army to fight for his claim. Unlike Sher Singh's, however, his army was met with unified resistance from Jindan's imperial troops. Greatly outnumbered on the battlefield, Pashaura was forced to surrender, but not before he made the regent promise to let him live out the rest of his life in peace and honour. In return, he vowed never again to challenge her son.

With the terms agreed, and on the pretext of escorting Prince Pashaura back to his home, Jawahar Singh, Jindan's brother, separated him from his soldiers and had him strangled to death. In the eyes of the high-born nobles, he had crossed an unforgivable line. He had reneged on a promise, and he had defied caste and honour by killing a prince of the royal blood. Jindan's brother would be made to pay for his treachery. On 21 September, now back in Lahore, Jawahar Singh was summoned to a meeting of the Sikh Khalsa, the spiritual leadership of Punjab.

The Khalsa acted as upholders of the Sikh moral code and were known to be uncompromising. Jawahar realised he was in danger, but could not ignore the summons from such an important group of men. He chose to meet the threat by riding out on the maharaja's own elephant, with Duleep sitting firmly in front of him on his lap.

His actions served as a very visual reminder to the Khalsa – Jawahar had the protection of his sister and her son. If they attacked him, they attacked their own sovereign. Thinking himself shielded, Jawahar lumbered towards the appointed meeting place, clinging to his little nephew. But he had underestimated the rage of his enemies. The Khalsa, along with a scattering of imperial guards, surrounded the elephant and rough hands reached up to pull his terrified, sobbing nephew from his arms. With the maharaja safely out of the way, the Khalsa then turned on Jawahar, tipping him from the jewelled howdah and throwing him into the dirt. As he lay there, pleading for his life, they hacked him to death.

Duleep, held out of danger by his own men, stood splattered with his uncle's warm blood. He saw every brutal blow, and the experience would haunt him all the days of his life. The screams of his mother, forced by durbar courtiers to watch, mingled with his own. After they were done, the vizier's killers bowed before the weeping child, assured him that he had never been the target of their anger, and that they would serve him loyally to the end of their days.

Jindan seemed to drown in her grief and terror for a time, and the nobles may have been forgiven for thinking they had rid themselves of her along with the malign influence of her brother. But her retreat to the *zenana*, the hidden women's apartments in the palace, was only temporary, and after a matter of weeks, defying all expectation, Jindan emerged from her quarters to resume her duties as regent. With a dignity that masked her inner turmoil, she took her place in the throne room, surrounded by the very men who had contrived to murder her brother and strongest ally. Hundreds of miles away from the unfolding drama, the British East India Company watched events with intense interest.

By the 1840s the British were the undisputed geopolitical masters of much of India. Through a mixture of trade and conquest, their territories expanded rapidly from Madras in the south-east of India all the way up to the Sutlej river, the natural boundary of the Sikh kingdom in the north. Ranjit Singh's strong army had stopped any further territorial gain, but his death and the years of turbulence which followed greatly weakened fortress Punjab.

In 1843, the very year that Duleep was anointed, East India Company troops began to build up south of the Sutlej. British agents tentatively approached Jindan, offering support to her regency, while at the same time making overtures to the most powerful men in the royal court, offering to help them topple her. Rani Jindan and Maharaja Duleep Singh were surrounded by embittered and ambitious men, and some of the most senior proved remarkably easy to turn.

Three months after the slaying of Duleep's uncle Jawahar, with resentment between Jindan and the Khalsa still simmering, the British made their move. Mobilising men from as far as West Bengal, they turned their comparatively small encampments by the Sutlej into an army. The Sikhs interpreted the unconcealed troop build-up as an act of aggression, and on 11 December 1845, Sikh cavalry crossed south over the Sutlej in order to push back the British encroachment. Two days later, claiming that his territory had been violated, the British governor general Sir Henry Hardinge declared war.

While the battles of the first Anglo-Sikh War raged, neither Duleep nor Jindan knew that two of the most powerful men in their court had already betrayed them. Lal Singh, who had replaced the slain Jawahar Singh as vizier, disclosed the position of Duleep's gun batteries to British spies and told them how many soldiers were in play and what they planned to do. Tej Singh, the commander of Duleep's armies, did far worse. The battle of Ferozeshah, which raged through

21–22 December 1845, was one of the hardest ever fought by the British army and their losses were heavy. Low on ammunition and food, governor general Hardinge found himself caught up on the front line. Continually battered by heavy guns all day, his men got no respite even when the sun went down. The Sikhs continued to pound his position with a 'terrific cannonade' that lit up the darkening sky. Hardinge described the long hours before dawn as 'a night of horrors'.[4] Expecting the Sikhs to overrun his position at any moment, he ordered the burning of his official documents: a protocol triggered when defeat was assured. He then presented his most precious personal possession, a sword which had once belonged to Napoleon Bonaparte, to his aide-de-camp.

This was the moment when the Sikhs ought to have delivered a decisive blow, but, instead of advancing, their general, Tej Singh, ordered a retreat. He would later claim he was trying to outflank his enemy, but most recognised his actions for what they were – a betrayal of his men and his maharaja. The Sikhs were cut to pieces by British reinforcements, who had been given ample time to muster thanks to Tej Singh's disastrous fallback.

Less than two months after the heavy defeat at Ferozeshah, on 10 February 1846, the Sikh army found itself pushed hard by freshly deployed, heavily armed British soldiers. To reorganise and rearm, Punjabi soldiers withdrew across the Sutlej river at every point except Sobaron, some forty miles south-east of Lahore. A single battalion of exhausted Sikhs was left to hold the bridgehead. Despite heavy fire, they refused to surrender or retreat. Superior numbers and greater firepower battered their position, yet they refused to give any ground. When they ran out of bullets, the Sikhs attacked with their swords, weaving through heavy artillery fire to attack the British at close quarters. For a while their bravery seemed to be turning the tide of battle, but at the very moment he should have been proudest of his men, General Tej Singh betrayed them again. Having himself crossed to the safety of the north bank of the river, he ordered the bridges across the Sutlej to be burned, cutting off any hope of reinforcement for his pinned-down soldiers. His men were now trapped between the British and the water, and their comrades were forced to watch the rout from the wrong side of the river. Though they knew their situation was hopeless, not one Sikh soldier surrendered that day. Backs to the torrent, they fought until British guns brought silence to the Sutlej. Sikh casualties are said to have numbered around 9,000.

Though they had emerged victorious in what became known as the First Anglo-Sikh War, the British were aware that they were still vastly outnumbered in the region. Entering Lahore as victors, Hardinge's men had to shore up their position, and they needed Duleep Singh to do that. So it was that the British hit upon an ingenious strategy. They assured a reeling Lahore that not only would they leave the maharaja on his throne but they would also safeguard his interests.

Signing the Treaty of Lahore with the child on 9 March 1846, the British vowed to stay only until Duleep reached the age of sixteen, as long as he in turn submitted to the presence of a resident, or local governor, who would have full authority to direct matters in all departments of the state. When Duleep turned sixteen, he would be old enough to govern for himself, and the British would leave as friends. The ink had barely had time to dry on the treaty when the British started to garrison their soldiers in Lahore, and draw up amendments to the legal document.

Ostensibly the British troops were protecting the boy king, and since they were there to serve him, Duleep was forced to foot the bill. He was, in effect, paying an occupying force to infiltrate his kingdom, while the resident worked to slash the size of his own imperial army within his realm. Outwardly in the durbar, things did not seem too different at first: Duleep remained on his throne, and the aristocrats of his court were allowed to continue in their positions too. The regent, Duleep Singh's mother, Rani Jindan, seemed to be the only one who could see what the British were doing.

Incandescent at the supine response of her advisers, she threw her bangles at them, accusing them of being weaker than women, taunting them for their stupidity. Could they not see that this was annexation by stealth? She railed impotently as the British carved up her son's kingdom and prepared to sell off parcels of land for war reparations. As amendments to the original agreement were pressed on her boy, like Cassandra, Jindan begged her nobles to see that their king was being deposed before their very eyes. Articles one and two of the treaty spoke of friendship and Duleep's right to rule, yet article three transferred control of his fortresses to the British. Articles four and five dealt with reparations that crippled Duleep's exchequer, and articles seven and eight decimated his army and gave away all his heavy guns. When the traitorous General Tej Singh was granted the Jagir of Sialkot, a district at the foot of the Kashmir hills, Jindan could stand it no more: the title would give the traitor all revenues from the district, and allowed him to parade around like a minor royal. Jindan could not allow her son to be debased in this way, and instructed him to defy the British and humiliate the treacherous general in front of all Lahore.

For the Sialkot title to be recognised, the maharaja himself needed to give Tej Singh his blessing by placing a mark of saffron and vermilion on his forehead. Jindan, fully aware of the defiance, told her son to resist no matter what his British advisers told him.

At a very public ceremony in Lahore, as Tej Singh knelt to receive his mark, Duleep Singh resolutely refused to dip his finger in the pot of colour held before him. His actions insulted Tej Singh and infuriated the British in equal measure. It was left to Sir Henry Lawrence, the new resident of Lahore, to deal with the problematic regent. In increasingly frustrated letters, complaints about Jindan's 'anti-English' behaviour and the 'scandalaous profligacy of her conduct' were scribbled and sent. Eventually a course of action was decided that took Jindan entirely by surprise: the British decided that she would have to be removed from Lahore and from Duleep completely. To make their decision more palatable, they attempted to conjure moral arguments for their decision. They were saving Duleep by taking his mother away from him: 'her general misconduct and habits of intrigue are sufficient to justify her separation from her son ... The British Government, being the guardian of the Maharajah, have the right to separate him from the contagion of her evil practice ...'[5]

In December 1847, when the maharaja was barely nine years old, he was sent to the Shalimar Gardens. Meanwhile, Jindan was torn screaming from her palace, fighting as she was dragged away, begging the Sikh men around her to wake up and fight. Not one man lifted a finger to help her.

Jindan was imprisoned in Lahore fort for ten days and then moved to a fortress in Sheikhupura, some twenty-five miles away. From the confines of her cell, she begged the British for the return of her only child:

> Why do you take possession of my kingdom by underhand means? Why do you not do it openly? ... You have been very cruel to me! ... You have snatched my son from me. For ten months I kept him in my womb ... In the name of the God you worship and in the name of the King whose salt you eat, restore my son to me. I cannot bear the pain of this separation. Instead you should put me to death ...[6]

She appealed to Henry Lawrence's humanity:

> My son is very young. He is incapable of doing anything. I have left the kingdom. I have no need of kingdom ... I raise no objections. I will accept what you say. There is no one with my son. He has no sister, no brother. He has no uncle, senior or junior. His father he has lost. To whose care has he been entrusted?[7]

Lawrence was decidedly uneasy. It was one thing to imprison meddlesome insurgents, quite another to keep a child from his mother. His superior, Sir Henry Hardinge, had no such misgivings: 'We must expect these letters in various shapes,' he assured Lawrence, 'which a woman of her strong mind and passions will assume as best suited either to gratify her vengeance or obtain her ends ...'[8]

With Jindan out of the way, the British were now free to do as they pleased in the maharaja's name. In 1848, they appointed a new governor general to replace the war-weary Hardinge. His name was James Andrew Broun Ramsay, the Earl of Dalhousie. His appointment would seal the fate of the maharaja and his entire kingdom.

Dalhousie in turn appointed Sir Frederick Currie as his new resident at the Sikh durbar. One of Currie's first acts was to raise taxes to refill depleted British coffers. The measure proved to be unpopular, and outlying areas of Punjab were hit hardest by the increasing demands. Multan, one of Punjab's largest and oldest cities, became a hotbed of resentment. Knowing that Diwan Mulraj, the governor of Multan, had always been fiercely loyal to Ranjit Singh and his family, the British resolved to replace him with an official more sympathetic to their needs. They chose Sardar Khan Singh, a little-known official from the court of Lahore, who had been most malleable.

Mulraj was ordered to hand over his city on 18 April 1848. Khan Singh presented himself at the gates, with a British political agent called Patrick Vans Agnew and a Lieutenant Anderson from the East India Company. What seemed at first to be a peaceful surrender proved to be anything but when the crowd, which had gathered to watch, turned into an angry mob. Whether what followed was pre-planned, or merely a reaction to the humiliation felt by the people of Multan, is hotly contested. What is not in dispute however is that Vans Agnew and Anderson were set upon and eventually hacked to death. This gave the British their *casus belli* and triggered an endgame that would ultimately lead to the total annexation of Punjab and the loss of the Koh-i-Noor.

Accused of orchestrating the violence, Mulraj became just the villain the East India Company, and more specifically Lord Dalhousie, had been looking for. The British declared war, and their troops swiftly converged on Punjab. Mulraj was painted as a bloodthirsty despot, intent on the overthrow of Duleep Singh and his British allies. By smearing Mulraj as an enemy of the maharaja it was hoped that the rest of Punjab would stay out of the conflict. But the British ploy had worn thin: soldiers from the old imperial army joined the Multan rebels, and conflict spread throughout the kingdom.

Lieutenant Herbert Edwardes, the British political agent in Bannu, was stationed near Multan, and sent his Pakhtun irregulars, and some Sikh regiments to drive back the rebels. Together, they engaged Mulraj's army at the Battle of Kineyri on 18 June 1848. The British Resident Currie then ordered a small force from the Bengal army to lay siege to the city of Multan, wanting to crush the centre of defiance once and for all. In November, the East India Company's armies also joined the war effort.

The battle of Chillianwala would prove the most bloody of the conflict. The fighting, which took place on 13 January 1849, would ultimately lead to the death of almost 2,000 East India Company troops. It occurred 250 miles north-east of Multan, in the same region where King Porus, an Indian ruler of Punjab, was once defeated by Alexander the Great in 326 BCE. Like Porus's troops before them, the Sikhs fought as if defeat were not an option, and their ferocity took many on the British side aback, as one eyewitness later reported: '[They] fought like devils, fierce and untamed ... Such a mass of men I never set eyes on and as plucky as lions: they ran right on the bayonets and struck their assailants when they were transfixed ...'[9]

Though Chillianwala ended with neither side gaining territory and both claiming victory, other battles were more decisive. More British troops, and soldiers from the East India Company, converged on Punjab by the day. Multan fell and eventually every rebelling force was either wiped out or forced to surrender. The final decisive battle took place in Gujrat and on 21 February 1849, British East India Company forces, armed with superior firepower, defeated what remained of the Sikh Empire's army.

The second Anglo-Sikh War had lasted almost a year, and at the end of it, Punjab was forced to watch what little was left of its imperial infrastructure destroyed.

This time, Dalhousie wanted the British conquest to be unmistakable, and under his direction the East India Company continued to pour men, artillery and logistics into the region. After the loss of thousands of lives, what was left of a rag-tag resistance surrendered on 12 March 1849. Rebel leaders, including Mulraj, were rounded up and sent to the Lahore dungeons to await trial and possible execution.

With all opposition now dead or in chains, on 29 March 1849 a new legal document was forced upon Duleep Singh, laying out stricter terms for surrender than any in Lahore had expected. The child, terrified by the recent fighting in his kingdom, separated from his mother and surrounded by foreigners and a smattering of Punjab nobles either too weak or too corrupt to stand up for him, was told he must sign over his kingdom, his fortune and his future. His British allies were all that stood between him and chaos, he was informed, and they now required nothing less than his complete acquiescence.

The Koh-i-Noor was high on the list of demands, and, with little choice, the ten-year-old obediently scratched his name on the document, agreeing to its uncompromising terms:

I. His Highness the Maharajah Duleep Singh shall resign for himself, his heirs, and successors all right, title, and claim to the sovereignty of the Punjab, or to any sovereign power whatever.

II. All the property of the State of whatever description and wheresoever found, shall be confiscated to the Honourable East India Company, in part payment of the debt due by the State of Lahore to the British Government and of the expenses of the war.

III. The gem called the Koh-i-Noor, which was taken from Shah Sooja-ool-mulk by Maharajah Runjeet Singh, shall be surrendered by the Maharajah of Lahore to the Queen of England.

IV. His Highness Duleep Singh shall receive from the Honourable East India Company, for the support of himself, his relatives and the servants of the State, a pension of not less than four and not exceeding five lakhs of the Company's rupees per annum.

V. His Highness shall be treated with respect and honour. He shall retain the title of Maharajah Duleep Singh Bahadoor, and he shall continue to receive during his life such portion of the above-named pension as may be allotted to himself personally, provided he shall remain obedient to the British Government, and shall reside at such place as the Governor-General of India may select.

With the signing of this, the final Treaty of Lahore, Punjab was now unquestionably a British territory; the Koh-i-Noor was British property; Maharaja Duleep Singh was a British problem. Such an outcome would have been unthinkable during the reign of Ranjit Singh, and had been brought about largely by the iron will of the new governor general of India.

When the thirty-five-year-old Earl of Dalhousie was named Hardinge's successor in 1847, he became the youngest ever governor general of India. His arrival in Lahore came a year after the signing of a document that had promised '... perpetual peace and friendship between the British Government on the one part, and Mahrajah Dhuleep Sing [sic] his heirs and successors on the other ...' The earlier treaty had also promised a British exit from Punjab when Duleep came of age. Such a return of territory did not fit with Dalhousie's view of imperial expansionism. Multan became not only his first real test in office, but also his first opportunity to challenge the agreements signed by his predecessors.

To some, including the former secretary of state for India, the Duke of Argyll, Dalhousie had shown the very best of British spirit: 'The history of the world presents no more splendid example of deserved success than the administration of the Punjaub under Lord Dalhousie. It displayed the highest virtues of a conquering and ruling race.'[10] To others, Dalhousie had behaved in a less than exemplary way, and had sowed the seeds of rebellion by his own hand. The poet and historian Edwin Arnold went as far as to suggest that the second Anglo-Sikh War had been caused by Dalhousie himself: 'The policy which afforded Moolraj time to turn a personal quarrel into a national revolt, and swelled the six thousand rabble of Mooltan into the thirty thousand warriors of Chillianwala, cannot be praised.' In words that stung Dalhousie's supporters, and drove the likes of Argyll to defend his conduct publicly, Arnold wrote: 'India was given to us, and will be kept, by men who, in the high mission of her mastery and redemption, are cautious in counsel without dulness, and swift in action without rashness.'[11]

When news reached Dalhousie that Duleep had signed the terms of surrender in 1849, he reacted with jubilation. Writing to a friend he declared: 'I had now "caught my hare".' The seizure of the Koh-i-Noor was as important as the annexation of the region. In the letter to his friend, Dalhousie added exultantly: 'the Council of the Regency and the Maharajah signed their submission to the British power, surrendered the Koh-i-Noor to the Queen of England; the British colours were hoisted on the Citadel of Lahore, and the Punjab, every inch of it, was proclaimed to be a portion of the British Empire in India.'[12]

With a characteristic flourish, he predicted the British government's response to his actions:

> If they sanction and approve (as unless they are maniacs they must do), their approval will be full and conspicuous. It is not every day that an officer of their Government adds four millions of subjects to the British Empire, and places the historical jewel of the Mogul Emperors in the Crown of his own Sovereign. This I have done. Do not think I unduly exult.[13]

The diamond's fate was settled and Duleep's fate was now entirely in Dalhousie's hands. The young maharaja had no way of knowing it, but even as he signed the treaty the governor general had already decided to send him away from Punjab, far from everything he had ever known. The Fategarh Hill Fort (in the Farrukhabad district of present-day Uttar Pradesh), almost 600 miles away, was chosen for Duleep's banishment, and de facto parents had even been selected to raise him. A Scottish doctor by the name of John Spencer Login and his wife Lena would look after the young maharaja until he became a man.

Lord Dalhousie, as he himself predicted, was eventually rewarded for his efforts and created a marquess. Because of him, the Koh-i-Noor was destined for England. India would never see its jewel again. Punjab would lose its king.

John Login was deemed by the British to be one of the most steadfast men in all India. Such was the faith placed in him that after the annexation he had been given the keys to the *toshakhana*. In the vaults, Login catalogued the Sikh Empire's treasures, including the Koh-i-Noor. Surrounded by piles of gold, he recorded descriptions, took measurements and estimated values for the East India Company. The assistant commissioner of Lahore, Robert R. Adams, watched him work and was amazed at Login's ability to resist the lures of his surroundings. As he wrote to Login's wife:

> I wish you could walk through that same Toshakhana and see its wonders! The vast quantities of gold and silver, the jewels not to be valued, so many and so rich! The Koh-i-noor, far beyond what I had imagined ... And all this made over to him, without any list, or public document of any sort, all put in his hands to set in order, value, sell, etc; that speaks volumes, does it not, for the character he bears with those whose good opinions are worth having? Few men, I fancy, would have been so implicitly trusted.[14]

Like Misr Beli Ram before him, Login took his duties in the vaults extremely seriously, personally foiling a plot by some of his own countrymen to steal from the treasury. One evening when he had been working late,

British soldiers successfully tunnelled into one of the darkened rooms containing treasure. They knocked a guard senseless and made off with whatever they could carry. The Koh-i-Noor, however, was safely out of their reach, in a special vault with a dedicated guard. Login not only raised the alarm, but personally led the hunting party which eventually tracked down the thieves. He also co-ordinated meticulous searches of the British barracks and nearby flowerbeds till he found every coin that had been taken.

Few were surprised by Login's dedication to his job. His association with India stretched back more than a decade and he had always conducted himself in an exemplary manner. He had served as a medic during the Afghan War of 1839–42, and then as a general adminis-trator for the growing British Empire. A man of faith, his unswerving Christian belief governed his every action.

Though Login recognised the honour of being trusted to guard the Koh-i-Noor, he did not relish the task. The men who had looked after it before him, Misr Beli Ram and his assistant, Misr Makraj, had whispered frequently of its dark power. Makraj, who had stayed on to assist Login in the *toshakhana*, was 'eloquent in his expressions of relief at being set free from the sole responsibility' for the diamond. As he handed it over to Login he reminded him: 'the Koh-i-noor had been fatal to so many of his family that he had hardly hoped ever to survive the charge of it!'[15]

Privately, Login hoped the diamond might be taken from his care too, as soon as possible, and preferably sold to the highest bidder. By his calculations, this would leave ample funds to replenish British war coffers and a considerable balance would also be left over which might be used 'in the improvement of the country from whence the Koh-i-noor came'.[16]

When Dalhousie made it clear that every last coin and trinket was to be sent back to England, and not a penny of gain spent on the natives, Login felt decidedly uneasy. Not only did it jar with his sense of Christian charity and fairness, he also harboured doubts about whether Dalhousie had had any legal or moral justification to start the second Anglo-Sikh War in the first place.

The governor general had blamed the 'villain Mulraj' for precipitating the conflict. The chieftain of Multan was painted as a cunning and ruthless warrior, hell-bent on the destruction of the British. The threat from such a malign figure had made the British cause seem righteous. However, Login had been given the keys to the citadel dungeons as well as to its vaults, and it was to one of these cells that Mulraj, the most wanted man in all India, was brought in chains. Login was entrusted with processing the prisoner and keeping him incarcerated till the date of his trial had been set.

Writing to his wife, Login confessed that Mulraj was nothing like the bloodthirsty rebel she may have read about in the papers, a man who had killed a friend of theirs, 'but rather a weak, chicken-hearted fellow, afraid to do what was right, and entirely in the hands of some resolute villains around him. I don't think he really intended any harm to dear Pat Vans Agnew ...'[17]

Login was left with no time to dwell on his misgivings, since in addition to his responsibility for the *toshakhana* he now also had to take charge of Duleep. Arrangements had to be made, and a little boy needed to be won over. He resolved to show his new ward nothing but kindness. He believed that a blameless boy was being punished for the actions of others. Login was not alone in feeling this way.

Sir Henry Lawrence, the resident of Lahore who had ignored the pleading letters from Rani Jindan, was also touched by Duleep Singh's plight. He had been against the military campaign from the start, and would have preferred to have left Duleep on the throne, forging a mutually beneficial alliance with the natives. As Lena Login later recalled: 'the Governor-General's [Dalhousie's] decision [to annex the kingdom] was a sore grief to the generous-hearted Resident, and a reversal of many cherished hopes and projects'.[18]

The British press had no such misgivings and crowed over the annexation, painting the boy king Duleep as the author of his own misfortune: '... this famous diamond (the largest and most precious in the world) forfeited by the treachery of the sovereign at Lahore,

[is] now under the security of British bayonets at the fortress of Goindghur ...' the *Delhi Gazette* said. 'It is hoped [it] will ere long, as one of the splendid trophies of our military valour, be brought to England in attention of the glory of our arms in India.'[19]

Duleep was as much 'under the security of British bayonets' as his Koh-i-Noor, and Dalhousie had little sympathy for him. The governor general described the maharaja as 'A child notoriously surreptitious, a brat begotten of a bhishti [water-carrier], and no more the son of old Runjeet than Queen Victoria is ...'[20] Despite his efforts to rubbish the boy and cast doubt on his legitimacy, Dalhousie still met with questions over his conduct towards a minor. He offered a shrug by way of explanation: 'He has a large territory but he is a boy ... I am sorry for him, poor little fellow, although it is a superfluous compassion ...'[21] Even the loss of the Koh-i-Noor, Dalhousie argued, would have little effect on the boy, who would in time grow to be grateful for what the British had done for him: 'He [Duleep] does not care two pence about it [the Koh-i-Noor] himself – he will have a good and regular stipend, ('without income tax') all his life, and will die in his bed like a gentleman; which under other circumstances, he certainly would not have done.'[22]

The *Mining Journal*, a dry technical publication, gave a more accurate representation of Duleep's plight than the governor general: 'The recent war in Mooltan, and disturbances in the Punjaub, have induced the British resident at Lahore to secure, as a hostage, the person of the boy King Maharajah Dhuleep Singh, and at the same time to seize the Koh-i-Noor.'[23]

Both Duleep and his diamond were now equally and entirely at the mercy of the British.

8

Passage to England

Duleep's new life began on 6 April 1849, the day he was formally introduced to his new guardian in Lahore. Login was more nervous than the child at their first meeting, and greatly relieved when it went better than he had dared to hope: 'The little fellow seemed very well pleased with me, and we got on swimmingly ... He seems a very fine-tempered boy, intelligent, and handsome.'[1]

In letters to his wife Login described the ten-year-old Duleep as 'very lovable'[2] and eager to please. With large dark eyes fringed by long curling lashes, he had inherited his mother's fine features. Duleep loved to paint and read books; but it was his passion for Persian poetry and hunting with hawks that made him unmistakably regal. Unlike many other children, from time to time Duleep would retreat into himself, preferring to be alone and quiet. Login attributed such episodes to the maharaja's contemplative nature rather than to any sadness. The pair assiduously avoided the topic of his mother or the Koh-i-Noor.

For his ward's eleventh birthday, the first since Duleep had lost his kingdom, Login decided to throw a large and colourful party: 'I should like to see as many children as possible, on the little fellow's account.'³ In order to make the day as perfect as he could, Login asked the British government if he might choose 'a lakh of rupees' worth' of Duleep's own jewels 'to select and present to him'.⁴

Had Duleep still reigned over his kingdom, his countrymen would have presented him with fabulous emeralds, rubies, diamonds and spinels to mark the day. Login wanted to approximate that experience, but could do so only by returning some of the gems which had been seized from the child, and which he himself had catalogued in the *toshakhana*. If Dalhousie gave consent, Duleep would be presented with precious baubles on his birthday, he would have his chance to look regal, and nobody needed to acknowledge that these trinkets had belonged to him only weeks before.

Though Dalhousie was adamant that Duleep's jewels were now the spoils of war, there were so many of them that the governor general could afford to be generous. John Login himself had catalogued the 'medley of articles', describing them as so numerous that they had often been treated with carelessness. He once told his wife: 'One of the largest emeralds ever seen was accidentally discovered set in the pommel of a saddle!

The saddle had been already condemned to be broken up or disposed of, when the piece of *green glass* (as it was supposed) was observed, set in the position in which the Sikh noblemen often carry a mirror when riding in full dress, to make sure that the turban and paraphernalia are all *en règle*.'[5]

The request for a few token trinkets was granted and the maharaja was duly presented with an assortment of gems. Though he was a king without a kingdom, on his birthday he looked like a maharaja. If Login's aim had been to distract the boy from his greater losses, his gambit did not entirely work. As he reported to his wife, Duleep 'innocently remarked that on his *last birthday* he had worn the Koh-i-noor on his arm'.[6]

John Login dreaded any mention of the Koh-i-Noor. He had been uneasy for some time about the way in which it had been appropriated. Nothing represented Duleep's downfall more eloquently than the loss of the legendary gem, and Login longed to put distance between the boy and his humiliation. A few weeks after the birthday party, Login heard some news that cheered him: 'There is a report going about since last mail that, much to the honour of "our dear little Queen," she has declined to accept the Koh-i-noor as a gift, under the circumstances in which it has been offered her; indeed I shall rejoice to hear that this is true, and I am sure that many of her subjects will rejoice with me.'[7]

Login hoped that Queen Victoria's misgivings about the diamond mirrored his own, and that they would force the British government to pay for the diamond if they wished to take it, making its transfer to the Tower of London feel a little less unjust: 'I feel certain that it would be easy to raise a sufficient sum to purchase it, and it would have more value in her eyes, given her in this way by her people, as a token of their respect and honour ...'[8]

In his excitement, Login even started spending the money that he thought the sale of the Koh-i-Noor would raise, the bulk of it 'to be spent for the good and benefit of her new subjects here, by making the Punjab to bloom like a garden ... giving employment to the 100,000 men who have been cast adrift, making roads, bridges, and canals, and establishing schools among them, and thus showing that we are above taking anything from them in a shabby way. This would be one way of converting the possession of the Koh-i-noor into a blessing instead of a curse ...'[9]

However, Login's hopes were soon dashed. They were based on nothing more than a rumour. Though the queen might have expressed private misgivings about the treatment of Duleep and the way in which his greatest treasure had been appropriated, she never went as far as to refuse the diamond, nor did she interfere with Dalhousie's plan for the maharaja's 'adoption' by the Logins. There was no question that he might be given back to his mother.

Meanwhile, over the course of several months, Jindan's reputation had been destroyed in dispatches shuttling between Lahore and London. She was painted as a sexual predator, described as the 'Messalina of Punjab' – evoking the promiscuous wife of the Roman emperor Claudius. It was suggested that she would use her beauty to bewitch men to follow her in an uprising. This was why she had to be locked away.

Having established Jindan as a whore, Dalhousie then set about attacking her parenting, knowing that this would poison the well at Buckingham Palace. He told Queen Victoria that Jindan was a cruel mother, who had physically abused her son. British intervention had saved the boy from such a woman: '[Duleep] has no desire to return to his mother, who "put discredit on him," he says, "by beating him every day" ...'[10]

Queen Victoria accepted Dalhousie's explanation; however, she also made it known that she wanted regular updates on the maharaja's welfare and progress, urging her representatives to treat him with kindness. Duleep was almost the same age as Victoria's eldest son, Bertie, the prince of Wales, and she was deeply touched by his plight.

While Login planned Duleep's birthday party, his mother, Jindan, marked her sixteenth month behind bars. Despite her subsequent move from Lahore to Sheikhupura, this was not far enough for Currie. In July 1848, he ordered Jindan to be transported hundreds of miles to a remote cell in Chunnar Fort, an ancient and imposing stone citadel, high on a rocky outcrop (in the Mirzapur district of modern Uttar Pradesh).

From her lonely, windswept prison, overlooking the vast Gangetic plains, Jindan pined for any scrap of information about her son. Only rage seemed to sustain her. That same passion threatened to drown her completely when she heard of the annexation of Punjab and the seizure of the Koh-i-Noor. Days after Duleep had signed the treaty, on 19 April 1849, Rani Jindan escaped from Chunnar Fort. Exchanging her clothes for the rags worn by a seamstress, a lowly servant who had come to Chunnar Fort to sew leaves into cups and plates, she fled under cover of darkness, taunting her British captors as she went. Jindan scrawled a note for guards to find: 'You put me in a cage and locked me up. For all your locks and your sentries, I got out by magic ... I had told you plainly not to push me too hard – but don't think I ran away. Understand well, that I escape by myself unaided ... don't imagine I got out like a thief.'[11]

Keeping to the wilderness paths, Jindan took a circuitous route of almost 800 miles to reach the Kingdom of Nepal. There, in the capital, Kathmandu, she threw herself on the mercy of the ruler Jung Bahadur. Unknown to her, British envoys had reached him first and instructed the Nepalese ruler to offer Jindan sanctuary as long as he also enforced a stringent set of conditions. He must forbid her from setting foot in India again. She must not attempt to contact her son. She must not attempt to stage an uprising in Punjab or challenge British rule in any way. Failure to comply with these rules would lead to her exile from Nepal and immediate incarceration in an Indian prison from which she would never escape again.

Physically and mentally battered, Jindan had no option but to accept.

While Jindan wasted away in Nepal, in early February 1850 the streets of her old capital, Lahore, were lined by tearful subjects. They watched as their maharaja's caravan left Punjab for the very last time, taking him into exile. He seemed to be taking the legacy of Ranjit Singh with him, and for many old sirdars it was almost too much to bear. John Login had tried his best to make the journey feel like an adventure to Duleep. His new home would be hundreds of miles away in Fategarh, and Login filled the boy's ears with promises of good hunting, new experiences and the prospect of a happy childhood with a 'normal' family.

The family Login offered was his own. His wife Lena would join them in Fategarh, as would his children, and there would be playmates and fun for the maharaja. After years of uncertainty and fear, Login offered him security, space to breathe and the freedom to act like a child.

Login's optimism was genuine. He felt that the more miles he could put between his ward and his old life, the better off he would be. Of late, his talks with Duleep had inspired him to think more ambitiously. Perhaps he might be able to remove the boy from India altogether. Much to Login's delight, the maharaja was beginning to show a fascination with England. He regularly asked about its people, culture and queen: 'I think the Maharajah shows a great desire to hear about England. Sir H[enry] Lawrence wished he could be educated there, and not left to grow idle and debauched in India with nothing to do, considering what he has *lost* and we have *gained*! ... he is young enough to mould.'[12] If his country could make room for Duleep's diamond, could it also make room for Duleep, Login wondered?

Though the British press was already clamouring for the great diamond to be brought to England it showed very little interest in the gem's previous owner: 'Are we really to see the Mountain of Light? ... is the renowned Koh-i-noor really on its way to England? Is the Tower of London actually to possess such a treasure?' asked *Lloyd's Weekly*, capturing the excited anticipation of the nation. Though the paper was delighted at the prospect of the Koh-i-Noor's arrival, it was less pleased about the role Dalhousie had played in its confiscation:

> Though the Marquis of Dalhousie has substantially made her Majesty a present of the gem, in point of form, the boy Dhuleep Singh ceded it to the Queen. But such a cession is a mockery; the lad did exactly what he was bid, and would have made it over with equal facility to the chief of the Cherokee Indians, had Lord Dalhousie directed him. He signed the paper placed before him quite regardless of its contents; and the responsibility of its terms rest [sic] entirely with the Governor General ...[13]

Painting an unflattering portrait of an arrogant man, the paper went on to charge Dalhousie with betraying his employers at the East India Company and overstepping his mandate in India. Dalhousie stood accused of unforgivable hubris, of acting as if he were the man presenting the diamond to the queen when he had no legal right to do so. The diamond, as with all else in the conquered territory of Punjab, belonged to the East India Company. It should have been in the Company's gift to present the gem to the sovereign, not some vain servant of that company, who sought only glory for himself.

Stung by the criticism, Dalhousie had to bear further insult when the East India Company insisted on leaving him out of any future presentation of the Koh-i-Noor to the queen. Though he had to accept their decision, Dalhousie did not do so graciously. In a letter to Sir John Hobhouse, the president of the Board of Control and ultimately the minister responsible for the East India Company, the governor general reminded him that not one man at Leadenhall Street, the Company's headquarters, had played a part in securing the diamond for Britain. Dalhousie and Dalhousie alone was responsible for the Koh-i-Noor making its way to the queen:

Whatever my 'affectionate friends' at Leadenhall Street should, or may, think, you at least will find no fault with my having regarded the Koh-i-Noor a thing by itself, and with my having caused the Maharajah of Lahore, in token of submission, to surrender it to the Queen of England. The Koh-i-Noor had become in the lapse of ages a sort of historical emblem of conquest in India. It has now found its proper resting place.[14]

Privately, Dalhousie was less polite, railing in a letter to a friend: 'I am much indebted to them for thinking me a blockhead. Our estimate of each other is mutual.'[15]

Though he would not be permitted to put the Koh-i-Noor directly into his queen's hands, Dalhousie still had to organise its safe passage to England. The Lahore vaults and their contents were now the responsibility of a Board of Administration, consisting of three men: Sir Henry Lawrence, the now former resident of Lahore, his younger brother John Lawrence, and Charles G. Mansell, a long-serving civil servant. Of the three, the tall, handsome John Lawrence was the most charismatic and contrary. He had served with distinction in the first Anglo-Sikh War, yet ever since the annexation he had won the esteem of the Punjab peasantry who hailed him as 'the saviour of Punjab'. Lawrence had fought to save them from punitive taxes, and though he represented the 'enemy' many poor Punjabis had grown to regard him as an ally.

John Lawrence was somewhat surprised when he, the man least impressed by princely baubles, was chosen to guard the Koh-i-Noor until such time as its passage to England could be arranged. Orders came in a letter, from Dalhousie, addressed to the three men just before Christmas in 1849. After they had read the governor general's wishes, the diamond was summoned up from the *toshakhana* and formally transferred into John's custody. If his official biographer is to be believed, John solemnly removed it from its casket, placed it in his waistcoat pocket, took it home and promptly forgot all about it.

Six weeks later, on 12 January 1850, a message arrived from Simla with Dalhousie's unmistakable signature. The time had come to send the great diamond to England and to Queen Victoria. As his brother Henry finished reading out the letter, John responded with a solemn but stirring: 'Send for it at once.' No sooner had the words left his lips than his brother exploded with an incredulous: 'Why, *you've* got it!'[16]

Like the absent-minded Mughal emperor Humayun who had left his bag of jewels, including Babur's Great Diamond, on a Persian riverbank while he bathed, John Lawrence had forgotten all about the jewel entrusted to him. Now, expected to produce the Koh-i-Noor, he realised he had absolutely no recollection of what he had done with it. John did his best to hide his panic and he left his companions, telling them blithely that he was just off to retrieve the Koh-i-Noor. In reality he had no earthly clue where it might be. 'Well, this is the worst trouble I have ever got you into!' he said to himself, as he desperately tried to remember the last time he had laid eyes on the stone.[17]

Reaching home, 'with his heart in his mouth', John Lawrence 'sent for his old bearer and said to him, "Have you got a small box which was in my waistcoat pocket some time ago?" "Yes, Sahib," the man replied, "I found it and put it in one of your boxes." "Bring it here," said the Sahib. Upon this, the old servant went to a battered tin box. "Open it," said John Lawrence, "and see what is inside."' John watched as the baffled bearer held up the Koh-i-Noor. 'There is nothing here, Sahib,' he said, 'but a bit of glass!'[18]

John Lawrence dined out on that story, although many of his contemporaries poured scorn on it. Lena Login, who usually kept controversial opinions to herself, scoffed at the idea that a man's waistcoat pocket could ever have held such a mighty gem. Whether the story of the lost Koh-i-Noor was true or not, it added another facet to the diamond's already colourful legend.

The Koh-i-Noor's ocean crossing was a straightforward proposition, but getting it to the port of Bombay was not. An overland trip of hundreds of miles would be fraught with risk and needed careful thought and preparation. Heavily guarded caravans would be too conspicuous. Small but swift cavalry escorts would be too vulnerable. Having considered all his options, Dalhousie decided that secrecy was more important than strength. Telling only a handful of his most trusted confidants, he decided that he would carry the diamond to Bombay himself. As a frequent visitor to Lahore, Dalhousie's swift arrival and departure would draw little attention. The very notion that the governor general might act as diamond courier was too ludicrous to be entertained, which is why he became convinced that it was the only plan that would work.

Keeping the circle of trust as small as he could, the governor general asked his wife, Lady Dalhousie, to stitch a small pouch for him. It was nondescript and just large enough to hold the diamond. She chose the softest kid leather she could find, material that would not chafe against her husband's skin when he hid it under his shirt. Lady Dalhousie also double-sewed the pouch on to the inside of a leather belt, which fitted snugly around her husband's waist, beneath his shirt. She attached a thin chain to the base of the bag, long enough to pull up over her husband's body and fasten around the back of his neck. Even if Dalhousie had cause to unbutton his shirt in the heat, the chain looked as if it might hold a locket or crucifix, and should have attracted no undue attention.

For the perilous journey to Bombay, Dalhousie chose Captain James Ramsay to accompany him. Not only was Ramsay an accomplished and decorated soldier, he was also Dalhousie's flesh and blood. The governor general's trusted nephew, Ramsay was the only other person who knew of Dalhousie's plan. Two other members of Dalhousie's household were also conscripted for the mission, though they probably were not aware of its importance. Dalhousie's pet dogs, Banda and Barron, would serve as ferocious guards, and were to be chained to his camp bed every night. Satisfied with his plan, at a small ceremony in Lahore on 7 December 1849, with John Lawrence, Henry Lawrence and Mansell in attendance, as well as Sir Henry Elliot, the secretary to the government of India, and John Login, Dalhousie signed a receipt for the Koh-i-Noor. Securing the diamond in his secret pouch, the governor general left Lahore for the long journey to Bombay.

Much to Dalhousie's relief, the trip was largely uneventful and he kept the Koh-i-Noor next to his skin. As he later confessed, 'It never left me, day or night.'[19] Only once was he forced to remove the pouch, and that was early on in his mission. Unavoidable government business required him to ride out from camp in a place called Dera Ghazi Khan, on the outskirts of Punjab territory. The terrain was notoriously treacherous and teeming with bandits. Dalhousie carefully unwound the Koh-i-Noor from his body and gave it to his nephew. As he later confessed to a friend in a letter, Ramsay was issued with some unusual instructions: 'I left it with Captain Ramsay (who now has joint charge of it) locked in a treasure-chest, and with strict instructions that he was to sit upon the chest until I came back! My stars! What a relief to get rid of it.'[20] One can only imagine how ridiculous Ramsay looked and felt, pistol in hand, sitting on a piece of luggage, all alone in a tent, for hours on end.

On 1 February, after nearly two months of travelling and tension, the Koh-i-Noor in its sweaty leather pouch finally reached Bombay. Though both Dalhousie and Ramsay were quite giddy with relief, it soon became clear that the diamond would have to stay hidden for a further two months. Dalhousie's hopes of putting the gem to sea immediately were thwarted when he found out that no suitable naval vessel would be available to carry the diamond to England for weeks. All appropriate vessels were fully committed in the Far East. Unable to expedite the process without drawing suspicion, Dalhousie resigned himself to another long stretch of anxiety.

First he placed the Koh-i-Noor in a small iron safe fitted with a sturdy lock. Then he placed the safe inside a red dispatch box, which also had a lock. This container was sealed with red tape and wax, making it look like a normal diplomatic pouch which might usually contain official papers bound for Westminster. The dispatch box was then placed in another chest, specially designed also to have two separate locks. The diamond in its multi-layered protection was then stored in the Bombay treasury, where it waited, under special guard, for the next leg of its journey.

On 6 April 1850, the Koh-i-Noor was finally taken aboard HMS *Medea*, a steam sloop in the charge of a seasoned naval commander named Captain William Lockyer. Lockyer watched the double-locked iron chest being loaded on to his vessel. It was not until his ship had weighed anchor that the importance of his cargo was made known to him. Dalhousie also sent his nephew, Captain Ramsay, to accompany the diamond on its final journey. The East India Company grandees in Leadenhall Street had demanded that one of their own men also be included in the diamond's entourage. Colonel J. Mackeson completed the trio of Koh-i-Noor escorts aboard *Medea*.

As the Bombay shoreline faded in the distance, Captain Ramsay produced four keys, each of which opened one of the locks in the chest, the dispatch box and the safe. He kept two keys for himself and gave the other two to Mackeson. Complicity between the three men would now be needed to free the diamond from its hiding place. With nothing but the deep blue sea around them, anyone thinking of stealing the gem would have nowhere to take it. The diamond was safe.

After around ten days at sea, Lockyer discovered another concealed passenger aboard his ship. *Medea* was carrying cholera. He found this out only when two of his 135 crewmen were found dead below decks and others started complaining of nausea and diarrhoea. Cholera outbreaks had wiped out entire crews in the past and, surrounded by the Indian Ocean, there was nothing Captain Lockyer could do to stop its deadly progress. He must have thanked his lucky stars that Mauritius, and the promise of medicine and treatment for his men, was close by. The captain did his best to reassure his men that fresh supplies and doctors would be with them soon.

However when *Medea* reached the coast, the Mauritians refused to have anything to do with the cholera-plagued ship. They demanded the immediate departure of *Medea* and her infected crew. When Lockyer refused to comply, the Mauritian authorities threatened to open fire and destroy the vessel, drowning the captain and all his men. After delicate negotiations between the ship and the shore, Lockyer finally convinced the Mauritians to part with 130 tons of coal to power the ship away from their coastline. Though the islanders threw in a small amount of medicine, it was hardly enough, and neither food nor water was provided.[21] Frightened and feverish, the crew of *Medea* had no choice but to continue on their way to England, praying for deliverance.

Deliverance did not come. Before long HMS *Medea*'s crew faced fresh peril as the ship sailed straight into a gale. High winds tossed the crew around for what seemed like an eternity. The rigging was stretched to snapping point, and the depleted men fought to save their mainsail from the waves. So severe was the storm that at one point *Medea* threatened to break entirely in half. Sailors prayed with renewed fervour, while

Lockyer, Mackeson and Ramsay, the three men who knew about the Koh-i-Noor and the dark curse that went with it, might have wondered whether the jewel was dragging them all to hell. The storm lasted for twelve hours before the skies cleared and the waters calmed.

Medea limped into Plymouth on 30 June 1850. By now, the press had been alerted to the Koh-i-Noor's arrival, and crowds gathered at the docks to greet it. The *Morning Post* had been one of the first newspapers to break the news. Though the rest of the ship's cargo was unloaded on the quay, the Koh-i-Noor stayed aboard: 'The priceless Koh-i-noor has arrived ... The jewel was not transhipped, but taken to Portsmouth in the *Medea*, where it remained on board last night ...'[22]

When *Medea* finally reached Portsmouth a day later, officers of the 22nd Foot, and a man called Onslow, private secretary to the chairman of the East India Company, were waiting to receive it. They took the diamond in its many layers of concealment and, accompanied by an exhausted Ramsay and Mackeson, sped away in a special train to London and the head-quarters of the East India Company in Leadenhall Street. There the wooden box and four keys were solemnly handed over to the Company's chairman, John Shepherd, who accepted them on behalf of his queen. With the Koh-i-Noor on British soil at last, the press were free to pore over the diamond's exotic and blood-soaked history. The newspapers were filled with stories of Ranjit Singh and his son, the boy king. The terrible curse, said to afflict the owners of the diamond, made for irresistible reading around the breakfast tables of Britain, and it was perhaps inevitable that recent worrying events were linked to its arrival.

While *Medea* was preparing to enter British territorial waters, Queen Victoria had been visiting her dying uncle in London. As she left his home, Cambridge House, a grand Palladian-style mansion in Piccadilly, a smartly dressed man approached her carriage and struck her over the head with a thin black cane with an iron handle. The blow was hard enough to crush her bonnet and draw blood. The attacker, Robert Francis Pate, a former British army officer, appeared to have no motive for his actions. The *Standard* was just one of the newspapers which ran the story of the Koh-i-Noor's arrival right next to a detailed account of the attack on the queen. Such juxtapositions in print merely fuelled the rumours about the diamond's dark powers.

Two days later, on 3 July, Queen Victoria greeted the president of the Board of Control, Sir John Hobhouse, and the chairman and deputy chairman of the East India Company, with a black eye and a prominent cut on her forehead where the cane had hit her. She would be left with the scar for years to come. Though she was receiving the most famous jewel in the world,

Victoria's mind seemed to be on other things. She was distracted by the death of her great confidant, the former prime minister Sir Robert Peel. A political giant of his day, Peel had served in high office for almost forty years, and had been prime minister twice. At the age of sixty-two, his death came entirely out of the blue. For his customary early evening ride on 29 June, Peel had chosen to saddle one of the newer horses in his stable, a thoroughbred hunter acquired only a few weeks before.

Although he did not know it, the horse had a reputation for kicking and bucking. It started acting up as he rode along Constitution Hill, near Buckingham Palace. Though he fought to control it, the horse threw him into the street. As Peel lay face down in the road, the skittish horse tripped over his body and fell on top of him, crushing him badly. Peel suffered broken ribs and a fractured collarbone. It later transpired that he also had severe internal bleeding. He died on 2 July, the very day the Koh-i-Noor reached London. On the 3rd, the day Hobhouse presented the great diamond to his queen, he did so against a backdrop of national mourning.

Queen Victoria's diary entry for that day is eight pages long, filled with her own personal grief for the man she described as 'so eminent a subject, so able a statesman, and so good a man'. Victoria was struggling to come to terms with her own pain as well as the grief of her husband, Prince Albert. Albert had been unpopular with her subjects after their marriage, and Sir Robert Peel had not only been a great adviser and ally to him, he had worked hard to give the prince a better reputation among his people. Summing up the mood of her people, Victoria wrote: 'From the highest to the lowest grief is shown and felt in a manner hardly ever before known for a person in his position. All the lower and middle classes realize that they have lost a father and a friend.'[23]

The Koh-i-Noor, by contrast, merited only a couple of paragraphs in her diary:

> We saw Sir J. Hobhouse who brought the two principal Members of the East Indian Company, Sir James Hogg & Mr Shepperd, who delivered up to me, with a short speech, the celebrated Koh-I-Noor, the largest diamond in the world, which comes from Lahore & belonged to Runjiet Sing, who took it from Shah Shoojah. It is estimated to be worth £500,000, & the two diamonds on either side, £10,000! Unfortunately it is not set 'à jour', & badly cut, which spoils the effect ...[24]

The Koh-i-Noor had finally made it into the queen's hands, but the Mountain of Light had spectacularly failed to shine in her eyes.

Back in India, Dalhousie was incandescent at the perceived ingratitude. Writing to a friend he fumed:

I received yesterday your letter of the 16th July. The several sad or foul [...] events in England on which it touches have been mentioned to me heretofore, and they are too sad to recur [sic] to. You add that these mishaps lie at my door, as I have sent the Koh-i-noor which always brings misfortune to its possessor. Whoever was the exquisite person from whom you heard this ... he was rather lame both on his history and tradition.

Dalhousie then went on to give a potted history of the diamond:

Without going back to the first emperors who held it, I would observe that Nadir Shah who took it was usually reckoned well to do in the world throughout his life; and that Runjeet Singh who also took it, and became, from the son of a petty zeminder, the most powerful native prince in India, and lived and died the power most formidable to England, and her best friend, has usually been thought to have prospered tolerably. As for tradition, when Shah Shoojah, *from whom it was taken*, was afterwards asked, by Runjeet's desire, 'what was the value of the Koh-i-noor?' he replied, 'Its value is *Good Fortune*; for whoever possesses it has been superior to all his enemies.'[25]

In closing, Dalhousie challenged the diamond's detractors to come up with sure-footed evidence if they wanted to malign his gift: 'Perhaps your friend would favour you with his authority, after this, for his opposite statement. I sent the Queen a narrative of this conversation with Shah Shoojah, taken from the mouth of the messenger.'[26]

With this, Dalhousie hoped to silence once and for all the rumours that had rumbled around the diamond since the fourteenth century. In later years he would become so exasperated by the recurring theme of the diamond's curse that he would write: 'if H.M. thinks it brings bad luck, let her give it back to me. I will take it and its ill-luck on speculation'.[27]

9

The Great Exhibition

As subdued as she had seemed in her journal upon receiving the Mountain of Light, Victoria was ebullient on the day the Koh-i-Noor, and other treasures, were to be revealed to the world: 1 May 1851 was to mark the most anticipated event in her reign. The queen, like the rest of her subjects, was beside herself with excitement at the mere thought of it: 'This day is one of the greatest and most glorious of our lives ... it is a day which makes my heart swell with thankfulness ...'[1]

Though the loss of Robert Peel had been felt keenly by both Queen Victoria and Prince Albert, an ambitious project had dragged them from their sadness. The Great Exhibition, or to give its full title, the Great Exhibition of the Works of Industry of All Nations, was to be the greatest show on earth, and it was to take place in London, the heart of Victoria's empire.

It had helped that Peel himself had been a champion of the Great Exhibition. He had devoted months of his time and expertise to the event, and had been at a planning meeting on the very day he was fatally thrown from his horse. Victoria and Albert were determined that his efforts should not have been in vain. The Great Exhibition was to be a showcase for the very best examples of culture, industry and beauty. Albert had been instrumental at every stage, coaxing and cajoling his way through British bureaucracy to bring the project from the page to Hyde Park.

The royal couple hoped that the Exhibition's success might increase Albert's popularity. Victoria's subjects deemed him to be beneath her, a minor royal from Saxe-Coburg-Gotha, an impoverished and undistinguished state, barely larger than a small English county.[2] Parliament also treated him with condescension, reducing his allowance from £50,000, the usual sum granted to a sovereign spouse, to £30,000, and refusing to grant him a peerage. Lord Melbourne, Peel's predecessor as prime minister, had personally thwarted the queen's desire to give her husband the title of 'king consort'. Albert was left feeling deeply undervalued as a result.

The Great Exhibition was his chance to show the country what he was really made of. In a letter to her uncle Leopold, the King of the Belgians, Victoria brimmed with pride for her husband: 'My Dearest Uncle – I wish you could have witnessed the 1st May 1851, the greatest day in our history, the most beautiful and imposing and touching spectacle ever seen

... truly it was astonishing, a fairy scene. Many cried, and all felt touched and impressed with devotional feelings ...'³

The venue for the Exhibition was the Crystal Palace, a vast edifice of glass and metal, specially constructed for the occasion. The complex, situated in one of London's largest areas of greenery, Hyde Park, was vast. Some 1,848 feet long and 408 feet wide, it covered around nineteen acres of land. The structure was big enough to incorporate a number of trees. Some 13,000 objects and curiosities had been shipped over from around the world and placed in tastefully curated galleries under the Crystal Palace's immense glass roof. Cutting through the structure, a large central boulevard dotted with trees, fountains and statues formed the backbone of the Exhibition, giving the space an altogether Parisian elegance. Though the uniquely beautiful building caused excitement, the promise of one particular exhibit eclipsed all other press coverage in the run-up to the opening. The Great Exhibition would provide Britons with their first chance to see the Koh-i-Noor diamond for themselves. The jewel was to be the star attraction, and its image and name were used liberally in the newspapers to drum up interest. Around six million people, a third of the entire population of Great Britain, were expected to attend the Exhibition between 1 May and 11 October 1851.⁴

On the day the Exhibition opened its doors, *The Times*, usually a sober and weighty newspaper, became positively effervescent:

> Never before was so vast a multitude gathered together within the memory of man. The struggles of great nations in battle, the levies of whole races, never called forth such an army as thronged the streets of London on the 1st of May ... The blazing arch of lucid glass with the hot sun flaming on its polished ribs and sides shone like the Koh-i-Noor itself.

The sun had not even risen when the British public began to converge on the Exhibition. By breakfast, there was hardly space to move on the streets surrounding Hyde Park, as the multitudes made their way to the great glass building: 'If a man ventured into the Strand or Holborn at eight o'clock with the intent to see the show, he felt half inclined to turn back with the idea that it would be useless to go where "all the world" would be before him.'[5]

Visitors from every social class came in their finest clothes. Aristocrats abandoned their carriages in the snarled-up streets and walked among the crush of commoners. The pilgrimage to the Crystal Palace was made in relentless drizzle, bedraggling rich and poor in equal measure. When the crowds finally reached the doors of the Exhibition, they had hours more to stand in the rain, which got heavier as the minutes ticked by. Undeterred, they waited patiently for the queen to arrive from Buckingham Palace. Just before noon, the sun broke through the clouds 'like a miracle' and 'to the Royal flourish of trumpets and the rolling of drums'[6] the queen in an open carriage, flanked by a 'troop of Life Guards at the trot', arrived at the Crystal Palace to a roar of 'God Save the Queen'. Visibly 'filled with emotion', Victoria declared the Great Exhibition open to the public.[7]

Many in the waiting crowd made straight for the Koh-i-Noor, which sat on a bolt of rich red velvet inside a gilded iron cage. Policemen, charged with keeping the crowds at bay, were almost lifted off their feet by the surge.

At the close of the first day, it became clear that something was very wrong with the Koh-i-Noor. Visitors who had managed to get near the exhibit left grumbling. The *Illustrated London News*, which had been one of the more excitable publications in the run-up to the Exhibition, expressed the disappointment of many:

A diamond is generally colourless, and the finest are quite free from any speck or flaw of any kind, resembling a drop of the purest water. The Koh-i-Noor is not cut in the best form for exhibiting its purity and lustre, and will therefore disappoint many, if not all, of those who so anxiously press forward to see it.[8]

The Koh-i-Noor had appeared dull in its captivity, and the bad publicity it was generating threatened to take the gleam off Prince Albert's finest moment. In a matter of days, he ordered gas lamps to be placed around the gem to help it shine for the visitors, but these failed to make much difference. Before long, visitors began turning their backs on the Koh-i-Noor, avoiding the exhibit altogether.

Disappointed and determined to change their minds, Prince Albert ordered work to begin on a new display setting for the Koh-i-Noor. While visitors squeezed past, men worked behind screens, creating a lattice of gas lamps and angled mirrors around the cage. Though such efforts helped, praise for the Koh-i-Noor remained lukewarm. More tinkering was needed.

On 14 June a dramatic new display was revealed to the public, one which Prince Albert was sure would save its reputation. To signify the importance of the Koh-i-Noor's re-entry into society, Queen Victoria, Prince Albert and their two eldest sons attended the unveiling of the freshened-up exhibit. A wooden cabin now surrounded the diamond, blocking out all the natural light streaming through the glass roof and windows of the Crystal Palace. This enabled the gas lamps and mirrors to do their work more efficiently. The original bolt of deep-red cloth which had been arranged beneath the diamond was now substituted with more vibrantly coloured velvet. Reporters bickered over its unusual shade, describing it as anything from shocking pink to imperial violet.

No other exhibit had received so much attention from the organisers, and early press coverage suggested that their efforts had not been in vain:

> One of the most extraordinary metamorphosis [sic] is the change that has come over the Koh-i-noor diamond. The doubts that have been thrown upon its value and authenticity and the difficulty of fully appreciating its brilliancy in the broad glare of day, have led to the enveloping of the cage and its contents in massive folds of crimson drapery, and showing its splendour by artificial light. The diamond has stood the test wonderfully, and has fully redeemed its character ... The difficulty of obtaining access to the cabin in which it is enshrined is little less than those encountered by Aladdin in his visit to the garden of diamonds, and has revived all the attraction and fascination of this famous gem.[9]

The reconfigured display made the diamond tantalisingly difficult to get to: 'You pass in singly – the cage, with the exception of about an eighth of its circumference, is enveloped in pink bolts of cloth; half a dozen jets of gas are arranged behind it, and the light from these is again reflected by more than a dozen small mirrors upon the diamond ...'[10]

The difficulty of access restored some of the lost mystery to the diamond. Also, in an attempt to reinstate the Koh-i-Noor's tarnished reputation, newspapers polished archive copy, reminding readers of the gem's exotic provenance and potent symbolism. The display and the diamond's mount became a metaphor for British supremacy:

> The two golden hands that slightly clasp its extreme points, and present it in gorgeous relief against the deep purple velvet background, are indicative of the graceful and delicate fingers which now hold it, while the massive and impenetrable safe by which it is surrounded illustrates the moral material power which defies the assaults of all enemies and secures it more efficiently than the triple ramparts of Lahore.[11]

The security provided for the Koh-i-Noor was substantial, and carried the name of Chubb.

From the moment he had patented his first 'detector lock' in 1817, Jeremiah Chubb gained a reputation for making unbreakable locks. His fame was such that his creations even figured in the stories of Sherlock Holmes as locks that could not be picked. So confident was Chubb of his workmanship that he offered £100 from his own pocket and a pardon from the government to one particular convict, a locksmith by trade, who had successfully cracked every lock he had ever been presented with. Though he toiled on Chubb's detector for three months, the convict could not pick it. Chubb's Koh-i-Noor safe was regarded as his best work to date: 'One of the peculiarities of Mr Chubb's wonderful safe is said to be that the moment the surrounding glass shade is touched, the diamond, like a sensitive plant, shrinks from the too near approach of a profane hand, and descends into its adamantine fastness.'[12] In reality, the diamond would not so much withdraw like a sensitive plant, but instead plop through a small trap door into a thick walled safe if anyone attempted to reach for it.

Although the celebrated changes drew fresh crowds, enthusiasm quickly evaporated, thanks to the unbearable temperatures inside the cabin. Gas lamps, mirrors and heavy fabric turned the display into a sauna, causing visitors to swoon after only a few minutes. The press began to blame the Koh-i-Noor for being difficult, as if it were some kind of contrary and disappointing child:

> There appears to be something impracticable about the gem, for the more it is lighted up, the less it is disposed to display its splendour. Those on Saturday, who were tempted to change the comparative coolness of the nave, with a temperature of 83 or 84, for the stifling heat of the diamond cavern, came away by no means satisfied with its appearance ...[13]

In October, the Great Exhibition ended, and the Koh-i-Noor was finally liberated from its iron cage and the withering estimation of the public, 'after having excited the wonder and the sneers of so many hundred thousand visitors, and to the great relief of the policeman who has been on duty beside the cage since 1st of May'.[14]

Spared any further public humiliation, the diamond was taken back to the vaults.

10

The First Cut

In Calcutta, Dalhousie had been following the Koh-i-Noor's debut with a mixture of disappointment and irritation. He had always described the gem in superlatives, and now stood accused of exaggeration as well as arrogance. He joined the choir of criticism, reproaching the diamond itself for its failed public debut: '[It] is badly *cut*: it is rose- not brilliant-cut, and of course won't sparkle like the latter.' Though Dalhousie did not dare name him directly, he also seemed to blame Prince Albert for the diamond's humiliation: 'it should not have been shown in a huge space. In the Toshakhana at Lahore Dr Login used to show it on a table covered with black velvet cloth, the diamond alone, appearing through a hole in the cloth, and relieved by the dark colour all around.'[1]

Albert too became preoccupied with the diamond's failure, and decided to do something about it. Summoning scientists and jewellers, he demanded to know what could be done to improve its appearance.

The eminent physicist Sir David Brewster was one of the most noteworthy men to be consulted on the matter. Known as the 'Father of modern experimental optics', Brewster had invented the kaleidoscope and had pushed at the boundaries of mineral analysis and the physics of light polarisation. After studying the Koh-i-Noor closely, Brewster came up with a damning verdict. The diamond was flawed at its very heart. Yellow flecks ran through a plane at its centre, one of which was large and marred its ability to refract light. If it had to be cut, the risk of destroying it in the process was high. At the very least, the diamond would lose a great deal of its mass if the flaws were to be dealt with adequately.

This was not the answer Prince Albert had wanted to hear, so he sent his expert's analysis to Messrs Garrard of London, jewellers to the queen, hoping for a more encouraging assessment. The Garrard family summoned the finest diamond-cutters in the world to give their opinion. Dutch craftsmen working for Mozes Coster, Holland's largest and most famous firm of diamond merchants, studied the scientific data and confirmed Brewster's opinion about its flaws. Unlike the scientist, however, they were sure they could cut the Koh-i-Noor. Not only would they make it glitter, they assured the prince, they would also preserve the diamond's majestic size. The royal couple ordered work on the Koh-i-Noor to begin.

A specially designed workshop was constructed at 25 Haymarket, in London's Piccadilly. Garrard hired Coster's two best diamond-cutters, Levie Benjamin Voorzanger and J. A. Feder, who travelled from Amsterdam to England.[2] The men were provided with a steam engine, designed by Maudslay Sons and Field, a firm of respected British marine engineers.[3] The engine powered fast-spinning grinders, vital precision-cutting tools used by the Dutch team. As engineers prepared for the cutting, clanking about the work-shop under the supervision of the queen's mineral-ogist, James Tennant, the Koh-i-Noor and its failings made their way into the headlines again: 'The precious stone, which was the cynosure of the world's exhib-ition of 1851, attracted from the multitudes who last year gazed upon it, disappointment at the somewhat dim radiance of its lustre ... not fulfilling the expec-tations entertained from the highflown descriptions which have given the Mountain of Light a title which many beholders held to be a misnomer.'[4]

Though there was little to see outside the heav-ily guarded Haymarket workshop, a steady trickle of onlookers started to arrive by the first week of July. Content merely to listen to the banging and whirring going on inside, they waited, like a crowd of concerned relatives outside an operating theatre. Finally, after weeks of anticipation, on 16 July 1852, the 'patient' was brought forth from the Tower of

London and presented to the Dutch craftsmen. Though the sight of the Koh-i-Noor's full military escort was impressive enough, spectators refused to leave even after the diamond had disappeared behind the heavily guarded gates. Rumours, fanned by the British press, had taken hold of the crowd. If they waited long enough, they were sure to be rewarded.

According to reports, no less than the 'Iron Duke', Wellington himself, hero of Waterloo and scourge of Napoleon, would inaugurate the cutting process. Some reports even suggested that his own battle-calloused hands would cut the Koh-i-Noor. The chance of seeing two legends meet, one diamond and one iron, was irresistible. The crowd stayed stubbornly where it was. It did not have long to wait. On 17 July, the eighty-three-year-old Wellington arrived on horseback to loud cheers. Adulation always caused the duke to feel uncomfortable, and he made his way stiffly through the guarded doors of the workshop with barely a nod to his admirers.

Thanks to his distinctive profile, the duke was affectionately referred to as 'Old Nosey', and people sang songs about his exploits in public houses up and down the realm. Small boys, rich and poor, played out his 1815 victory at Waterloo with tin soldiers. Though thirty-seven years had passed since he had vanquished Napoleon, that victory remained vivid to patriotic Britons. Most would have been baffled by the great warrior's interest in a piece of jewellery.

To Wellington, however, the Koh-i-Noor was so much more. The diamond was India, and India had been the making of him. In 1769, eleven years before the birth of Maharaja Ranjit Singh, the Duke of Wellington had been plain old Arthur Wellesley, born into an aristocratic Anglo-Irish family. Unlike his elder brother Richard, Arthur showed little promise as an Eton schoolboy, causing his mother to worry constantly about her awkward son.

When he turned sixteen, his father died, leaving the family in a financially precarious situation. Wellesley was encouraged by his mother to join the army and make his own fortune. After a stuttering start, at the age of twenty-four Wellesley joined the 33rd Regiment of Foot. In May 1796, Wellesley's 33rd Regiment arrived in Calcutta. The British had been embroiled in a vicious struggle against the Kingdom of Mysore, and though they were not actually at war, three previous conflicts had taught the British to prepare for a rapid escalation of the conflict.

Rancour between the East India Company and the sultan of Mysore, Hyder Ali, dated back more than three decades. By the time Wellesley reached India, Hyder Ali had already died, but his son, Tipu Sultan, was proving to be an even more ferocious adversary. Tipu hated the British, and seized any opportunity to show it, entertaining his guests with a life-size mechanical tiger that appeared to be chewing on the throat of a British soldier. Clever hidden cogs and pipes made the man groan and his arm flail as the tiger sank its teeth in.

Seringapatam, a town nine miles from Mysore, was the centre of hostilities. Twenty-four thousand British troops were deployed by the time Wellesley and his 33rd Regiment reached them in August 1798. With Wellesley leading from the front, the 33rd fought valiantly, forcing Tipu's army into retreat. Buoyed by their success, in April 1799, the governor general, Lord Mornington, who also happened to be Arthur's elder brother, ordered Wellesley to take part in a final push on Seringapatam. Under the command of General George Harris, a combined force of 50,000 native and British soldiers, including Wellesley and his regiment, pounded the fortress town.

The British had made a small breach in the walls of the fortress, and on 4 May a final, decisive assault was launched. Seventy-six men, fortified with whisky and dry biscuits, led the bayonet charge into the citadel. Arthur Wellesley and his 33rd went in after them. During the subsequent fighting in the citadel, Tipu Sultan was killed. Though he had not struck the fatal blow, Wellesley was swiftly at the scene, bending over the sultan's body to make sure he was dead. The Fourth Anglo-Mysore War was over.

Wellesley went on to distinguish himself further in India, serving as the governor of Mysore and later successfully leading his men in battle against the Marathas of the Deccan Plateau. The Marathas were a proud and martial people and, of all the battles he ever fought, Wellesley would describe his fight against them at the Battle of Assaye as 'the bloodiest for the numbers that I ever saw'.[5]

In India, Wellesley earned his spurs. The recognition he received put him in the front line of battle against Napoleon's army years later. His subsequent success against the French gave him the title of Duke of Wellington. Without India, he might never have had the chance to shine, and awareness of his debt to India perhaps added to his fascination with its most infamous diamond: 'His Grace the Duke of Wellington, having manifested great interest in the precious gem, so associated with the land of the East, where his first, and not least glorious, laurels were won, attended several times during the progress of preparations ...'[6]

The idea, though, that he might have some part in the reshaping of the gem seemed fanciful. At the Garrard workshop, the Dutch jewellers spent weeks trying to come up with a way for the octogenarian to cut the first facet without wrecking the diamond. In the end, they embedded the entire Koh-i-Noor in lead, 'with the exception of one small salient angle intended to be first submitted to the cutting operation'.[7] 'His Grace placed the gem upon the *scaife*[8] – a horizontal wheel revolving with almost incalculable velocity – whereby the exposed angle was removed by friction and the first facet of the new cutting was effected ...'[9] Having performed his duty, the duke left the diamond where it lay, walked out of the workshop, remounted his ageing white horse and rode away, barely acknowledging the near-hysteria outside.

Inaugural cut complete, the Dutch masters were allowed to continue with their work. The crowds dwindled and eventually disappeared, and infrequent updates about the Koh-i-Noor made it to the back pages of the papers. The Iron Duke himself never lived to see the completed Koh-i-Noor. Eight weeks and four days after he had cut its face, on 14 September 1852, he suffered a fatal stroke, and died a day later.

The diamond was finished days after Wellington's death. The bill for the recutting came to £8,000 – the equivalent of more than a million pounds in today's money. Despite all the assurances from Coster and Garrard, the Koh-i-Noor did not retain its size. Instead, what was left was unrecognisable. The cut had practically halved the Koh-i-Noor's 190.3 metric carats to 93 metric carats. It now sparkled brilliantly, but could lie meekly in the palm of a hand. News of the reduction left Prince Albert shaken and he braced himself for savage criticism from the press and the public.

In the event, however, and perhaps because the diamond had been so poorly received in its original form, Prince Albert got off lightly. All but a few newspapers praised the new and improved Koh-i-Noor. It was flatter than its original egg shape, cut into what jewellers called an 'oval stellar brilliant'. Traditionally such diamonds were given thirty-three facets on top in 'the table' of the gem, and twenty-five facets below, 'in the pavilion'. However, the Dutch cutters had given the Koh-i-Noor perfect symmetry with thirty-three facets both on top and underneath. In the pale light of the English sun, the Koh-i-Noor had at last learned to shine.

As news of its beauty spread, for the first time since its arrival in Britain the diamond seemed to have been cut free of its bad luck. Instead of the curse being mentioned in the same breath as the diamond, the name Koh-i-Noor began to be associated with good fortune. Ships were christened *Koh-i-Noor*. Newspaper advertisements encouraged students to buy 'Kohinoor lead pencils' for their exams. In May 1853, the Cheshire Stakes, a popular and lucrative fixture in the flat-racing calendar, was won by a horse called Koh-i-Noor. Fictional works like Wilkie Collins's *The Moonstone*, where a cursed Indian diamond is given to an innocent

English girl who is, as a result, then pursued by angry Hindu priests, and Benjamin Disraeli's *Lothair*, where the plot follows a bag of uncut diamonds once belonging to an Indian maharaja, became hugely successful.

The diamond was now a celebrity in its own right, and had been set free of its foreignness. It was a British jewel for a British queen. Few thought about the boy who had once owned it. If they did, they would have known that while the world's attention was on the Garrard workshop, Duleep Singh too had been 'recut'.

———

In 1852, while the Koh-i-Noor was being transformed on the scaife, Duleep Singh was undergoing a similar process in India. He had by now been in the care of the Logins for three years, and as a boy of thirteen had come to regard them as his parents. John Login's opinion mattered to Duleep above all else, and he tried to please his guardian by studying diligently, maintaining a cheery demeanour and joining in parlour games. Over time, Duleep developed genuine fondness for the couple, referring to John as his 'MaBaap'[10] – a peculiarly Indian concept of 'universal and complete parent'.

Lena Login, who kept a meticulous diary of her time with the deposed Sikh sovereign, often thought about all that had been snatched from him: 'One could not but have great sympathy for the boy, brought up from

babyhood to exact the most obsequious servility ...'[II]
If Duleep missed his old life, he rarely said so; there
were intense flashes of anger or bitterness, but they did
not last long. Under the tutelage of the Logins, Duleep
learned to speak like a 'Britisher'. He read his Bible,
swapped Persian verses for English ones and devoured
tales of life in 'Blighty'.

In time he even took a blade to his long hair, which
had remained uncut since birth in the tradition of the
Sikh religion. Having shorn away the outward signs of
his origins, it became easier for Duleep to contemplate
a more profound metamorphosis. Just over a year after
the Koh-i-Noor had emerged from its workshop completely changed, Duleep asked his guardians whether
he might rid himself of his old faith entirely. Duleep
Singh wanted to become a Christian.

Lord Dalhousie greeted the news with mixed emo-
tions. If Punjab perceived that its young maharaja had
been forced to convert, this might become the spark
for an uprising. Dalhousie demanded evidence that
Duleep's Christian revelation was real and was his
alone. Writing to a friend, the governor general confided his unease:

My little friend Duleep has taken us all aback lately
by declaring his resolution to become a Christian.
The pundits, he says, tell him humbug – he has had
the Bible read to him, and he believes the Sahib's

religion ... Politically we could desire nothing better, for it destroys his possible influence forever. But I should have been glad if it had been deferred, since at present it may be represented to have been brought about by tampering with the mind of a child. This is not the case – it is his own free act, and apparently his firm resolution.[12]

Later in the same letter, Dalhousie recounted a story that may well have been allegorical if it was not actually true, describing it to his friend as 'a sad thing'. 'A coolie went up to an elephant and took away some sugar-cane which it was eating. The beast seized him round the neck with his trunk, put the man's head under his forefoot, and leaning on it, crushed it like an egg-shell. The animal was quite quiet; but if even a dog will not part with his bone, why should the Behemoth of the land?'[13] Dalhousie mused. 'It is well these monsters do not know their strength, or fear to use it.'

On 8 March 1853, Maharaja Duleep Singh, aged fourteen years and six months, converted to Christianity at a quiet ceremony in his home in Fategarh. Punjab greeted news of Duleep's conversion with grief rather than anger. The feared uprising did not occur. The behemoth truly did not know its own strength.

Far away in England, Victoria rejoiced at the salvation of the maharaja's soul. From the time of his exile, she had keenly awaited updates on Duleep's progress.

These she read with great care and growing interest. The more she learned about him, the more fascinated she became. The maharaja was also curious about the queen across the water. When he turned fifteen, he asked his guardians if he might ever be able to visit England. Despite receiving ample discouragement from her ministers, who felt such favour might go to the maharaja's head, Victoria enthusiastically granted permission. Duleep packed his belongings and made the long voyage with his guardians, the Logins, by his side.

Queen Victoria's 'Loyal Subject'

From the moment he set foot in her court, Duleep became Victoria's favourite. Her praise for him was frequent and enthusiastic: 'He is extremely handsome and speaks English perfectly, and has a pretty, graceful and dignified manner. He was beautifully dressed and covered with diamonds ... I always feel so much for these poor deposed Indian Princes ...'[1]

In the bustling life of the English court, the maharaja enjoyed the status of a senior aristocrat. Behind the closed doors of the palace, he soon became a member of Victoria's family. Though Dalhousie and others counselled the queen against showing him too much favour, she ignored them, showering the maharaja with lavish presents of jewellery, cameos of herself and even a thoroughbred horse. The two spent hours sketching each other at Buckingham Palace and at Osborne House, her Isle of Wight sanctuary, and Victoria was deeply touched by the kindness Duleep showed her children, particularly her youngest son, Prince Leopold.

Leopold was a haemophiliac and frequently suffered from fits and poor health. Though his own brothers gave little concession to his frailty, Duleep would invariably scoop up the child and put him on his shoulders, ensuring that he never felt left out of their games. Prince Albert also grew genuinely fond of the maharaja and designed a coat of arms for him to use in England. It comprised a lion standing beneath a coronet surmounted by a five-pointed star. Albert even chose the motto: *Prodesse quam conspici*, meaning 'to do good rather than be conspicuous'. As one of the only brown faces at court, however, Duleep would only ever be conspicuous, and as time went by he grew to crave the attention.

On 10 July 1854, Duleep was standing on a specially constructed stage set up in the White Drawing Room of Buckingham Palace, trying very hard not to move. Queen Victoria had asked the celebrated court painter Franz Xaver Winterhalter to capture Duleep's likeness for her on canvas. She intended to display it at Osborne House. In silk pyjamas, a heavy gold-embroidered shirt and fine jewellery, Duleep looked every inch a king. On his feet he wore embroidered slippers which curled at the toe, and on his head he sported a turban dripping with emeralds. At his throat hung an ivory miniature of Victoria, set in diamonds, and another was pinned by his heart, out of sight. As Queen Victoria recorded in her journal, 'Winterhalter was in ecstasies at the beauty and nobility of the young Maharajah.'[2]

There was, however, one item conspicuously absent from all Duleep's finery. The amulet that had been strapped to his bicep as a child was missing. The loss of the Koh-i-Noor had always hurt him deeply and it was also preying on Queen Victoria's mind. While Winterhalter tinkered at his easel, Queen Victoria beckoned Lady Login to follow her into a corner of the drawing room; she wished to talk in private. Lena Login recorded the conversation in her diaries: 'She had not yet worn it [the Koh-i-Noor] in public, and, as she herself remarked, had a delicacy about doing so in the Maharajah's presence. "Tell me, Lady Login, does the Maharajah ever mention the Koh-i-Noor? Does he seem to regret it, and would he like to see it again?"'[3]

Victoria ordered Lady Login to find out before the next sitting, though Lena already knew exactly how he felt:

> There was no other subject that so filled the thoughts and conversation of the Maharajah, his relatives and dependants as the forsaken diamond. For the confiscation of the jewel which to the Oriental is the symbol of sovereignty of India, rankled in his mind even more than the loss of his kingdom, and I dreaded what sentiments he might give vent to were the subject once re-opened![4]

Despite her fears, Lady Login dutifully brought up the subject while out riding with Duleep in Richmond Park a few days later. How would he feel if he saw the Koh-i-Noor again? 'I would give a good deal to hold it again in my own hand! I was but a child, an infant, when forced to surrender it by treaty; but now that I am a man, I should like to have it in my power to place it myself in Her Majesty's hand!'⁵

This was exactly the answer Victoria would have wanted to hear. But was it true? The next day, while Duleep posed for the German artist at the palace once more, a pantomime of sorts was enacted. Lena Login watched as an emissary from the Tower of London, escorted by yeoman warders, entered the drawing room. He carried a small casket in his hands, which the queen opened delicately. She showed the open box to Albert and together they walked over to where Duleep stood on the dais. Looking up at him, she called: 'Maharajah, I have something to show you!' Duleep Singh stepped down and moved towards her, not knowing what to expect. She took the jewel from its box and dropped it into his outstretched hand, asking him 'if he thought it improved, and if he would have recognised it again?'⁶

The maharaja walked towards the window, and held the diamond to the sunlight. It was so much smaller than he remembered. It was the wrong shape. It felt so much lighter in his hand. However, it was still the

Maharaja Kharak Singh, 1801–40.
Son of Ranjit Singh; poisoned to death.

Maharaja Nau Nihal Singh, 1821–40.
Son of Kharak Singh; killed by falling
masonry as he returned from his
father's cremation.

Maharani Chand Kaur (regent), 1802–42.
Wife of Kharak Singh; bludgeoned
to death by her maids.

Maharaja Sher Singh, 1807–43.
Son of Ranjit Singh; shot dead.

Maharaja Duleep Singh seated on a chair with attendants.
Lithograph on paper, 1849, from an original sketch by Lady Helen C. Mackenzie.

James Andrew Braun-Ramsay, Earl of Dalhousie.
Governor-General of India, 1838–49.

Sir John Spencer Login, Guardian of Maharaja Duleep Singh.
Engraved print, c. 1860.

The submission of the Maharaja Duleep Singh to the Governor-General, Sir Henry Hardinge, after defeat in the First Anglo-Sikh War.
Engraving by J. & F. Tallis, London, c. 1850.

Portrait of Rani Jindan (1817–63) by George Richmond. Oil on canvas, 1862 – one year before Jindan died in London.

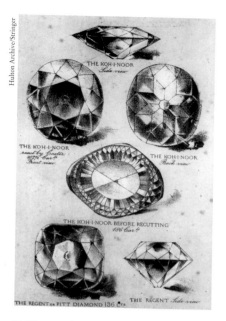

Different views of the Koh-i-Noor, before and after cutting.

John Lawrence, who claimed to have lost the Koh-i-Noor for a time after he was entrusted with its safekeeping.

THE POOR OLD KOH-I-NOOR AGAIN!

1. THE KOH-I-NOOR.
2 2. THE DUTCH ARTISTS.
3 3 3. THE REQUISITE MACHINERY.

4. THE "DOOK" MANIFESTING GREAT INTEREST IN THE PRECIOUS GEM.
5 5 5. EMINENT SCIENTIFIC MEN WATCHING PROCEEDINGS.

An 1852 *Punch* cartoon depicting the Duke of Wellington making the first cut to the Koh-i-Noor.

The opening of the Great Exhibition at the Crystal Palace, 1 May 1851. This was the first time the Koh-i-Noor would be seen by the British public.

Maharaja Duleep Singh, attending court at Buckingham Palace in March 1879. Though the maharaja still appeared close to Queen Victoria, he was now questioning his treatment at her hands.

Portrait of Maharaja Duleep Singh by Franz Xaver Winterhalter. Oil on canvas, 1854. While posing for the portrait, the maharaja held the Koh-i-Noor for what would be the last time.

Portrait of Queen Victoria by Franz Xaver Winterhalter. Oil on canvas, 1856.
The queen would wear the Koh-i-Noor to all her important engagements.

Duleep Singh, c. 1865. Though living the life of a British aristocrat, Duleep Singh was on a collision course with the monarchy.

The Koh-i-Noor took centre stage at the 1902 coronation of King Edward VII in Queen Alexandra's specially designed crown.

Queen Mary opted for a simplified crown for the coronation of her husband, George V, in 1911. The Koh-i-Noor was retained at the heart of the design.

Koh-i-Noor, and the very touch of it transported him: 'for all his air of polite interest and curiosity,' wrote Lena Login, 'there was a passion of repressed emotion in his face ... evident, I think, to Her Majesty, who watched him with sympathy not unmixed with anxiety ...'

Time seemed to slow, as the awkwardness in the room grew. 'At last, as if summoning up his resolution after a profound struggle and with a deep sigh he raised his eyes from the jewel ...' I was prepared for almost anything,' recalled Lena Login, 'even to seeing him, in a sudden fit of madness, fling the precious talisman out of the open window by which he stood! [My own and] the other spectators' nerves were equally on edge – [as] he moved deliberately to where her Majesty was standing ...' Bowing before her, Duleep gently put the gem into Queen Victoria's hand. 'It is to me, Ma'am, the greatest pleasure thus to have the opportunity, as a loyal subject, of *myself* tendering to *my Sovereign* – the Koh-i-Noor!!'[7] The maharaja had presented to the queen something that no longer belonged to him. Neither Duleep, nor any of his family, would ever come so close to the diamond again.

12

The Jewel and the Crown

Though the handover ceremony in the drawing room at Buckingham Palace was more an act of performance than permission, the maharaja had set Victoria free. The manner in which it had been taken from him, coupled with her genuine fondness for the maharaja, had been enough to prevent her from wearing her most fabulous jewel. After Duleep's handover, she took to wearing the Koh-i-Noor frequently and conspicuously. One of the jewel's earliest and most spectacular outings took place just over a year later. In 1855, Queen Victoria announced plans to travel to France for a state visit. This was momentous news, for not only would this be the first state visit to France by a British sovereign in more than 400 years, it would also cement an historic alliance between France and Britain in the Crimean War.

The French had never had an easy relationship with monarchy. They had gone through a cycle of removing and reinstating their kings with a frequency that alarmed other sovereigns of Europe. In 1792, Louis XVI of the

House of Bourbon was not merely dethroned, he was decapitated. A series of bloody purges followed, and as the people took power, France's First Republic was born. The country remained without a monarch until Napoleon Bonaparte morphed from military dictator to emperor in 1804. His reign lasted only eleven years, and was ended by the decisive British victory under the Duke of Wellington at the battle of Waterloo. Napoleon was exiled to the damp and windswept island of St Helena in the South Atlantic in 1815, where he died miserably of stomach cancer in 1821.

After 1814, three more kings ruled France until 1848, when the Second Republic was established. In 1852, however, France lurched from republicanism to monarchy again, declaring Bonaparte's nephew, Napoleon III, the new emperor. Unlike his predecessor, this Napoleon was an anglophile and was keen on an alliance with Queen Victoria. To prove his friendly intentions, Napoleon III entreated Victoria to visit him in Paris. To make his invitation impossible to resist, the emperor decided to throw a grand ball in her honour at the Palace of Versailles. It was to be an event so opulent that even the Bourbons would have approved.

Victoria arrived in Paris on 18 August 1855 to an enthusiastic reception, and made a grand entrance at the ball a week later. Around 1,200 guests had been invited, representing the cream of European aristocracy, art and music. Four separate orchestras had been positioned at each corner of the spectacular gardens, one of them conducted by the celebrated Austrian composer Johann Strauss. Musicians' stands had been concealed in the shrubs and 'harmony seemed to proceed from invisible instruments through a bower of dahlias, roses, and other flowers'.[1]

If the gardens were enchanting, the inside of the palace was nothing short of magical. A vast array of chandeliers and candelabras had been positioned to reflect in the 357 mirrors of Versailles' famous Galerie des Glaces: 'Thousands of lustres and torches, reflected in mirrors, threw streams of light upon the rich garments of the guests, covered in gold and ornamented with diamonds.'[2]

Victoria's sartorial choices usually failed to impress the stylish Parisian elite, but on the night of the great ball on 25 August she outshone them all. In a billowing white satin gown, designed by Prince Albert, Victoria swept in to gasps of appreciation. Though the delicate golden flowers embroidered on her skirts and the vividly contrasting blue sash across her shoulder were much admired, it was the 'diadem' or crown upon her head that eclipsed all else. The work of Garrard, the diadem's gold and silver trellis of interweaving flowers was inlaid with hundreds of small pearls and almost 3,000 small diamonds. They caught the candle flames in a myriad of tiny sparkles, but were themselves rendered dull by what lay in the cross pattée at the front of the crown.³ Sitting above Victoria's brow, the legendary Koh-i-Noor gleamed like a third eye.

The crown had been crafted a full twelve months *before* the maharaja had made the token gesture of personally handing over the diamond to Queen Victoria, implying that she had been determined to keep and wear the Koh-i-Noor, despite her guilt over the manner in which the gem had been taken, and no matter what the response of Duleep might have been.

Garrard's invoice for the crown revealed not only the cost but also the intricate craftsmanship that had gone into its manufacture:

> Setting a brilliant royal tiara consisting of four Maltese crosses and four Fleurs de Lis with a jointed circlet of two rows of diamonds enclosing large diamonds and small crosses. The large crosses and Fleurs de Lis arranged to be removed at pleasure from the circlet by double springs and sockets and have also movable jointed stems and hooks to form a brooch when required.⁴

Both the crown and the brooch were designed exclusively to show off the newly cut Koh-i-Noor to its best advantage. The 'springs and sockets' referred to ingeniously engineered clasps, strong enough to hold the Koh-i-Noor securely, yet clever enough to release it when the queen wished to transfer the diamond to her brooch. According to the Garrard paperwork, there were '2203 brilliant-cut' and '662 rose-cut' diamonds in the crown, augmenting the Koh-i-Noor. The price and origin of these tiny stones were not itemised, suggesting that the palace had supplied them, or had prised them from existing crown jewels. Duleep Singh's Mountain of Light had found its new home in one of the most beautiful crowns in all Europe.

Notwithstanding the weight and value of the treasure on her head, Queen Victoria waltzed with Emperor Napoleon III in Versailles till the early hours of the morning.

Six years later, at the end of 1861, such tragedy struck Queen Victoria that Paris seemed like a distant dream. At the age of just forty-two, Prince Albert contracted typhoid and, after weeks of suffering, died in the Blue Room of Windsor Castle with his inconsolable wife and five of his nine children at his side. With his death, Queen Victoria lost not only a consort, but also her lover and her best friend. Without Albert, all colour seemed to drain from her life. She shut herself away from the world and wrapped herself tightly in despair. Servants were instructed to put away all her exquisite gowns and jewels, because she could not imagine ever wearing them again. Instead, Victoria put on a simple black dress trimmed with white crepe, and on her forty-two-year-old head, she wore a widow's cap. She would dress this way until the day she died.

Victoria's grief did not diminish as the months went by, even preventing her from carrying out mandatory royal duties. While Albert lived, she, like every monarch who preceded her, had been obliged to attend the State Opening of Parliament in Westminster. The event marked the beginning of the parliamentary year in Great Britain, and a number of arcane rituals, performed to this day, took place accompanied by much fanfare. Before her loss, Victoria had participated in the ceremonies and rituals with gusto. On the appointed day, her coach of state, in its distinctive livery of midnight blue, jet black and gold, drawn by four horses, would make its way to Westminster, escorted by the distinctive coats and gold brocade of the Household Cavalry. Marching music kept the horses and soldiers in step, as the procession wound its way through the streets of London, her cheering subjects lining the route. The State Opening was the monarch's chance to show her respect for parliamentary democracy, and her people's chance to show their love for their queen.

After Albert had died, Victoria could not bear to carry out the task. Her ministers warned her that her prolonged absence might leave her people feeling abandoned. It might even make the monarchy obsolete. Victoria ignored their entreaties. After three years of absence, there was widespread speculation that she had been driven mad by grief. It became known that Prince Albert's rooms were maintained exactly as they had been when he was alive. Servants, it was said, still brought hot water into his dressing room every day, ready for a morning shave that would never happen.

For five long years Victoria remained in seclusion, and it was not until 1866 that she was shaken out of her depression. When she finally agreed to take her place in Parliament, she let it be known that she was less than happy about it, and imposed a set of non-negotiable conditions. There were to be no trumpet fanfares and no pageantry. There were to be no grand coaches, and no royal robes or crowns of state. The queen would wear her widow's cap, a long black dress and a veil. She would not deliver the monarch's speech in person, but merely nod at the lord chancellor, who would read on her behalf.

When Victoria made her appearance in Parliament, one piece of jewellery stood out against the blackness of her widow's weeds – the Koh-i-Noor, pinned to the top of her sash, wordlessly conveying a sense of the power and reach of the British monarch. The diamond might once have graced the most formidable potentates in the world, but now it, and most of their dominions, belonged to her.

Duleep Singh too seemed to be waking from a trance. From the moment he arrived in England, he had believed that Victoria was his friend – more than a friend, a surrogate mother. He had lived for almost seven years as an English aristocrat, invited to all the parties that mattered, and had been befriended by the most powerful men in the realm. However, when he turned twenty-one, Duleep's thoughts drifted towards his real mother.

Rani Jindan had been fading away in her de facto Nepalese prison, and the years had taken a terrible toll. Jindan had aged dramatically. She had lost weight, and had been progressively losing her sight. The India Office and palace officials had made every effort to insulate the maharaja from the depressing news of his mother's decline, yet in 1860 worrying rumours filtered through to him. Perhaps knowing that his new friends would not approve, Duleep attempted to contact his mother in secret, sending a letter through a trusted servant.

When they intercepted the letter, the British found themselves facing a quandary. Could they block the son from speaking to his mother? The maharaja was one of Queen Victoria's favourites. He had committed no crime. Should he suffer because his mother had been a problem so many years before?

After much diplomatic toing and froing, the British decided that little could be done to stop Duleep re-establishing ties with Jindan. Though they could not prevent it, they might be able to control it. Duleep Singh was given permission to travel to India to meet his mother for the first time since she had been dragged to the tower. With great care, the authorities selected a

place as far away from Punjab as possible for the reunion. Spence's Hotel in Calcutta was one of the finest
hotels in the world in the 1860s and it was there that
Duleep, flanked by representatives of the Raj, waited
for his mother on 16 January 1861.

According to Punjabi folklore, when the rani was
brought in to see him, she said not a word, but instead
ran her hands all over her son's face and body. The last
time they had been together, he had been her glittering
boy. Now almost blind, she relied on her fingertips to
reveal who her son had become, and as she reached
up to touch his face, they told her Duleep was a man.
It was only when Jindan stroked the hair on Duleep's
head that she let out the howl of grief and rage she had
suppressed for so long.

Jindan railed at her son: though she had known they
had taken away his kingdom and his Koh-i-Noor,
never could she have believed he would let them take
his religion too. When Jindan finally calmed herself,
she turned to Duleep's British escort and declared
she would never again be parted from her son. They
would have to let her travel back with him to England,
the land she had loathed for so long.

A hesitant Duleep wrote almost apologetic letters
to the palace and his former guardians, the Logins,
explaining his mother's wishes, and sheepishly saying
that he might as well go along with the idea. He was
perhaps rather taken aback when the British told the

rebel queen that she *would* be able to sail to England. Though they still treated her with a mixture of suspicion and derision, having Jindan on British soil served their purpose: in one fell swoop they could remove her from India, and any chance of her stirring insurrection there, and keep her under close watch. If the British needed a reminder of how potent Jindan was in the eyes of fellow Punjabis, they got it at the reunion itself.

A troopship filled with Sikh soldiers returning from the second Opium War happened to be sailing up Calcutta's Hooghly River. Rumours spread among the crew that their lost maharaja had returned to India, and that Rani Jindan, his much-wronged mother, was back at his side. In no time at all, hundreds of exhausted and emotional soldiers gathered around Spence's Hotel. Their bellowing salute to their fallen sovereigns shook the walls: 'Jo Bole So Nihal, Sat Sri Akal!' – 'Whoever says these words will know true joy. Eternal is the Lord God!'

After that, the British could not get the pair on a boat fast enough.

***

From the moment of her return, Jindan filled her son's ears with tales of his 'stolen' Koh-i-Noor. Under the rani's influence, Duleep slowly changed, turning from a favourite pet of the royal court into a man who dared to defy its wishes. The more Duleep's friends gossiped about his mother, the closer he seemed to draw to her. Lady Normanby counted herself as an ally and confidante of the maharaja. She regularly leased her ancestral home, Mulgrave Castle, to Duleep whenever he wished to hunt. The rugged 16,000-acre estate in Yorkshire allowed him to indulge his passions for shooting and for throwing lavish parties. When Duleep chose to bring his mother with him to Mulgrave, Lady Normanby poured scorn on Jindan behind his back. Writing to her own son, she gossiped: 'She ... sometimes dresses in a dirty sheet and a pair of cotton stockings, sometimes decked out in a Cloth of Gold and covered with jewels ... It rather seems to me when I see queer Indian figures flitting about that "The Heathen are come in to mine inheritance."'[5]

Duleep, who must have been aware of the whispering, refused to be swayed by it. Instead, he chose to purchase a house for his mother in an exclusive part of London, opposite Hyde Park, at 1 Lancaster Gate. Duleep himself lived just around the corner, in a smart residence at Number 3. Passers-by often pressed their noses to the windows of the mysterious rani's house, drawn by the exotic smell of spiced dishes bubbling in the kitchen vats.

Not long after their return to London, the maharaja began to question the terms of the settlement he had been forced to sign, all those years ago. These were awkward missives, which caused consternation at the highest levels. Sir John Login, formerly Duleep's

'Ma-Baap', received one such letter from Duleep: 'I very much wish to have a conversation with you about my private property in the Punjab and the Koh-i-noor diamond.'[6] Realising the delicacy of the situation, Login immediately referred the letter to Buckingham Palace.

By now, Victoria was too deep in mourning for her dead husband to show much interest, so it was left to her adviser, the keeper of the privy purse, Sir Charles Phipps, to address the situation. Phipps wrote back to Login, echoing his concern: 'I am very sorry to hear what you say about the Maharajah – nothing could be so destructive to him as that he should succumb to his mother's, or any other native influence. He is too good to be so lost ...'[7] Phipps urged Login to break Jindan's spell over her son by becoming more involved in the maharaja's life. Duleep had once trusted him above all others; he would do so again. In the meantime Phipps assured Login that plans were being drawn up to have the maharaja married off. If Duleep had a wife and family of his own to occupy him, Jindan's influence would diminish. The India Office went as far as to identify a country estate far away from London that might be perfect for the maharaja and his new life.

Behind the scenes, there was also talk of sending Jindan back to Asia, perhaps even locking her up again. But on 1 August 1863, before the British could put any such plans into action, Rani Jindan died peacefully at her home in London. She was only forty-six. She looked much older.

If the British thought their problems had ended with the death of Duleep's mother, they were mistaken. Jindan had successfully sown seeds of doubt in her son's mind, and it was only after she died that they truly began to flourish. Outwardly, it seemed as if Duleep was still following the wishes of the palace, but everything now seemed a little subverted. On 7 June 1864, Duleep dutifully took a wife and started a family, much to the satisfaction of the India Office and men like Phipps. His choice, though, was bizarre to say the least: Bamba Müller was a beautiful sixteen-year-old, little educated, illegitimate daughter of a German merchant and an Abyssinian slave. She had lived in the cloistered environment of a Christian mission in Cairo from the moment she was born, and spoke not one word of English. Duleep had rejected Queen Victoria's suggested match, of a fellow deposed Indian royal who, like him, had embraced Christianity: Princess Gowramma of Coorg. Instead, he took pains to find a person who would least fit in with court life. He was beginning to feel like an outsider, and wanted a woman who would understand that and even share his sense of alienation. Without Victoria's knowledge, Duleep had contacted a Christian mission in Cairo, one he had visited when his ship had stopped to take on supplies during his first voyage to England. He asked the missionaries there to find him a virginal girl, a good Christian who might be moulded by him. They immediately thought of Bamba. She had grown up behind the high walls of the mission and knew nothing of the world, let alone the rarefied circles in which her future husband moved.

Duleep also purchased the home identified for him by the India Office when Login had warned them of Jindan's hold on him. It was a handsome estate on the Norfolk–Suffolk border, not far from the Sandringham home of his close friend the Prince of Wales. Duleep spent the next five years, and a considerable fortune, tearing down the existing mansion and rebuilding it in such a flamboyant style that locals referred to it as 'the Wedding Cake'. Inside, the house, Elveden Hall, resembled a Mughal palace, replete with carved marble, gilt and fine silk rugs. Outwardly, he had never been more settled in his life. Inwardly, he would never again be the contented, carefree young man who had laughed and played in the bosom of Queen Victoria's family.

Soon after his marriage, Duleep, who had always been a bon vivant, took to drinking heavily, and carousing with even more dancing girls and women of ill repute than he had in his bachelor days. His antics caused acute embarrassment both to his new wife, who seemed permanently pregnant, producing six children in the first ten years of her marriage, and to Queen

Victoria. Even when he asked Victoria to become god-
mother to Sophia, the youngest of his children borne
by the maharani, instead of following convention
and naming her Victoria he allowed her to be named
after her slave grandmother Sofia, albeit with a different spelling. He was being subversive even when he
appeared most loyal.

Queen Victoria had tolerated reports of his shocking behaviour for over a decade. It had been the
subject of concern from the moment she had come
out of her mourning for Albert. Duleep was throwing money around in a calamitous fashion, drunk-
enly handing out jewels to dancing girls at the seedy
Alhambra, a music hall in London's West End, as
if they were sweets. His profligate spending grated
on the India Office. They kept receiving outrageous
bills, which were resented. In some cases they simply refused to settle them as an expression of their
disgust. Simultaneously, Elveden was haemorrhaging
funds, as Duleep ploughed a fortune into the barren
landscape, attempting to turn it into the best hunting
estate in all England. The maharaja was living as if he
still possessed Punjab. Victoria gently chided him for
his excesses and asked him to temper both his conduct and his expenditure. For the first time in their
warm relationship, he ignored her.

By 1877 things had deteriorated to such an extent
that the British government stopped bankrolling the

maharaja. Returning his invoices unpaid, its representatives presented him with a stark choice – either he changed his ways, or he faced bankruptcy and ruin. Duleep responded by going on a spending spree, challenging the India Office to return almost half a million pounds' worth of family jewels, which he now insisted had never been subject to the treaty he had been forced to sign. He also threw in a demand for over a million pounds' worth of ancestral lands.

The stakes kept ratcheting higher. The India Office refused to settle a bill for Duleep Singh's children's clothes. Undeterred, Duleep directed a lengthening line of creditors to their door. Though he appeared bullish and belligerent, the stress of conflict was taking its toll. The once beautiful young man who had sent the painter Winterhalter into raptures was now a bad-tempered, paunchy, balding drunk. He neglected his young family at Elveden, and drove his wife to the bottle too. Though his eldest sons were at boarding school and protected from the mounting chaos, the younger children were left to run wild as Elveden disintegrated around them.

In the early months of 1880, the British government offered Duleep a one-off, interest-free sum of £57,000, enough to pay his debts and save him from bankruptcy. But the loan came with a condition. Elveden would have to be sold upon his death and all proceeds paid back to the British government. The maharaja was devastated. The terms would render him unable to leave any inheritance to his children. They would, in effect, be homeless and at the mercy of the same state he now believed had robbed him. With creditors refusing to provide further goods and services till they were paid, and banks refusing to lend him any more money, Duleep had only one roll of the dice left. He wrote directly to Queen Victoria and pleaded with her to let him keep Elveden. He wrote:

> It breaks my heart to think my eldest son will have to be turned out of his house and home and leave the place with which his earliest associations in life are connected. No one knows but myself, my Sovereign, the agony that I suffered when I was turned out of my home and exiled from the land of my birth and I shudder to think of the sufferings the poor boy may undergo.[8]

Queen Victoria's reply was warm, but offered little solace:

> Dear Maharajah,
>
> I have to acknowledge your letter of the 13th which has pained me so much. You know how fond I have always been of you, and how truly I felt for you, knowing how completely innocent you were of the unfortunate circumstances which led to you

leaving your own country. I have at once written to Lord Hartington [the secretary of state for India] to see what can be done to ensure your own comfort and a proper position for your children. As I once or twice mentioned to you before, I think you were thought extravagant and that may have led to a want of confidence as regards the future ... Trusting that the Maharanee and your dear children are well ...[9]

The Duleep Singhs were far from well, and things were about to get much worse for them all.

———

The maharaja turned to his influential friends for support, but most of them abandoned him, embarrassed by what he had become. He then threatened to go to the courts, but gave up on legal process when a book he wrote highlighting his legal argument against the Treaty of Lahore was ridiculed by those whose opinion carried the most weight. Duleep then turned to the press, begging the British people directly through their pages to put pressure on their government. Though the newspapers published his letters, they simultaneously mocked him for his increasing desperation.

All the while, Victoria, the woman he had once loved like a mother, watched silently, unable or unwilling to wade in on his behalf. Hurt and angry, Duleep wrote to the queen, reminding her of what had brought him to this dire point:

> From childhood I have been absolutely in the hands of the government without a will or independent action of my own – trusting implicitly to their good faith. Now there appears to have been a deliberate intention from the first, merely to do what least might suffice to answer my urgent demands and leave my children and family to gradually sink in the world.[10]

With no help forthcoming, Duleep decided to hit Victoria where he knew it would hurt her the most. He suggested he might renounce the Christianity she had so prized in him:

> My Sovereign … I embraced Christianity because those by whom I was surrounded at the time happened to be so consistent in their conduct. We Sikhs though savages by nature implicitly act up to the (such as it is) morality of our faith. We do not profess one thing and do the other.[11]

To her courtiers he made even more dire threats. If the British government continued to thwart him, he might try and forge an alliance with Britain's old enemy, Russia, and go to war, with an army of avenging Sikhs behind him.

In January 1886, the maharaja put the entire contents of Elveden Hall up for auction. Through the bricks and mortar had been seized by the government in lieu of his debts, everything from the fixtures in the house to the few remaining pheasant eggs in the hatchery was priced up and catalogued for a quick sale. Duleep had spent five fruitless years trying to extract the funds he thought he deserved, a fraction of what had been taken from him when he was a boy. The money raised from the sale at Elveden would buy tickets for him and his family to return to India. Secretly he harboured dreams of taking his old kingdom by force. By Duleep's calculations, his loyal subjects would rise up on his return, and Russian troops, anxious to help him, would pour in from Afghanistan.

Duleep never made it beyond Aden. He and his family were arrested on 21 April 1886 at Port Said, before their ship could reach the Suez Canal. Though he would eventually be released, his obsession had consumed him, wrecked his family and broken his health.

On 21 October 1893 Duleep Singh died penniless and alone in a shabby Parisian hotel. He was fifty-three. Since none of his children would ever have heirs of their own, his very name died with him. It is a tragedy still keenly felt in Punjab today.

13

'We Must Take Back the Koh-i-Noor'

When news of Duleep's demise became public, talk of the curse of the Koh-i-Noor was revived; and when Queen Victoria died in 1901, the Koh-i-Noor passed not to her son, the new emperor of India, King Edward VII, but to her daughter-in-law, Queen Alexandra. Somehow a belief had taken root that women could wear it with impunity but that it would destroy any man who dared. Though nobody seemed to know the provenance of the superstition, in view of what had happened to Duleep Singh, it was felt unwise to court the possibility.

Beautiful, with snow-white complexion, deep chestnut curls and an elegant swan neck, Queen Alexandra had a passion for jewels unsurpassed in British consorts past or present. For her coronation on 9 August 1902, Queen Alexandra's skirts were pinned with diamond bows, each with a large gem suspended from it. A diamond-encrusted girdle wound about her slender waist, and her jewelled bodice was obscured by the fabulous Dagmar necklace, comprising 2,000 diamonds and 118 pearls set in gold. The Dagmar was also said to contain a splinter of wood from the cross of Jesus Christ. Around her neck, Queen Alexandra wore a large diamond cockade[1] that fought for attention among several strings of ostentatious pearls. The queen consort's neck also somehow managed to support the weight of Queen Victoria's coronation necklace, a spectacular piece boasting twenty-six giant diamonds.

The item which attracted the most attention, however, was Queen Alexandra's newly designed consort's crown. Refashioned from the crown Queen Victoria had worn at Versailles in 1855, its 3,000 diamonds had been configured into eight sweeping arches meeting high in a diamond-encrusted globe. At the front and centre of the Coronation Crown, once again, the Koh-i-Noor took pride of place.

In the decades that followed, the Koh-i-Noor diamond found itself at the coronation of two other British queen consorts. The wife of the future King George V, Princess Mary, found her mother-in-law's crown too ostentatious and asked Garrard to fashion a simpler crown for her coronation in 1911. Sporting 2,200 small diamond embellishments, the crown was made so that, after her investiture, Queen Mary could remove parts and wear the rest as a circlet. One facet remained constant. Like Queen Alexandra, and Queen

Victoria before her, Queen Mary opted to keep the Koh-i-Noor at the very centre of her crown. When King George V promised to 'Govern the People of this Kingdom of England and the Dominions thereto belonging according to the Statutes in Parliament Agreed on and the Laws and Customs of the same ...'[2] he did so under the gaze of the Koh-i-Noor.

So did his son, King George VI. Never born to be king, George stepped into the void left by his love-struck brother Edward, who had abdicated to pursue his relationship with the American divorcee Wallis Simpson. For George VI's coronation, Elizabeth, his queen, had the consort's crown refashioned again. The new crown was framed in platinum with 2,800 diamonds, mainly cushion-shaped with some rose-cut and some brilliant-cut. A band of glittering crosses and rectangles was interrupted at the front by a large diamond, given to Queen Victoria in 1856 by the sultan of Turkey. Above this, four fleurs-de-lis and four crosses pattées stretched around her head, interrupted by a larger cross at the front and centre, in which was embedded the Koh-i-Noor. She would wear the crown at each of her husband's State Openings of Parliament, and also at her own daughter's coronation, when the present monarch Queen Elizabeth II took the throne on 2 June 1953.

Though the British had come to believe that the Koh-i-Noor's curse would only bring down a male monarch, it seems Queen Elizabeth II is taking no chances, and she has refrained from wearing the jewel. It now sits on display at the Jewel House in the Tower of London, but retirement for the Koh-i-Noor has not been altogether peaceful.

In 1947 the government of a newly independent India asked for the return of the Koh-i-Noor. Simultaneously, the Congress ministry of Orissa made its own claim, citing the deathbed bequest of Maharaja Ranjit Singh to the Jagannath Temple in Puri. Both demands were dealt with curtly. The British government stated that the diamond had been formally presented to the then sovereign, Queen Victoria, by its rightful owner, the maharaja of Lahore. To draw a line under the matter, the government added that this situation was 'non-negotiable'.

At the time of the coronation of Queen Elizabeth II, when the Koh-i-Noor made its appearance in her mother's crown, India put forward another request, perhaps hoping the new sovereign would be more amenable. That too was turned down flatly.

In 1976, Britain experienced its hottest summer since records began. Water was rationed, and hospitals placed on alert due to a spike in emergency admissions and a 20 per cent increase in 'excess deaths'. The hot weather also gave rise to a plague of ladybirds, usually friendly-looking insects with distinctive crimson and black-spotted backs. Some twenty-four billion of them swarmed across the skies as crops failed and tinder-dry forest caught fire. Staff at the House of Commons, forbidden from taking off their distinctive green jackets despite the temperatures, made history when they walked out in disgust, and the clock of Big Ben suffered its first and only major breakdown. Its chimes were silent for three weeks, adding to the growing feeling that some dark power had Britain in its grasp.

In August of that same year, on the eve of Pakistan's Independence Day celebrations, as temperatures in London climbed to their highest levels yet, Zulfikar Ali Bhutto, the prime minister of Pakistan, wrote to James Callaghan, his British counterpart, and demanded the return of the Koh-i-Noor. His claim was based on the belief that the jewel was part of Lahore's heritage, having been taken from the treasure house of that city.

In his letter, the Pakistani premier decried the disappearance of 'the unique treasures which are the flesh and blood of Pakistan's heritage'. The Koh-i-Noor's return to Pakistan 'would be a convincing demonstration of the spirit that moved Britain voluntarily to shed its imperial encumbrances and lead the process of decolonisation'. Bhutto added that the diamond's repatriation 'would be symbolic of a new international equity strikingly different from the grasping, usurping temper of a former age'.

The claim had come completely out of the blue and gave an already sweltering government even more reason to perspire. It took Callaghan about a month to reply, but when he did, the answer was a firm no once again. He said that 'explicit provision' had been made for the Koh-i-Noor's 'transfer to the British Crown ... in the peace treaty with the Maharajah of Lahore, which concluded the war of 1849'. He went on: 'In the light of the confused past history of the Koh-i-Noor diamond, the clear British title to it and the multiplicity of claims which would undoubtedly be made to it if its future were ever thought to be in doubt, I could not advise Her Majesty the Queen that it should be surrendered to any other country.'

Civil servants opened a file on the matter, and Bhutto's letter and Callaghan's uncompromising reply were placed inside. A potted history of the Koh-i-Noor was also added, in which a Whitehall scribe noted that the queen mother had worn the diamond fairly recently at the coronation of her daughter. 'I thought it was very awkward!' scribbled Callaghan.

Bhutto might have pursued the matter further had he not been deposed in a military coup a year later, and hanged two years after that.

In 1990, Kuldip Nayar, then high commissioner for India in London, raised the question of the Koh-i-Noor's return. Like Bhutto, he condemned the way in which the diamond had been appropriated, describing it as state-sponsored theft. Nayar insisted that the rightful claim was India's and India's alone. As he would later recall:

> During my short stint in the U.K., I found that the British would be embarrassed whenever I talked to them about the Kohinoor. When I visited the Tower of London with my family to see Indian diamonds, including the Kohinoor ... British officials, who showed us around, were very apologetic. They said: 'We feel ashamed to show them [diamonds] because they are from your country.' I recall the remark, which our old servant, Murli, made after seeing the diamonds: 'We must take back the Kohinoor when we return to India.' His words reflected the popular Indian opinion.[3]

Nayar's request too went nowhere. When he became a member of the Rajya Sabha (India's upper house in Parliament) in 2000, he raised the issue again:

> I got a petition signed by some 50 M.P.s – Opposition leader Manmohan Singh was one of them – to request the Government of India to ask the British government to return the Kohinoor. Jaswant Singh, the then Foreign Minister, assured me that the government would take up the matter with London forthwith. I presumed that he had done so.[4]

It later transpired that he had done no such thing.

The Koh-i-Noor had turned from an ancient gem with legendary powers into a live diplomatic grenade. After Bhutto and Nayar, neither the Indian nor the Pakistani government seemed keen to jeopardise relations with Great Britain over the Koh-i-Noor. All other attempts to repatriate the diamond have been instigated by members of the public, often to the embarrassment and irritation of those who sit in Delhi and Islamabad.

Calls to give back 'the stolen diamond' were not restricted to India and Pakistan either. In November 2000, the Taliban demanded that Queen Elizabeth hand the Koh-i-Noor to them, 'as soon as possible'. Presumably, they wished to display it in the bombed-out museum of Kabul. The Taliban's foreign affairs spokesman, Faiz Ahmad Faiz, insisted that the diamond was the 'legitimate property' of Afghanistan, adding that 'many other things' stolen from Afghanistan during the colonial period should be returned in order for the Taliban to reconstruct their war-torn country. Faiz went on: 'The history of the diamond shows it was taken from us to India, and from there to Britain. We have a much better claim than the Indians.' Unsurprisingly, nothing came of the Taliban request, and no further approach has been made by the Afghan government.

Indians and Pakistanis, in contrast, have not given up. Every so often an event will stoke their zeal once more. In 2002, Britain's queen mother died and her crown, containing the Koh-i-Noor, was placed on her coffin as she lay in state. This time British Sikhs took to the airwaves to condemn the flaunting of 'stolen goods' right under their noses. There were demands for the diamond to be returned to the Golden Temple in Amritsar, because, as one caller to a phone-in put it, 'the diamond belonged to a Sikh maharaja, and India did not even exist as a sovereign nation in those days'.[5]

Time has done nothing to dampen the passions of Indians and Pakistanis wanting the jewel back. In 2010, David Cameron, the then prime minister, made an official visit to Punjab. He was confronted by the Indian media, which suggested that by giving back the diamond, Britain could begin to atone for its exploitation of India during the Raj. 'If you say yes to one you suddenly find the British Museum would be empty,' explained the prime minister, perhaps having in mind the controversies surrounding the Rosetta Stone and the Elgin Marbles. 'I am afraid to say, it is going to have to stay put.'

It does not seem to matter how many British prime ministers say no, nor how many times they say it, the Koh-i-Noor continues to attract claims, with 2015 being a particularly active year.

In July, a group calling themselves the 'Mountain of Light' announced their intention to sue the British Crown for the return of the diamond. The consortium, made up of businessmen and Bollywood actors, said they would make their claim under the common law doctrine of 'trespass to goods', arguing that the British government had wrongfully taken possession of the diamond. If need be, they would be taking their claim to the international courts. Actress Bhumika Singh, part of the consortium, said: 'The Koh-i-Noor is not just a 105-carat stone but part of our history and culture and should undoubtedly be returned.'[6]

The campaign received the whole-hearted support of Keith Vaz, the son of Goan parents, and then a senior British MP in the House of Commons. 'These are genuine grievances which must be addressed. Pursuing monetary reparations is complex, time-consuming and potentially fruitless, but there is no excuse for not returning precious items such as the Koh-i-Noor diamond, a campaign I have backed for many years,' said Vaz.

His comments came just as Narendra Modi prepared for a three-day state visit to Britain. 'What a wonderful moment it would be, if and when Prime Minister Modi finishes his visit, which is much overdue, he returns to India with the promise of the diamond's return,' said Vaz.

The Modi visit came and went in November 2015, and the prime minister refrained from raising the issue of the diamond in his many speaking and media appearances around the country. Despite his diplomatic silence, just weeks later, in December, the Koh-i-Noor was in the news again. A Pakistani citizen had approached the Lahore High Court asking it to help him get the Koh-i-Noor back for his own country. In his petition, Jawaid Iqbal Jaffrey described the Koh-i-Noor as a 'Pakistan asset' in 'illegal possession' of Britain.

According to a report in one British newspaper, 'In the last half-century, Mr Jaffrey has written more than 786 letters to the Queen and various Pakistani officials asking for the diamond's return. His High Court petition notes that his letters have never been acknowledged, except once by the Queen through her principal private secretary.'[7] The newspaper might not have realised the significance of 786, but Muslims all over the world would have seen it. The Arabic letters of the opening words of the Quran, 'Bismillah ir-Rahman ir-Rahim' (In the name of Allah, the most Merciful, the most Beneficent), add up to the numerical value 786.[8]

Not even the invocation of Allah could move the British on this matter, and since no formal governmental request had been made, the authorities shrugged off these demands with ease. In 2016, the stakes became somewhat higher.

In April that year, the Indian government found itself in the middle of a cyclonic controversy. An Indian NGO had filed a petition asking the Supreme Court to direct the Indian government to bring back the diamond. Representing the government, the solicitor general, Ranjit Kumar, said it was pointless to pursue such a claim since the Koh-i-Noor was 'neither stolen nor forcibly taken'. Instead Kumar suggested that the diamond had been 'gifted' to the East India Company by Ranjit Singh in 1849. With one simple statement he opened the floodgates, and a number of old wounds. A deluge of mockery followed. How could Ranjit Singh have handed over the diamond, unless he had done so through astral projection? He had been dead for a decade. The notion of it being a 'gift' was also dissected, as the sorry saga of the deposed boy king was repeatedly examined on the twenty-four-hour news cycle. Acres of print and opinion were published on the way in which the diamond had been appropriated. The conclusion of the Indian media was straightforward. There was no way this was a gift.

Hours later, the Indian government seemed to perform a volte face. In a statement issued to the press, the Ministry of Culture distanced itself from the solicitor general's comments: 'The government of India further reiterates its resolve to make all possible efforts to bring back the Kohinoor diamond in an amicable manner …' The ministry added that the diamond was a 'valued piece of art with strong roots in our nation's history' and that Narendra Modi, the Indian prime minister, was determined to bring it back.

In September 2016, the government submitted an affidavit to the court. It stated that it did not believe it had legal grounds to pursue a return, but might resort to diplomatic means to seek its retrieval from Britain. It stressed that according to India's Antiquities and Art Treasures Act 1972, the country of origin of an antique could not invoke its right of retrieval if the article had left the country before the law came into force. In addition, the UNESCO convention, the affidavit said, could not come to the Indian government's aid since the convention was signed by Britain and India long after the diamond had been taken from Duleep Singh.

So the impasse continues. The Indian government maintains that it will try and bring the diamond back one way or another. The British government remains adamant that the stone is staying in London.

What should happen to this supposedly cursed diamond? Some have suggested creating a museum for the stone at the Wagah border between India and Pakistan, a unique institution, accessible from both sides. Others have suggested that it be cut up once again and a piece each given to all those countries that make a credible argument for its return – including modern-day Iran and Afghanistan. But it is most unlikely that such Solomonic wisdom would ever be entertained by the British, nor indeed would it satisfy any of the various parties involved.

The question of whether or not the Koh-i-Noor was cursed greatly exercised the proudly rational Victorians. As we have seen, Lord Dalhousie firmly believed that the great diamond was not cursed, and he used to quote Shah Shuja who told Ranjit Singh that it brought only good fortune 'as those who possess it have it in their power to subdue their enemies'. He pointed out that the diamond had belonged to some of the luckiest, richest and most powerful monarchs in history and scoffed at the notion that a curse was even possible.

Yet as this story also shows, many owners of the Koh-i-Noor – Shah Shuja among them – have indeed suffered in the most appalling ways. Its owners have variously been blinded, slow-poisoned, tortured to death, burned in oil, threatened with drowning, crowned with molten lead, assassinated by their own family and bodyguards, or have lost their kingdoms and died in penury. Even inanimate objects associated with the gem seem to have been struck down – witness the cholera epidemic and storms that nearly sank *Medea* as it brought the Koh-i-Noor to England, scything through passengers and crew.

Although it was not the largest diamond in Mughal hands – the Darya-i-Nur and the Great Mughal diamond were probably both originally around the same weight, and today, after Prince Albert's cut, there are at least eighty-nine diamonds larger than the Koh-i-Noor – it retains a fame and celebrity unmatched by any of its larger or more perfect rivals. This more than anything else has made it the focus of recent demands for compensation for colonial looting, and set in motion the repeated attempts to have it returned to its various former homes.

The story of the Koh-i-Noor continues to raise not only important historical issues but contemporary ones too, being in many ways a lightning rod for attitudes towards colonialism. The diamond's very presence in the Tower of London poses the question: what is the proper response to imperial looting? Do we simply shrug it off as part of the rough-and-tumble of history or should we attempt to right the wrongs of the past?

What is certain is that nothing in the immediate future is likely to prise this diamond from its display case. It awaits a new queen consort, and one day it may well sit on the head of Queen Camilla, wife of the future King Charles III. But given the diamond's violent and often tragic history, she, indeed the very monarchy itself, may well want to avoid the risk.

For nearly 300 years after Nader Shah carried the great diamond away from Delhi, fracturing the Mughal Empire as he did so, and 170 years after it first came into British hands, the Koh-i-Noor, like the legendary Syamantaka gem before it, has lost none of its power to create division and dissension. At its very best, it seems to bring mixed fortunes to whoever wears it, wherever it goes.

Notes

INTRODUCTION

1. *Papers Relating to the Punjab 1847–9*, London, 1849, f. 693.
2. James Andrew Broun Ramsay, Marquess of Dalhousie, *Private Letters*, London, 1911, p. 62.
3. Dalhousie to Hobhouse, 9 April 1849. In Michael Alexander and Sushila Anand, *Queen Victoria's Maharajah: Duleep Singh 1838–93*, London, 1980, p. 13.
4. Sir Penderel Moon, *The British Conquest and Dominion of India*, London, 1990, p. 616.
5. Christy Campbell, *The Maharajah's Box*, London, 2000, pp. 40–2.
6. National Archives of India, Foreign Dept, Political, Foreign 1849 Dept Pol Consultation 22 Dec, No. 11. Orders for the collection of information about the history of the Koh-i-Noor.
7. Ibid.
8. National Archives of India, Foreign Dept, Political, 1850, 14 June No. 72, item 14. Theophilus Metcalfe to Sir Henry Elliot, 7 January 1849.
9. I go by the figures given in Ian Balfour, *Famous Diamonds*, London, 2009; and Anna Malecka, 'The Great Mughal and the Orlov: One and the Same Diamond', *Journal of Gemmology* 35, no. 1 (2016): 56–63.

10. At least judging by the table in Balfour, *Famous Diamonds*, pp. 320–1. There have apparently been a rash of new large diamond discoveries in South Africa since Balfour drew up his table of diamond sizes, so it is quite possible that the Koh-i-Noor now ranks below 100.

11. Mohammad Kazem Marvi, *Alam Ara-ye Naderi* (three volumes), edited by Mohammad Amin Riyahi, Tehran (third edition), 1374/1995, Vol. 2, p. 739n.

1. THE INDIAN PREHISTORY OF THE KOH-I-NOOR

1. Borneo became quite a major source of diamonds in the seventeenth century – indeed, the East India Company were exploiting Borneo diamonds prior to the Indian ones. See Jack M. Ogden, *Diamonds, Head Hunters and a Prattling Fool: The British Exploitation of Borneo Diamonds* in *Gems and Jewellery*, September 2005, Vol. 14, No. 3, pp. 67–9.

2. Godehard Lenzen, *The History of Diamond Production and the Diamond Trade*, London, 1970, pp. 1–7. See also P. J. Lu, Y. Nan Yao, J. F. So, G. E. Harlow, J. Lu, G. Wang, and P. M. Chaikin, *Earliest Use of Corundum and Diamond in Prehistoric China* in *Archaeometry*, 2005, Vol. 47, pp. 1–12.

3. *The Garuda Purana*, primary source edition, edited and translated by Manmatha Nath Dutt, Calcutta, 1908.

4. Raja Sourindro Mohum Tagore, *Mani-masa or A Treatise on Gems*, Calcutta, 1881, Pt 1, p. 17.

5. *Bhagavad Purana*, Chapter 56, 'The Syamantaka Jewel'. Also in Tagore, *Mani-masa*, Pt 1, p. 9.

6. Tagore, *Mani-masa*, Pt 1, p. 17.

7. Gyula Wojtilla, 'Ratnasastra in Kautilya's *Arthasastra*', *Acta Orientalia Academiae Scientiarum Hungaricae* 62, no. 1 (2009): 37–44.

8. Radha Krishnamurthy, 'Gemmology in Ancient India', *Indian Journal of the History of Science* 27, no. 3 (1992): 251–60.

9. Daud Ali, *Courtly Culture and Political Life in Early Medieval India*, Cambridge, 2004, p. 164.

10. Vidya Dehejia, *The Body Adorned: Dissolving Boundaries between Sacred and Profane in Indian Art*, Ahmedabad, 2009, p. 38.

11. Ibid.

12. *The Kautilya Arthasastra*, translated by R. P. Kangle, New Delhi, 2004, pp. viii–ix.

13. Adapted from E. Hultzsch, *South Indian Inscriptions*, Vol. 2, New Delhi, 1992 (reprint), Pt 1, Inscription No. 8, pp. 87–8. Also Vidya Dehejia, *The Sensuous and the Sacred: Chola Bronzes from South India*, Seattle, 2002.

14. Adapted from Hultzsch, *South Indian Inscriptions*, Vol. 2, Pt 1, Inscription No. 8, pp. 87–8. Also Dehejia, *The Sensuous and the Sacred*.

15. *India in the Fifteenth Century, Being a Collection of Narratives of Voyages to India*, edited by Richard Henry Major, London, 1857, pp. 23–5.

16. Garcia da Orta, *Colloquies on the Simples and Drugs of India*, translated by Clements Markham, London, 1913.

17. Jonathan Gil Harris, *The First Firangis*, Delhi, 2014, p. 37.

18. Ibid., p. 41.

19. Da Orta, *Colloquies*, pp. 342–52.

2. THE MUGHALS AND THE KOH-I-NOOR

1. Babur, *The Babur Nama or Journal of the Emperor Babur*, translated from the Turkish by Annette Susannah Beveridge, London, 2006.

2. Ibid.

3. 1 misqal = 6.22 grams or 0.22 ounces.

4. BM Ms Or 1717, Rieu's catalogue III, 9565 Treatise on Precious Stones by Mohammad, son of Ashraf al-Hussaini. Quoted by H. Beveridge, 'Babar's Diamond: Was It the Koh-i-Nur', *Asiatic Quarterly Review* (April 1899), pp. 370–89.

5. Abu'l Fazl, *The History of Akbar*, Vol. 1, translated by Wheeler M. Thackston, Cambridge, MA, 2015, p. 549.

6. Jauhar, *The Tezkereh al-Vakiat or Private Memoirs of the Emperor Humayun*, translated by Charles Stewart, Edinburgh, 1832, p. 90.

7. Ibid., p. 91.

8. BM Persian Mss Or 53, Rieu's Catalogue. Quoted by Beveridge, 'Babar's Diamond', p. 381.

9. BM Ms. Add. 9997, Rieu's catalogue 314b, p. 266. Quoted by Beveridge, 'Babar's Diamond', p. 382. The return of the diamond to India is also referred to in *Tarikh-i-Firishta*: see Abdul Aziz, *The Imperial Treasury of the Indian Mughals*, New Delhi, 2009, p. 188.

10. Quoted by Beveridge, 'Babar's Diamond', p. 379.

11. Susan Stronge, *Bejewelled Treasures: The Al Thani Collection*, London, 2015, pp. 24–5.

12. Assadullah Souren Melikian-Chirvani, 'The Red Stones of Light in Iranian Culture', *Bulletin of the Asia Institute* 15 (2001): 82.

13. Da Orta, *Colloquies*, p. 342.

14. 'Allami, Abul Fazl, *The A'in-i Akbari*, translated and edited by H. Blochmann, New Delhi 1977, Vol. 1, 'The Treasury for Precious Stones', p. 15.

15. Ibid.

16. Sir William Foster, *The Embassy of Sir Thomas Roe to India 1615–19, as Narrated in his Journal and Correspondence*, New Delhi, 1990, p. 270.

17. Quoted in Stronge, *Bejewelled Treasures*, p. 29.

18. Jahangir, *Tuzuk-i-Jahangiri or Memoirs of Jahangir*, translated by Alexander Rogers, edited by Henry Beveridge, London, 1919, p. 317.
19. Aziz, *Imperial Treasury*, p. 173; Jahangir, *Tuzuk-i-Jahangiri*, p. 320.
20. Jahangir, *Tuzuk-i-Jahangiri*, p. 320.
21. Ebba Koch, 'The Mughals and their Love of Precious Stones', in *Halqeh-ye Nur Astaneh-ye Ferdaws*, London, 2012.
22. Niccolao Manucci, *Storia do Mogor or Mogul India*, translated by William Irvine (four volumes), London, 1907, Vol. 1, p. 222.
23. Jean Baptiste Tavernier, Baron of Aubonne, *Travels in India* (1676), translated by V. Ball (two volumes), London, 1889, Vol. 1, p. 233.
24. Ibid.
25. Inayat Khan, *The Shah Jahan Nama of Inayat Khan*, edited by W. E. Begley and Z. A. Desai, New Delhi, 1990, p. 511.
26. Manucci, *Storia do Mogor*, Vol. 1, p. 227; and Khan, *Shah Jahan Nama*, p. 533.
27. Aziz, *Imperial Treasury*, pp. 190–8.
28. Much has been written on the Peacock Throne, but much the most interesting essay is the magisterial study by Susan Stronge, 'The Sublime Thrones of the Mughal Emperors of Hindustan', *Jewellery Studies* 10 (2004): 52–65.
29. See Bruce Wannell's 'Two Versions of a Book of Jewels in Persian: On the Jawahir Nama, or Book of Jewels' for the Simon Digby Memorial Festschrift (forthcoming).
30. Stronge, 'Sublime Thrones', p. 56.
31. Khan, *Shah Jahan Nama*, p. 147.
32. Tavernier, *Travels in India*, Vol. 1, p. 315.
33. Ibid., p. 316.
34. Balfour, *Famous Diamonds*, pp. 81–5, 173. Balfour accepts the theory of V. B. Meen and A. D. Tushingham in *Crown*

Jewels of Iran, Toronto, 1968, that Tavernier's Great Table diamond was split in two, possibly by accident, and now makes up the Darya-i-Noor and the Nur al-Ain, or Light of the Eye.

35. See, for example, Balfour, *Famous Diamonds*, p. 174; and Malecka, 'Great Mughal'.

3. NADER SHAH: THE KOH-I-NOOR GOES TO IRAN

1. Dargah Quli Khan, *The Muraqqa' e-Dehli*, translated by Chander Shekhar, New Delhi, 1989. For Ad Begum, p. 107; for Nur Bai, p. 110.
2. Père Louis Bazin, 'Mémoires sur dernières années du règne de Thamas Kouli-Kan et sa mort tragique, contenus dans une lettre du Frère Bazin', 1751, in *Lettres édifiantes et curieuses écrites des missions étrangères*, Paris, 1780, Vol. 4, pp. 277–321. These passages are at pp. 314–15, 316–18.
3. Michael Axworthy, *The Sword of Persia: Nader Shah from Tribal Warrior to Conquering Tyrant*, London, 2006, p. 182.
4. Willem Floor, 'New Facts on Nader Shah's Indian Campaign', In *Iran and Iranian Studies: Essays in Honour of Iraj Afshar*, edited by Kambiz Eslami, Princeton, 1998, p. 200.
5. Anand Ram Mukhlis, *Tazkira*, in Sir H. M. Elliot and John Dowson, *The History of India as Told by its own Historians*, London, 1867–77, Vol. 8, p. 77.
6. Sanjay Subrahmanyam, 'Un Grand Derangement: Dreaming of an Indo-Persian Empire', in *Journal of Early Modern History*, Vol. 4, Issue 3, 2000, pp. 337–78, p. 357.
7. Floor, 'New Facts', p. 210.
8. Mukhlis, *Tazkira*, pp. 82–3.
9. Axworthy, *Sword of Persia*, p. 207.

10. Michael Edwards, *King of the World: The Life and Times of Shah Alam, Emperor of Hindustan*, London, 1970, p. 15.
11. Mukhlis, *Tazkira*, p. 86.
12. Syed Ghulam Hussain Khan, *Seir Mutaqherin or Review of Modern Times* (four volumes), Calcutta, 1790, Vol. 1, pp. 316–17.
13. Ibid., p. 315.
14. Ibid.
15. Floor, 'New Facts', p. 217.
16. Elliot and Dowson, *History of India*, Vol. 8, p. 90.
17. Mirza Mahdi Astarabadi, *'Tarikh-e Jahangosha-ye Naderi*: The Official History of Nader's Reign', Bombay lithograph 1849/1265, p. 207.
18. *The Memoirs of Khojeh Abdulkurreem*, translated by Francis Gladwin, Calcutta, 1788, p. 26.
19. Syed Hasan Askari, *Raja Jugal Kishore Despatch Regarding the Sack of Delhi by Nadir Shah, Indian Historical Records Association: A Retrospect 1919–1948*, Vol. 25, Dec 1948. See also Abhishek Kaicker, *Unquiet City: Making and Unmaking Politics in Mughal Delhi, 1707–39*, unpublished PhD, Columbia University, p. 562.
20. Abd ol-Karim Kashmiri, *Bayan-e-Waqe'*, translated by H. G. Pritchard, BM Mss Add 30782, ff. 86–7.
21. Marvi, *Alam Ara-ye Naderi*, Vol. 2, p. 739n.
22. Elliot and Dowson, *History of India*, Vol. 8, p. 93.
23. Mark Zebrowski, *Gold, Silver and Bronze from Mughal India*, London, 1990, p. 52 (from Simon Digby's unpublished translation of Mirza Mahdi Astarabadi, *Tarikh-e-Jahangoshay-e-Naderi*).
24. *The Memoirs of Khojeh Abdulkurreem*, p. 26.
25. Axworthy, *Sword of Persia*, p. 167.
26. Ibid., pp. 231–40.
27. Ibid., pp. 278–9.
28. Bazin, *Mémoires*, pp. 320–1.

29. Ibid., pp. 321–2.
30. Ibid., pp. 322–3.
31. Robert McChesney, the brilliant translator of the *Siraj ul-Tawarikh*, kindly sent me this note about Fayz Muhammad's account of the assassination and Ahmad Shah Abdali's seizure of the Koh-i-Noor: 'Other Afghan sources tend to be circumspect about how Ahmad Shah got the diamond. His own chronicler, Mahmud Husayni Jami, speaks only of turmoil in the army camp after the assassination (see Jami, *Tarikh-i Ahmad Shahi*, Tehran, 2005 edition). But the modern editor of this edition, Ghulam Hosein Zargari Nizhad, says in his introduction (p. 15), "on the very day of the assassination, Ahmad Khan who had seized the Koh-i Noor diamond from the women of Nader Shah's harem and, along with that had taken other precious objects from the shah's household, after reaching Naderabad [i.e. Qandahar] began the work needed to establish his rule over the Afghans." He cites no source for this, of course, but as an Iranian he has no trouble believing it. A source contemporary with the *Tarikh-i Ahmad Shahi*, the *Tarikh-i Husayni* (or *Husayn Shahi*) written during Zaman Shah's reign, likewise says only that after the assassination Ahmad Shah "headed for Qandahar" (p. 22; this is a manuscript in the archives in Kabul). *Tarikh-i Sultani*, to the best of my knowledge, says nothing at all about the diamond. The only Afghan source, Shayr Muhammad Khan Gandapur of Dera Isma'il Khan, writing in the mid-19th century (he died in 1885), refers vaguely to the Koh-i Noor speaking of the turmoil and fighting between units of Nader Shah's army on learning of his death. He says only that Ahmad Khan first strove to "fulfill the rights of his salt" (i.e. suggesting as a bodyguard of Nader Shah he was obliged to protect the household) but then says

"As for the Afghans, having beaten back [the Uzbeks and Afsharis who were attacking them] they plundered the shah's household and seized many precious things and set off for Qandahar" (*Tarikh-i Khurshid-i Jahan*, Lahore, 1894, p. 169). The long and short of it is that I don't know where Fayz Muhammad got his information. However, I can see Fayz Muhammad putting the best spin on it by suggesting Ahmad Shah was rewarded for his service defending the harem rather than suggesting he or other Afghans forcibly took it.'

32. James Baillie Fraser, *Narrative of a Journey into Khorasan, in the Years 1821 and 1822*, London, 1825, Appendix B, p. 43.

33. Michael Axworthy, *Iran: Empire of the Mind: A History from Zoroaster to the Present Day*, London, 2007, p. 173; also Balfour, *Famous Diamonds*, p. 176.

34. Balfour, *Famous Diamonds*, p. 214.

4. THE DURRANIS: THE KOH-I-NOOR IN AFGHANISTAN

1. Ganga Singh, *Ahmad Shah Durrani*, Delhi, 1925, pp. 25–6.

2. Mountstuart Elphinstone, *An Account of the Kingdom of Caubul*, London, 1819, Vol. 2, pp. 281–4.

3. Mir, *Zikr-I Mir: The Autobiography of the Eighteeenth Century Mughal Poet, Mir Muhammad Taqi 'Mir'*, translated, annotated and introduced by C. M. Naim, New Delhi, 1998, pp. 83–5, 93–4.

4. Singh, *Ahmad Shah*, p. 260.

5. Translated by A. Habibi, in Louis Dupree, *Afghanistan*, Oxford, 1973, p. 337.

6. Jonathan Duncan, 'Purn Puri', *Asiatic Researches* (1792), Vol. 5 (1799), pp. 37–49.

7. Singh, *Ahmad Shah*, p. 326.

8. Mirza Ata Muhammad, *Naway Ma'arek* (The Song of Battles), Published as *Nawā-yi ma'ar-ik. Nuskha-i*

khat.t.ī-i Mūza-i Kābul mushtamal bar wāqi'āt-i 'as.r-i Sadōzā'ī u Bārakzā'ī, ta'līf-i Mīrzā Mīrzaā 'At.ā'-Muh.ammad, Kabul, 1331 AH/1952 (*Nashrāt-i Anjuman-i tārīkh*, No. 22 [with a preface by Ah.mad-'Alī Kohzād, without index]; idem: *Āryānā*, VIII (1328–9 AH /1950), Introduction, pp. 1–9.

9. Robert Byron, *The Road to Oxiana*, London, 1937, p. 90.

10. Fayz Muhammad, *Siraj ul-Tawarikh* (The Lamp of Histories), Kabul, 1913, translated by R. D. McChesney (2013), Vol. 1, p. 63.

11. Olaf Caroe, *The Pathans*, London, 1958, p. 262; Syad Muhammad Latif, *History of the Punjab*, New Delhi, 1964, p. 299; Robert Nichols, *Settling the Frontier: Land, Law and Society in the Peshawar Valley 1500–1900*, Oxford, 2001, p. 90.

12. Muhammad, *Naway Ma'arek*, Introduction, pp. 1–9.

13. Sohan Lal Suri, *Umdat-ut-Tawarikh: An Original Source of Punjab History: Chronicles of the Reign of Maharaja Ranjit Singh 1831–1839 by Lala Sohan Lal Suri*, translated by V. S. Suri, Delhi, 1961; Amritsar, 2002, p. 33.

14. H. T. Prinsep, *History of the Punjab, and of the rise, progress, & present condition of the sect and nation of the Sikhs* [based in part on the 'Origin of the Sikh Power in the Punjab and political life of Muha-Raja Runjeet Singh'], London, 1846, Vol. 1, p. 260; Muhammad, *Siraj ul-Tawarikh*, Vol. 1, p. 84; Elphinstone, *Kingdom of Caubul*, Vol. 1, p. 317.

15. Muhammad, *Siraj ul-Tawarikh*, Vol. 1, p. 88.

16. Muhammad, *Naway Ma'arek*; Shah Shuja, *Waqi'at-i-Shah Shuja*, Introduction, pp. 1–9.

17. Sultan Mohammad Khan ibn Musa Khan Durrani, *Tarikh-i-Sultani*, began writing on 1 Ramzan 1281 AH (Sunday, 29 January 1865) and published first on 14 Shawwal 1298 AH (Friday, 8 September 1881), Bombay, p. 212.

18. Ibid., p. 217.
19. Muhammad, *Naway Ma'arek*, p. 5.
20. *Tarikh-i-Sultani*, p. 219.
21. Elphinstone, *Kingdom of Caubul*, Vol. 1, pp. 67–8.
22. Fraser Papers, Inverness, Vol. 30, p. 171. WF to his father, 6 March 1809.
23. Ibid., pp. 201–6. WF to his father, 19 June and 6 July 1809.
24. Muhammad, *Naway Ma'arek*, pp. 10–12.
25. Shuja, *Waqi'at-i-Shah Shuja*, The 26th Event; also Muhammad, *Siraj ul-Tawarikh*, Vol. 1, p. 122.
26. Alexander Burnes, *Travels into Bokhara, Being the Account of a Journey from India to Cabool, Tartary and Persia, also a Narrative of a Voyage on the Indus from the Sea to Lahore* (three volumes), London, 1834, Vol. 2, pp. 309–10.
27. Shuja, *Waqi'at-i-Shah Shuja*, The 26th Event.
28. Muhammad, *Naway Ma'arek*, pp. 13–15, 35–6, for the promised Rs 200,000.
29. Shuja, *Waqi'at-i-Shah Shuja*, The 26th Event.
30. Punjab Archives, Lahore, from Ochterlony in Ludhiana to John Adam, Calcutta, 23 April 1813, Book 13, No. 42, No. 164, p. 98.
31. Prinsep, *History of the Sikhs*, Vol. 2, pp. 14–15.

5. RANJIT SINGH: THE KOH-I-NOOR IN LAHORE

1. The Hon. Emily Eden, *Up the Country: Letters Written to her Sister from the Upper Provinces of India*, London, 1930, pp. 198–9.
2. National Archives of India, Foreign Political Dept, 1850, 14 June No. 74, 75 Subject: Account of the KOHINUR while it was in the possession of the Lahore Durbar previously. Duplicate Copy. No. 174 of 1850 From Major Macgregor CB, Deputy Commissioner, Lahore. To P. Melville Esquire, Secretary to the Board of Administration for the Affairs of the Punjab, Lahore, April 20 1850.

3. Ibid.
4. Ibid.
5. Ibid.
6. Bhai Nahar Singh and Kirpal Singh (eds), *History of the Koh-i-Noor, Darya-i-Noor and Taimur's Ruby*, New Delhi, no date, p. 33.
7. Eden, *Up the Country*, p. 209.
8. Ben Hopkins, *The Making of Modern Afghanistan*, London, 2008, p. 51.
9. Burnes, *Travels into Bokhara*, Vol. 1, p. 143.
10. Ibid., p. 144.
11. Khushwant Singh, *Ranjit Singh: Maharaja of the Punjab*, London, 1962.
12. Ibid., p. 257.
13. Prinsep, *History of the Sikhs*, Vol. 2, p. 158.
14. Eden, *Up the Country*, p. 235.
15. Singh, *Ranjit Singh*, p. 257.
16. Jagannath/Juggernaut or 'Lord of the Universe' is a deity worshipped by Hindus and Buddhists.
17. Suri, *Umdat-ut-Tawarikh*, p. 694.

6. CITY OF ASH

1. Prince Alexis Soltykoff, *Voyages dans l'Inde*, Paris, 1858.
2. J. Limbird, *The Mirror of Literature, Amusement, and Instruction*, containing original papers, Vol. 8, London, 1845, p. 230.
3. *Satis* or *suttees*, according to ancient Hindu custom, are married women burned alive on the pyres of their dead husbands.
4. Sohan Lal Suri, *Umdat-ut-Tawarikh*, translated by V. S. Suri (Amritsar, Guru Nanak Dev University 2002), verse 3, lines 484–9.

5. Ibid., 3 (v.) p. 489.
6. John Martin Honigberger, *Thirty-Five Years in the East: Adventures, Discoveries, Experiments, and Historical Sketches, Relating to the Punjab and Cashmere; in Connection with Medicine, Botany, Pharmacy, &c.*, London, 1852, p. 100.
7. Ibid.
8. Ibid., p. 47.
9. Ibid., p. 53.
10. Ibid., p. 54.
11. Ibid.
12. Jean-François Allard (French), Paolo di Avitabile (Italian, Naples), Claude Auguste Court (French) and Jean-Baptiste Ventura (Italian, Modena) were all generals in Ranjit Singh's army.
13. Honigberger, *Thirty-Five Years in the East*, p. 57.
14. Ibid., p. 58.
15. Hindu priests.
16. *Asiatic Journal and Monthly Register for British India and its Dependencies* 28 (1839).
17. *Era*, 20 October 1839.
18. Lady Login, *Sir John Login and Duleep Singh*, London, 1890, p. 196.
19. Stephen Howarth, *The Koh-i-noor Diamond*, London, 1980, p. 112.
20. Fakir Syed Aijazuddin, *The Resourceful Fakirs*, Delhi, 2014, p. 253.
21. Honigberger, *Thirty-Five Years in the East*, p. 104.
22. George Monro Carmichael Smyth, *A History of the reigning family of Lahore, with some account of the Jummoo rajahs, the Seik soldiers and their sirdars*, Calcutta, 1847, pp. 32, 33.
23. Honigberger, *Thirty-Five Years in the East*, p. 102.
24. Ibid., p. 103.

25. To this day the gate is known as Khooni Dharwaza – the murder gate.
26. The golden throne of Punjab is now in the Victoria and Albert Museum in London.

7. THE BOY KING

1. Honigberger, *Thirty-Five Years in the East*, p. 111.
2. Prinsep, *History of the Sikhs*, p. 276.
3. Honigberger, *Thirty-Five Years in the East*, p. 112.
4. *The Indian Mutiny, to the Evacuation of Lucknow: To which is Added, a Narrative of the Defence of Lucknow, and a Memoir of General Havelock*, compiled by the Former Editor of the *Delhi Gazette*, London, 1858, p. 194.
5. Letter from Hardinge to Lawrence quoted in Michael Alexander and Sushila Anand, *Queen Victoria's Maharajah: Duleep Singh 1838–93*, London, 1980, p. 7.
6. *Maharajah Duleep Singh Correspondence*, edited by Ganda Singh, Patiala, 1972, p. 90.
7. Rani Jindan to J. Lawrence, undated, translated from Punjabi, in ibid., p. 26.
8. Letter from Hardinge to Eliot, 27 August 1847, in ibid., p. 32.
9. Kushwant Singh, *A History of the Sikhs: 1839–2004*, Vol. 2, Delhi, 2004, p. 78.
10. The Duke of Argyll, *India under Dalhousie and Canning*, London, 1865, p. 9.
11. Edwin Arnold, *The Marquis of Dalhousie's Administration of British India* (two volumes), London, 1862, Vol. 1, p. 103.
12. James Andrew Broun Ramsay, Marquess of Dalhousie, *Private Letters*, London, 1911, p. 62.

13. Ibid.
14. Letter from Robert R. Adams, Assistant Comissioner of Lahore, to Lena Login, 2 November 1849. Reproduced in Lady Login, *Lady Login's Recollections: Court Life and Camp Life 1820–1904*, London, 1917, p. 80.
15. Ibid., pp. 76–7.
16. Login, *Sir John Login and Duleep Singh*, p. 217.
17. Ibid., p. 166.
18. Ibid., p. 128.
19. *Delhi Gazette*, quoted in the *Kendal Mercury*, 30 September 1848.
20. Broughton Mss, Dalhousie to Hobhouse, 22 December 1848, British Library (BL) 36456–36483.
21. Ibid.
22. Broughton Mss, Dalhousie to Hobhouse, 4 April 1849, BL 36456–36483.
23. *Mining Journal*, 13 January 1849.

8. PASSAGE TO ENGLAND

1. Login, *Sir John Login and Duleep Singh*, p. 154.
2. Ibid., p. 155.
3. Ibid., p. 174.
4. Ibid., p. 175.
5. Lady Login, *Recollections*, p. 83.
6. Login, *Sir John Login and Duleep Singh*, p. 175.
7. Ibid., p. 177.
8. Ibid.
9. Ibid.
10. Alexander and Anand, *Queen Victoria's Maharajah*, p. 19.
11. Avtar Singh Gill, *Lahore Darbar and Rani Jindan*, Ludhiana, 1983, p. 231.
12. Login, *Sir John Login and Duleep Singh*, p. 157.

13. *Lloyd's Weekly Newspaper*, 1 July 1849.
14. Quoted in Alexander and Anand, *Queen Victoria's Maharajah*, p. 13.
15. Dalhousie, *Private Letters*, p. 124.
16. Reginald Bosworth Smith, *Life of Lord Lawrence*, London, 1912, p. 175.
17. Ibid.
18. Ibid.
19. Dalhousie, *Private Letters*, p. 124.
20. Ibid.
21. Howarth, *The Koh-i-noor Diamond*, p. 138.
22. *Morning Post*, 1 July 1850.
23. Ibid.
24. Ibid.
25. Dalhousie, *Private Letters*, p. 139.
26. Ibid.
27. Dalhousie, *Private Letters*, p. 396.

9. THE GREAT EXHIBITION

1. Queen Victoria's Journals, 1 May 1851, Royal Archives (RA).
2. Roger Fulford, *The Prince Consort*, London, 1949, p. 45.
3. Juliet Gardiner, *Queen Victoria*, London, 1997, p. 79.
4. John Loadman and Francis James, *The Hancocks of Marlborough: Rubber, Art and the Industrial Revolution – A Family of Inventive Genius*, Oxford, 2010, p. 127.
5. *The Times*, 2 May 1851.
6. Ibid.
7. *Glasgow Herald*, 5 May 1851.
8. Quoted in *The North American Miscellany*, Boston, 1851, Vol. 2, p. 334 (Vol. 939 of *American Periodical Series 1800–1850*).
9. *London Evening Standard*, 16 June 1851.

10. Ibid.
11. Ibid.
12. Ibid.
13. *London Evening Standard*, 23 June 1851.
14. *London Evening Standard*, 14 October 1851.

10. THE FIRST CUT

1. Dalhousie, *Private Letters*, p. 172.
2. Cyril Davenport, *The English Regalia*, London, 1897.
3. *Illustrated London News*, 24 July 1852.
4. *Morning Chronicle*, 19 July 1852.
5. Louis J. Jennings (ed.), *The Correspondence and Diaries of the Late Right Honourable John Wilson Croker*, Cambridge, 2012, p. 354.
6. Ibid.
7. Ibid.
8. Traditional horizontal plate used for diamond cutting, made from a special hard and porous cast iron.
9. *Morning Chronicle*, 19 July 1852.
10. Login, *Sir John Login and Duleep Singh*, p. 180.
11. Login, *Lady Login's Recollections*, p. 88.
12. Dalhousie, *Private Letters*, p. 156.
13. Ibid., p. 157.

11. QUEEN VICTORIA'S 'LOYAL SUBJECT'

1. Queen Victoria's Journals, 6 July 1854, RA.
2. Ibid., 10 July 1854.
3. Login, *Lady Login's Recollections*, p. 123.
4. Ibid., pp. 123–4.
5. Ibid., p. 124.
6. Ibid.
7. Ibid., pp. 125–6.

12. THE JEWEL AND THE CROWN

1. Login, *Lady Login's Recollections*, pp. 125–6.
2. Ibid.
3. A cross pattée (or 'cross patty', known also as 'cross formée/formy') is a type of cross that has arms narrow at the centre and often flared in a curved or straight line, so that they are broader at the perimeter.
4. Garrard's invoice, reproduced in Suzy Menkes, *The Royal Jewels*, London, 1985, p. 12.
5. Lady Normanby to Lord Mulgrave, 2 July 1861, Normanby Archives.
6. Login, *Sir John Login and Duleep Singh*, p. 463.
7. Ibid., p. 470.
8. Duleep Singh to Queen Victoria, 13 Sep 1880, QVM, p. 138.
9. Queen Victoria to Duleep Singh, 18 Sep 1880, QVM, p. 139.
10. Duleep Singh to Palace, Memo 15 December 1883, Vic Add N2/145, RA.
11. Duleep to Queen Victoria, 16 September 1884, Vic Add N2/176, RA.

13. 'WE MUST TAKE BACK THE KOH-I-NOOR'

1. A cockade is a circular arrangement of gems, made to look a little like a rosette.
2. Coronation Oath Act 1688, Section III.
3. Kuldip Nayar, *Tribune*, 17 July 2005.
4. Ibid.
5. Taken from a programme presented by Anita Anand in 2002.
6. This is the non-metric measurement system, current in the nineteenth century, for the 108.93 carat Koh-i-Noor.
7. *Daily Telegraph*, 4 December 2015.
8. In the Abjad system, the twenty-eight letters of the Arabic alphabet are assigned numerical values.

Bibliography

I. MANUSCRIPT SOURCES IN EUROPEAN LANGUAGES

Bodleian Library

Kimberley Papers

British Library

Broughton Diaries and Memorandum: Add Mss 43744
Broughton Papers: Add Mss 36456–83
Broughton Papers: Add Mss 46915
Duleep Singh Family Papers: Mss Eur E377
Wellesley Papers: Add Mss 37274–318

National Archives of India, New Delhi

Foreign Dept, Political, Foreign 1849 Dept Pol Consultation
  22 Dec, No. 11. Orders for the collection of information re
  the history of the KOHINUR
Foreign Political Dept, 1850 Dept, 14 June No. 72, 74, 75
Subject: Account of the KOHINUR while it was in the possession of the Lahore Durbar previously. Duplicate Copy.
  No. 174 of 1850

Punjab Archives

Delhi Residency Papers

Private Archives

The Fraser Papers, Inverness
The Letters of Queen Victoria, Project Gutenberg,
eBook, Vol. 2

Royal Archives

Queen Victoria's Journals
The Letters of Queen Victoria, Windsor Castle, via Project
Gutenberg

2. PERSIAN, URDU AND SANSKRIT SOURCES

Manuscripts

Oriental and India Office Collections, British Library
(formerly India Office Library), London
BM Persian Mss Or 53 Letters of Khur Shah
BM Ms Or 1717, Treatise on Precious Stones by Mohammad,
son of Ashraf al-Hussaini
Kashmiri, Abd ol-Karim, *Bayan-e-Waqe'*, translated by H. G.
Pritchard, BM Mss Add 30782.

Published Texts

Askari, Syed Hasan, *Raja Jugal Kishore Despatch Regarding
the Sack of Delhi by Nadir Shah, Indian Historical Records
Association: A Retrospect 1919–1948*, Vol. 25, Dec 1948.
Astarabadi, Mirza Mahdi, '*Tarikh-e Jahangosha-ye Naderi:*
The Official History of Nader's Reign', Bombay
lithograph 1849/1265.

Babur, *The Babur Nama or Journal of the Emperor Babur*, translated from the Turkish by Annette Susannah Beveridge, London, 2006.

Durrani, Sultan Mohammad Khan ibn Musa Khan, *Tarikh-i-Sultani*, began writing on 1 Ramzan 1281 AH (Sunday, 29 January 1865) and published first on 14 Shawwal 1298 AH (Friday, 8 September 1881), Bombay.

Fazl, Abu'l, *The History of Akbar*, Vol. 1, translated by Wheeler M. Thackston, Cambridge, MA, 2015.

Garrett, Lt Col. H. L. O., and G. L. Chopra, *Events at the Court of Ranjit Singh 1810–1817*, Lahore, 1935.

The Garuda Purana, Primary source edition, edited and translated by Manmatha Nath Dutt, Calcutta, 1908.

Hultzsch, E., *South Indian Inscriptions*, Vol. 2, New Delhi, 1992 (reprint).

India in the Fifteenth Century, Being a Collection of Narratives of Voyages to India, edited by Richard Henry Major, London, 1857.

Jahangir, *Tuzuk-i-Jahangiri or Memoirs of Jahangir*, translated by Alexander Rogers, edited by Henry Beveridge, London, 1919.

Jauhar, *The Tezkereh al-Vakiat or Private Memoirs of the Emperor Humayun*, translated by Charles Stewart, Edinburgh, 1832.

The Kautilya Arthasastra, translated by R. P. Kangle, New Delhi, 2004.

Khan, Dargah Quli, *The Muraqqa' e-Dehli*, translated by Chander Shekhar, New Delhi, 1989.

Khan, Inayat, *The Shah Jahan Nama of Inayat Khan*, edited by W. E. Begley and Z. A. Desai, New Delhi, 1990.

Khusrau, Amir, *The Campaigns of Alauddin Khalji, being the Khazainul Futuh (Treasures of Victory) of Hazrat*

Amir Khusrau of Delhi, translated by Habib Muhammad, Madras, 1931.

Limbird, J., *The Mirror of Literature, Amusement, and Instruction*, containing original papers, Vol. 8, London, 1845.

Marvi, Mohammad Kazem, *Alam Ara-ye Naderi* (three volumes), edited by Mohammad Amin Riyahi, Tehran (third edition), 1374/1995.

The Memoirs of Khojeh Abdulkurreem, translated by Francis Gladwin, Calcutta, 1788.

Mir, *Zikr-I Mir: The Autobiography of the Eighteeenth Century Mughal Poet, Mir Muhammad Taqi 'Mir'*, translated, annotated and introduced by C. M. Naim, New Delhi, 1998.

Muhammad, Fayz, *Siraj ul-Tawarikh* (The Lamp of Histories), Kabul, 1913, translated by R. D. McChesney (forthcoming).

Muhammad, Mirza Ata, *Naway Ma'arek* (The Song of Battles), published as *Nawā-yi ma'ar-ik. Nuskha-i khat.t.ī-i Mūza-i Kābul mushtamal bar wāqi'āt-i 'as.r-i Sadōzā'ī u Bārakzā'ī, ta'līf-i Mīrzā Mīrzaā 'At.ā'-Muh.ammad*, Kabul, 1331 AH/1952 (*Nashrāt-i Anjuman-i tārīkh*, No. 22 [with a preface by Ah.mad-'Alī Kohzād, without index]; idem: *Āryānā*, VIII (1328–9 AH/1950), Nos. 7–10 (pp. 41–8), No. 11 (pp. 46–8), No. 12 (pp. 49–56); IX (1329–30 AH/1951), Nos. 1–12 (pp. 41–8); X (1330–1 AH/1952), Nos. 1–9 (pp. 41–8), No. 10 (pp. 49–56).

Mukhlis, Anand Ram, *Tazkira*, in Sir H. M. Elliot and John Dowson, *The History of India as Told by its own Historians* (eight volumes), London, 1867–77.

Shuja, Shah, *Waqi'at-i-Shah Shuja* (Memoirs of Shah Shuja), written in 1836, supplement by Mohammad Husain Herati, 1861; published as *Wāqi'āt-i Shāh-Shujā'. Daftar-i avval, duvvum: az Shāh-Shujā'. Daftar-i sivvum: az Muh. ammad-H.usain Harātī*, Kabul, 1333 AH/1954 (*Nashrāt-i*

Anjuman-i tārīkh-i Afgānistān, No. 29) [published after the text of the Kabul manuscript, without notes or index, with a preface by Ah.mad-'Alī Kohzād]. Idem: *Āryānā,* X (1330–1 AH/1952), No. 11 (pp. 33–40), No. 12 (pp. 33–40); XI (1331–2 AH/1953), Nos. 1–4 (pp. 49–56), No. 5 (pp. 49–51), Nos. 6–11 (pp. 49–56).

Suri, Sohan Lal, *Umdat-ut-Tawarikh: An Original Source of Punjab History, Chronicles of the Reign of Maharaja Ranjit Singh 1831–1839 by Lala Sohan Lal Suri,* translated by V. S. Suri, Delhi, 1961; Amritsar, 2002.

3. CONTEMPORARY WORKS AND PERIODICAL ARTICLES IN EUROPEAN LANGUAGES

'Allami, Abul Fazl, *The A'in-i Akbari,* translated and edited by H. Blochmann, New Delhi, 1977.

Archer, Major, *Tours in Upper India,* London, 1833.

Argyll, The Duke of, *India under Dalhousie and Canning,* London, 1865.

Arnold, Edwin, *The Marquis of Dalhousie's Administration of British India* (two volumes), London, 1862.

Asiatic Journal and Monthly Register for British India and its Dependencies 28 (1839).

Ballantyne Press, *The Maharajah Duleep Singh and the Government: A Narrative,* London, 1884.

Bazin, Père Louis, 'Mémoires sur dernières années du règne de Thamas Kouli-Kan et sa mort tragique, contenus dans une lettre du Frère Bazin', 1751, in *Lettres édifiantes et curieuses écrites des missions étrangères,* Paris, 1780, Vol. 4, pp. 277–321.

Bell, Evans, *The Annexation of the Punjab and the Maharajah Duleep Singh,* London, 1882.

Bernier, François, *Travels in the Mogul Empire, 1656–68,* edited by Archibald Constable, translated by Irving Brock, Oxford, 1934.

Burnes, Alexander, *Travels into Bokhara, Being the Account of a Journey from India to Cabool, Tartary and Persia, also a Narrative of a Voyage on the Indus from the Sea to Lahore* (three volumes), London, 1834.

Connolly, Arthur, *Journey to the North of India, 1829–31* (two volumes), London, 1838.

Dalhousie, James Andrew Broun Ramsay, Marquess of, *Private Letters*, Edinburgh and London, 1910; London, 1911.

Davenport, Cyril, *The English Regalia*, London, 1897.

Duncan, Jonathan, 'Purn Puri', *Asiatic Researches* (1792).

Eden, Emily, the Hon. *Letters from India*, edited by Eleanor Eden, London, 1872.

—, *Miss Eden's Letters*, edited by Violet Dickinson, London, 1927.

—, *Up the Country: Letters from India*, London, 1930.

Eden, Fanny, *Tigers, Durbars and Kings: Fanny Eden's Indian Journals 1837–1838*, transcribed and edited by Janet Dunbar, London, 1988.

Edwards and Merivale, *Life of Sir Henry Lawrence*, London, 1873.

Elphinstone, Mountstuart, *An Account of the Kingdom of Caubul, and its Dependencies in Persia, Tartary, and India; Comprising a View of the Afghaun Nation, and a History of the Dooraunee Monarchy*, London, 1819.

Foster, Sir William, *The Embassy of Sir Thomas Roe to India 1615–19, as Narrated in his Journal and Correspondence*, New Delhi, 1990.

Fraser, James, *The History of Nadir Shah*, London, 1742.

—, *Narrative of a Journey into Khorasan, in the Years 1821 and 1822*, London, 1825.

Griffin, Lepel, *Ranjit Singh and the Sikh Barrier between our Growing Empire and Central Asia*, Oxford, 1892.

Hanway, Jonas, *An Historical Account of the British Trade over the Caspian Sea ... to which are added The Revolutions of Persia during the present Century, with the particular History of the great Userper Nadir Kouli* (four volumes), London, 1753.

Harlan, J., *A Memoir of India and Afghanistan, with Observations on the Present Exciting and Critical State and Future Prospects of those Countries*, Philadelphia, 1842.

Honigberger, John Martin, *Thirty-Five Years in the East: Adventures, Discoveries, Experiments, and Historical Sketches, Relating to the Punjab and Cashmere; in Connection with Medicine, Botany, Pharmacy, &c.*, London, 1852.

Hügel, Baron Charles, *Travels in Kashmir and the Panjab*, translated by Maj. T. B. Jervis, London, 1845.

The Indian Mutiny, to the Evacuation of Lucknow: To which is Added, a Narrative of the Defence of Lucknow, and a Memoir of General Havelock, compiled by the Former Editor of the *Delhi Gazette*, London, 1858.

Jacquemont, Victor, *Letters from India (1829–32)* (two volumes), translated by Catherine Phillips, London, 1936.

Jennings, Louis J. (ed.), *The Correspondence and Diaries of the Late Right Honourable John Wilson Croker*, Cambridge, 2012.

Khan, Syed Ghulam Hussain, *Seir Mutaqherin or Review of Modern Times* (four volumes), Calcutta, 1790.

The Letters of Queen Victoria: A Selection from Her Majesty's Correspondence between the Years 1837 and 1861, Vol. 2: *1844–1853*, edited by Arthur C. Benson and Viscount Esher, London, 1908.

Login, Lady, *Lady Login's Recollections: Court Life and Camp Life 1820–1904*, London, 1917.

—, *Sir John Login and Duleep Singh*, London, 1890.

Malleson, George Bruce, *History of Afghanistan from the Earliest Period to the Outbreak of War of 1878*, London, 1879.

Manucci, Niccolao, *Storia do Mogor or Mogul India* (four volumes), translated by William Irvine, London, 1907.

Marshman, John Clark, *The History of India from the Earliest Period to the Close of Lord Dalhousie's Administration* (three volumes, original edition 1863–7), full text available online www.ibiblio.org.

The North American Miscellany, Vol. 2, Boston, 1851 (Volume 939 of *American Periodical Series 1800–1850*).

Orta, Garcia da, *Colloquies on the Simples and Drugs of India*, translated by Clements Markham, London, 1913.

Osborne, W. G. *The Court and Camp of Runjeet Sing*, London, 1840.

Papers Relating to the Punjab 1847–9, London, 1849.

Parkes, Fanny, *Wanderings of a Pilgrim in Search of the Picturesque*, London, 1850.

Polier, Antoine, *Shah Alam II and his Court*, Calcutta, 1947.

Prinsep, Henry Thoby, *History of the Punjab, and of the Rise, Progress and Present Condition, of the Sect and Nation of the Sikhs* [based in part on the 'Origin of the Sikh Power in the Punjab and Political Life of Muha-Raja Ranjeet Singh'], London, 1846.

Records of the Ludhiana Agency, Lahore, 1911.

Roset, Hipponox, *Jewellery and Precious Stones ... Including Particularly a Consideration of the Koh-i-Noor's Claim to Notoriety*, Philadelphia, 1856.

Singh, Bhai Nahar, and Kirpal Singh (eds), *History of the Koh-i-Noor, Darya-i-Noor and Taimur's Ruby*, New Delhi, no date.

Sleeman, Major General Sir W. H., *Rambles and Recollections of an Indian Official*, Oxford, 1915.

Smith, Reginald Bosworth, *Life of Lord Lawrence*, London, 1912.

Smyth, George Monro Carmichael, *A History of the reigning family of Lahore, with some account of the Jummoo rajahs, the Seik soldiers and their sirdars*, Calcutta, 1847.

Soltykoff, Prince Alexis, *Voyages dans l'Inde*, Paris, 1858.

Tagore, Raja Sourindro Mohum, *Mani-masa or A Treatise on Gems*, Calcutta, 1881.

Tavernier, Jean Baptiste, Baron of Aubonne, *Travels in India* (two volumes), 1678, translated by V. Ball, London, 1889.

Vigne, Godfrey, *A Personal Narrative of a Visit to Ghuzni, Kabul, and Afghanistan and of a Residence at the Court of Dost Mohamed with notices of Runjit Singh, Khiva, and the Russian Expedition*, London, 1840.

Wade, Sir C. M., *A Narrative of the Services, Military and Political, of Lt Col. Sir C. M. Wade*, Ryde, 1847.

4. SECONDARY WORKS AND PERIODICAL ARTICLES

Aijazuddin, Fakir Syed, *The Resourceful Fakirs*, Delhi, 2014.

—, *Sikh Portraits by European Artists*, New York, 1979.

Alam, Muzaffar, *The Crisis of Empire in Mughal North India: Awadh and the Punjab 1707–1748*, New Delhi, 1986.

Alexander, Michael, and Sushila Anand, *Queen Victoria's Maharajah: Duleep Singh 1838–93*, London, 1980.

Ali, Daud, *Courtly Culture and Political Life in Early Medieval India*, Cambridge, 2004.

Amini, Iradj, *The Koh-i-Noor Diamond*, New Delhi, 1994.

Anand, Anita, *Sophia, Princess, Suffragette, Revolutionary*, London, 2015.

Archer, Mildred, and Toby Falk, *India Revealed: The Art and Adventures of James and William Fraser 1801–35*, London, 1989.

Avery, Peter, Gavin Hambly and Charles Melville, *The Cambridge History of Iran*, Vol. 7: *From Nadir Shah to the Islamic Republic*, Cambridge, 1991.

Axworthy, Michael, *Iran: Empire of the Mind: A History from Zoroaster to the Present Day*, London, 2007.

—, *The Sword of Persia: Nader Shah from Tribal Warrior to Conquering Tyrant*, New York, 2006.

Aziz, Abdul, *The Imperial Treasury of the Indian Mughals*, New Delhi, 2009.

Babu, T. M., *Glorious Indian Diamonds*, New Delhi, 2015.

Balfour, Ian, *Famous Diamonds*, London, 2009.

Bance, Peter, *Sovereign, Squire and Rebel: Maharajah Duleep Singh*, London, 2009.

—, *The Duleep Singhs: The Photographic Album of Queen Victoria's Maharajah*, London, 2004.

Banerjee, A. C., *Anglo-Sikh Relations: Chapters from J. D. Cunningham's History of the Sikhs*, Calcutta, 1949.

—, *The Khalsa Raj*, New Delhi, 1985.

Banerjee, Himadri, *The Sikh Khalsa and the Punjab: Studies in Sikh History, to the 19th Century*, New Delhi, 2002.

Bansal, Bobby Singh, *The Lion's Firanghis: Europeans at the Court of Lahore*, London, 2010.

Barfield, Thomas J., *Afghanistan: A Cultural and Political History*, Princeton, 2010.

— 'Problems of Establishing Legitimacy in Afghanistan', *Iranian Studies* 37, no. 2 (June 2004): 263–93.

Beveridge, H., 'Babar's Diamond: Was It the Koh-i-Nur', *Asiatic Quarterly Review* (April 1899): 370–89.

Bosworth, Edmund, and Carole Hillenbrand, *Qajar Iran*, Edinburgh, 1983.

Butler, Iris, *The Elder Brother: The Marquess Wellesley 1760–1842*, London, 1973.

Campbell, Christy, *The Maharajah's Box*, London, 2000.

Caroe, Olaf, *The Pathans*, London, 1958.

Carvalho, Pedro Moura, *Gems and Jewels of Mughal India*, London, 2010.

Chandra, Satish, *Parties and Politics at the Mughal Court 1717–1740*, New Delhi, 1972.

Cheema, G. S., *The Forgotten Mughals: A History of the Later Emperors of the House of Babar 1707–1857*, New Delhi, 2002.

Chopra, Barkat Rai, *Kingdom of the Punjab 1839–45*, Hoshiarpur, 1969.

Crill, Rosemary, John Guy, Susan Stronge and Deborah Swallow, *Arts of India 1550–1900*, London, 1990.

Dalrymple, William, *City of Djinns: A Year in Delhi*, London, 1992.

—, *The Last Mughal: The End of a Dynasty, Delhi 1857*, London, 2006.

—, *Return of a King*, London, 2012.

—, and Yuthika Sharma, *Princes and Poets in Mughal Delhi 1707–1857*, Princeton, 2012.

David, Saul, *Victoria's Wars: The Rise of Empire*, London, 2006.

Dehejia, Vidya, *The Body Adorned: Dissolving Boundaries between Sacred and Profane in Indian Art*, Ahmedabad, 2009.

—, *The Sensuous and the Sacred: Chola Bronzes from South India*, Seattle, 2002.

Dickinson, Joan Y., *The Book of Diamonds*, London, 1965.

Dunbar, Janet, *Golden Interlude: The Edens in India 1836–1842*, London, 1955.

Dupree, Louis, *Afghanistan*, Oxford, 1973.

Edwards, Michael, *King of the World: The Life and Times of Shah Alam, Emperor of Hindustan*, London, 1970.

Ferrier, Joseph Pierre, *A History of the Afghans*, London, 1858.

Fisher, Michael H., *Beyond the Three Seas: Travellers' Tales of Mughal India*, New Delhi, 1987.

Floor, Willem, 'New Facts on Nader Shah's Indian Campaign', in *Iran and Iranian Studies: Essays in Honour of Iraj Afshar*, edited by Kambiz Eslami, Princeton, 1998, pp. 198–220.

Fraser-Tytler, Sir Kerr, *Afghanistan: A Study of Political Developments in Central Asia*, Oxford, 1950.

Fulford, Roger, *The Prince Consort*, London, 1949.

Gardiner, Juliet, *Queen Victoria*, London, 1997.

Gill, Avtar Singh, *Lahore Darbar and Rani Jindan*, Ludhiana, 1983.

Gommans, Jos J. L., *The Rise of the Indo-Afghan Empire c. 1710–1780*, New Delhi, 1999.

Gregorian, Vartan, *The Emergence of Modern Afghanistan: Politics of Reform and Modernization 1880–1946*, Stanford, 1969.

Guise, Lucien de, *Jewels without Crowns: Mughal Gems in Miniatures*, Kuala Lumpur, 2010.

Haidar, Navina Najat, and Courtney Ann Stewart, *Treasures from India: Jewels from the Al-Thani Collection*, New York, 2015.

Haroon, Sana, *Frontier of Faith: Islam in the Indo-Afghan Borderland*, London, 2007.

Harris, Jonathan Gil, *The First Firangis*, Delhi, 2014.

Hart, Matthew, *Diamond: The History of a Cold-Blooded Love Affair*, New York, 2002.

Heathcote, T. A., *The Afghan Wars 1839–1919*, Staplehurst, 2004.

Hopkins, Ben, *The Making of Modern Afghanistan*, London, 2008.

Hopkirk, Peter, *The Great Game*, London, 1990.

Howarth, Stephen, *The Koh-i-noor Diamond*, London, 1980.

Ingram, Edward, *The Beginning of the Great Game in Asia 1828–1834*, Oxford, 1979.

Kaicker, Abhishek, *Unquiet City: Making and Unmaking Politics in Mughal Delhi, 1707–39*, unpublished PhD, Columbia University.

Keay, Anna, *The Crown Jewels*, London, 2012.

Keene, Manuel, *Treasury of the World: Jewelled Arts of India in the Age of the Mughals*, London, 2001.

Koch, Ebba, 'The Mughals and their Love of Precious Stones', in *Halqeh-ye Nur Astaneh-ye Ferdaws*, London, 2012.

Khalidi, Omar, *Romance of the Golconda Diamonds*, London, 1999.

Krishnamurthy, Radha, 'Gemmology in Ancient India', *Indian Journal of the History of Science* 27, no. 3 (1992): 251–60.

Krishnan, Usha R. Bala, and Meera Sushil Kumar, *Dance of the Peacock: Jewellery Traditions of India*, Mumbai, 1999.

Kulkarni, Uday S., *Solstice at Panipat, 14 January 1761*, Pune, 2011.

Lafont, Jean-Marie, *Fauj-i-Khas: Maharaja Ranjit Singh and his French Courtiers*, Amritsar, 2002.

—, *Maharaja Ranjit Singh: Lord of the Five Rivers*, New Delhi, 2002.

—, *La Présence française dans la Royaume Sikh de Penjaub 1822–1849*, Paris, 1992.

Latif, Momin, 'The Golden Age of Jewellery', in *A Kaleidoscope of Colours: Indian Mughal Jewels from the 18th and 19th Centuries*, Antwerp, 1997.

—, *Mughal Jewels*, Brussels, 1982.

Latif, Syad Muhammad, *History of the Punjab*, New Delhi, 1964.

Lee, J. L., *The 'Ancient Supremacy': Bukhara, Afghanistan & the Battle for Balk 1731–1901*, Leiden, 1996.

Lenzen, Godehard, *The History of Diamond Production and the Diamond Trade*, London, 1970.

Lockhardt, Laurence, *Nadir Shah*, London, 1938.

Losty, J. P., and Malini Roy, *Mughal India: Art, Culture and Empire*, London, 2012.

Lunt, James, *Bokhara Burnes*, London, 1969.

Maharajah Duleep Singh Correspondence, edited by Ganda Singh, Patiala, 1972.

Malecka, Anna, 'The Great Mughal and the Orlov: One and the Same Diamond', *Journal of Gemmology* 35, no. 1 (2016): 56–63.

Malik, Zahir Uddin, *The Reign of Muhammad Shah 1719–1748*, Aligarh, 1977.

Meen, V. B., and A. D. Tushingham, *Crown Jewels of Iran*, Toronto, 1968.

Melikian-Chirvani, Assadullah Souren, 'The Jewelled Objects of Hindustan', *Jewellery Studies* 10 (2004): 9–32.

—, 'The Red Stones of Light in Iranian Culture', *Bulletin of the Asia Institute* 15 (2001): 77–110.

Menkes, Suzy, *The Royal Jewels*, London, 1985.

Moon, Sir Penderel, *The British Conquest and Dominion of India*, London, 1990.

Nichols, Robert, *Settling the Frontier: Land, Law and Society in the Peshawar Valley 1500–1900*, Oxford, 2001.

Noelle, Christine, *State and Tribe in Nineteenth-Century Afghanistan: The Reign of Amir Dost Muhammad Khan (1826–1863)*, London, 1997.

Owen, Sidney J., *The Fall of the Mughal Empire*, London, 1912.

Prior, Mary Ann, *An Indian Portfolio: The Life and Work of Emily Eden*, London, 2012.

Reshtia, Sayed Qassem, *Between Two Giants: Political History of Afghanistan in the Nineteenth Century*, Peshawar, 1990.

Rizvi, Sayid Athar Abbas, *Shah Walli-Allah and his Times*, Canberra, 1980.

Roberts, Hugh, *The Queen's Diamonds*, London, 2011.

Rushby, Kevin, *Chasing the Mountain of Light*, London, 1999.

Saddozai, Wg Cdr Sardar Ahmad Shah Jan, *Saddozai: Saddozai Kings & Viziers of Afghanistan 1747–1842*, Peshawar, 2007.

Sarkar, J. N., *Nadir Shah in India*, Calcutta, 1973.

Shukla, M. S., *A History of the Gem Industry in Ancient and Medieval India*, Varanasi, 1972.

Singh, Captain Amarinder, *The Last Sunset: The Rise & Fall of the Lahore Durbar*, New Delhi, 2010.

Singh, Bhai Nahar, and Kirpal Singh, *The History of Koh-i-Noor, Darya-i-Noor and Taimur's Ruby*, New Delhi, 1985.

Singh, Ganga, *Ahmad Shah Durrani*, Delhi, 1925.

Singh, Khushwant, *Ranjit Singh: Maharaja of the Punjab*, London, 1962.

—, *The Fall of the Kingdom of the Punjab*, Telangana, 1962.

Singh, Patwant, *Empire of the Sikhs: The Life and Times of Maharajah Ranjit Singh*, New Delhi, 2008.

Sinha, Narendra Krishna, *Ranjit Singh*, Calcutta, 1933.

Spear, Percival, *The Nabobs*, Cambridge, 1963.

Streeter, E., *Great Diamonds of the World*, London, 1882.

Stronge, Susan, *The Arts of the Sikh Kingdoms*, London, 1999.

—, *Bejewelled Treasures: The Al Thani Collection*, London, 2015.

—, 'The Myth of the Timur Ruby', *Jewellery Studies* 7 (1996): 5–12.

—, 'The Sublime Thrones of the Mughal Emperors of Hindustan', *Jewellery Studies* 10 (2004): 52–65.

—, Nima Smith and J. C. Harle, *A Golden Treasury: Jewellery from the Indian Subcontinent*, London, 1988.

Subrahmanyam, Sanjay, *Un Grand Derangement: Dreaming of an Indo-Persian Empire*, in *Journal of Early Modern History*, Vol. 4, Issue 3, 2000.

Sucher, Scott D., and Dale P. Carriere, 'The Use of Laser and X-Ray Scanning to Create a Model of the Historic Koh-i-Noor Diamond', *Gems and Gemology* (Summer 2008): 124–41.

Swamy, K. R. N., and Meera Ravi, *The Peacock Thrones of the World: A Reference Anthology*, Bombay, 1993.

Sykes, Sir Percy, *A History of Persia* (two volumes), London, 1963.

Tanner, Stephen, *Afghanistan: A Military History from Alexander the Great to the Fall of the Taliban*, Cambridge, MA, 2002.

Tobias, Marc Weber, *Locks Safes and Security: An International Police Reference* (two volumes, second edition), Springfield, IL, 2000.

Untracht, Oppi, *Traditional Jewellery of India*, London, 1997.

Wannell, Bruce, 'Two Versions of a Book of Jewels in Persian: On the Jawahir Nama, or Book of Jewels' for the Simon Digby Memorial Festschrift (forthcoming).

Wojtilla, Gyula, 'Indian Precious Stones in Ancient East and West', *Acta Orientalia Academiae Scientiarum Hungaricae* 27, no. 2 (1973): 211–24.

—, 'Ratnasastra in Kautilya's *Arthasastra*', *Acta Orientalia Academiae Scientiarum Hungaricae* 62, no. 1 (2009): 37–44.

Yogev, Gedalia, *Diamonds and Coral: Anglo-Dutch Jews and Eighteenth-Century Trade*, Leicester, 1978.

Zebrowski, Mark, *Gold, Silver and Bronze from Mughal India*, London, 1990.

Acknowledgements

I'd like to thank the following authorities on Indian gems who kindly shared their learning with me: Susan Stronge, Navina Haidar, Courtney Stewart, Momin Latif, Ebba Koch, Derek Content, Iradj Amini, Amin Jaffer, Alan Hart and Jack Ogden. Bruce Wannell, Michael Axworthy, Katherine Butler-Schofield, Robert McChesney, Ursula Sims-Williams and Saqib Baburi all gave crucial and generous advice on the Persian sources that hold the key to unravelling the forgotten twists of the Koh-i-Noor's history. Navtej Sarna, Lily Tekseng, Riya Sarkar and Ian Trueger provided invaluable assistance with various bits of research and editing. Nandini Mehta, Parth Mehrotra and Chiki Sarkar, at Juggernaut, and Alexandra Pringle and Mike Fishwick, at Bloomsbury, have all been wonderful to work with, as has my brilliant, kind and ingenious agent, David Godwin. Together they helped turn a momentary jeu d'esprit into a book. My lovely family – Olivia, Ibby, Sam and Adam – have kept me sane and happy during this long summer and autumn of writing. Finally, I'd like to thank my wonderful co-writer, Anita – a diamond geezer if ever there was one.

William Dalrymple

My thanks to Peter Bance for being so generous with his time and expertise and in giving access to his extraordinary Duleep Singh archive. Many of the images in this book are from his collection, and I can think of nobody else who has devoted so much care and time to conserving the artefacts of the Ranjit Singh/Duleep Singh era. He has always been a tremendous support. Thanks also to Alan Hart, chief executive of the Gemmological Association of Great Britain, for his guidance and extraordinary knowledge. From the corner of a dimly lit pub in west London he illuminated the Koh-i-Noor story. My thanks to Sue Woolmans – a jewellery expert right under my nose! Also an enthusiastic supporter. I will always be deeply indebted to F. S. Aijazuddin, not only one of the foremost authorities on the Lahore Darbar, but a man whose family history and very DNA is entwined around the history of Ranjit Singh and his heir. His generous guidance has proved to be invaluable. Thanks also to the British Library and its ever helpful archivists, to the Royal Archive and to Amandeep Madra for being my Sikh history guide. Thanks too to Navtej Sarna, who has done so much to put flesh on the Duleep Singh story, and to Patrick Walsh, my agent and wise friend. Thanks to Chiki Sarkar, Ameena Syed, Alexandra Pringle and Michael Fishwick for their enthusiasm for this project, and special thanks to Nandini Mehta for helping to birth this baby. Thanks to my late father, who first took me by the hand to visit the Koh-i-Noor when I was a child of six, and talked about its loss with such passion that the diamond burned bright in my imagination ever after; and to my husband and sons – Simon has captained our little ship heroically while I have been crossing oceans for this book. I could not have written it without his patience and support. Finally, thanks to Willie Dalrymple – what a joy to work with you. Shine on, you crazy diamond!

Anita Anand

Index

A Note on the Authors

William Dalrymple wrote the highly acclaimed bestseller *In Xanadu* when he was just twenty-two. Since then, he has had seven more books published and has won numerous awards for his writing, including the *Sunday Times* Young British Writer of the Year Award, the Duff Cooper Memorial Award, the Hemingway Prize and the Ryszard Kapuściński Award for Literary Reportage. He lives with his wife and three children on a farm outside Delhi.

Anita Anand has been a radio and television journalist for over twenty years. On BBC television she has presented, among other shows, *Daily Politics*, *The Heaven and Earth Show* and *Newsnight*. She is currently the presenter of *Any Answers* on BBC Radio 4. Her first book, *Sophia: Princess, Suffragette, Revolutionary*, received widespread acclaim. She lives in London with her husband and two children.

A Note on the Type

The text of this book is set in Linotype Stempel Garamond, a version of Garamond adapted and first used by the Stempel foundry in 1924. It is one of several versions of Garamond based on the designs of Claude Garamond. It is thought that Garamond based his font on Bembo, cut in 1495 by Francesco Griffo in collaboration with the Italian printer Aldus Manutius. Garamond types were first used in books printed in Paris around 1532. Many of the present-day versions of this type are based on the *Typi Academiae* of Jean Jannon cut in Sedan in 1615.

Claude Garamond was born in Paris in 1480. He learned how to cut type from his father and by the age of fifteen he was able to fashion steel punches the size of a pica with great precision. At the age of sixty he was commissioned by King Francis I to design a Greek alphabet, and for this he was given the honourable title of royal type founder. He died in 1561.